BERLITZ®

Russian
PHRASE BOOK & DICTIONARY

Easy to use features

- Handy thematic colour coding
- Quick Reference Section – opposite page
- Tipping Guide – inside back cover
- Quick reply panels throughout

How best to use this phrase book

• We suggest that you start with the **Guide to pronunciation** (pp. 6–9), then go on to **Some basic expressions** (pp. 10–15). This gives you not only a minimum vocabulary, but also helps you get used to pronouncing the language.

• Consult the **Contents** pages (3–5) for the section you need. In each chapter you'll find travel facts, hints and useful information. Simple phrases are followed by a list of words applicable to the situation.

• Separate, detailed contents lists are included at the beginning of the extensive **Eating out** and **Shopping guide** sections (Menus, p. 39, Shops and services, p. 97).

• If you want to find out how to say something in Russian, your fastest look-up is via the **Dictionary** section (pp. 162–189). This not only gives you the word, but is also cross-referenced to its use in a phrase on a specific page.

• If you wish to learn more about constructing sentences, check the **Basic grammar** (pp. 157–161).

• Note the **colour margins** are indexed in Russian and English to help both listener and speaker. And, in addition, there is also an **index in Russian** for the use of your listener.

• Throughout the book, this symbol ☛ suggests phrases your listener can use to answer you. If you still can't understand, hand this phrase book to the Russian-speaker to encourage pointing to an appropriate answer.

 Library of Congress Catalog Card No. 86-72022

Revised edition—5th printing 1993 Printed in Switzerland

Contents

Guide to pronunciation 6

Some basic expressions 10

Arrival 16

16 Passport control
17 Customs
18 Baggage—Porters
18 Currency exchange
19 Where is...?
19 Hotel reservation
20 Car hire (rental)
21 Taxi

Hotel—Accommodation 22

23 Checking in—Reception
25 Registration
26 Hotel staff
27 General requirements
28 Telephone—Post (Mail)
28 Difficulties
29 Laundry—Dry cleaner's
30 Hairdresser—Barber
31 Checking out
32 Camping

Eating out 33

34 Meal times
34 Eating habits
35 Russian cuisine
36 At the restaurant
37 Diet
38 Breakfast
39 What's on the menu?
41 Starters (Appetizers)
42 Salads
43 Cheese and dairy products
44 Soups
45 Fish and seafood
47 Meat
49 Game and poultry
50 Vegetables
51 Cereals, rice, potatoes
51 Sauces
52 Fruit
53 Dessert
55 Drinks
55 Wine
56 Beer
57 Vodka
58 Other alcoholic drinks
59 Tea
59 Kvass
60 Other beverages
61 Complaints
62 The bill (check)
62 Snacks—Picnic

Travelling around 65

65 Plane
66 Train
67 Information
69 Tickets
70 On the train
71 Baggage and Porters
72 Public transport
72 Underground (Subway)
73 Bus—Tram (Streetcar)
74 Ship
75 Car
76 Asking the way
77 Parking
78 Breakdown—Road assistance
79 Repair
79 Accident
79 Road signs

Sightseeing 80

81 Where is...?
82 Admission
83 Who—What—When?
84 Religious services
85 Countryside

Relaxing 86

86 Cinema (Movies)—Theatre
87 Circus
87 Opera—Ballet—Concert
88 Nightclubs—Discos
89 Sports
90 On the beach
91 Winter sports

Making friends 92

92 Introductions
94 The weather
94 Invitations
95 Dating

Shopping guide 97

98 Shops and useful addresses
100 General expressions
102 Paying
104 Bookshop—Stationer's
106 Camping equipment
108 Chemist's (Drugstore)
112 Clothing
112 Size
113 Colour
114 Fabric/Material
116 Clothes
118 Shoes
119 Electrical appliances
120 Grocery
121 Jeweller's—Watch-maker's
123 Optician
124 Photography
126 Tobacconist's
127 Souvenirs
127 Records—Cassettes
128 Toys

Your money: banks—currency 129

130 At the bank
131 Business terms

At the post office 132

133 Telegrams
134 Telephone

Doctor 137

137 General
138 Parts of the body
139 Accident—Injury
140 Illness
141 Women's section
143 At the doctor's—Treatment
144 Fee
144 Hospital
145 Dentist

Reference section 146

146 Countries
147 Numbers
149 Year and age
150 Seasons
150 Months
151 Days and date
152 Public holidays
152 Greetings and wishes
153 Time
154 Abbreviations
154 Signs and notices
155 Emergency
155 Lost property—Theft
156 Conversion tables

Basic Grammar 157

Dictionary and index (English-Russian) 162

Russian index 190

Map of western Russia 192

Acknowledgments
We are particularly grateful to Eva Antonnikov for her help in the preparation of this book, and to Dr. T.J.A. Bennett who devised the phonetic transcription.

Guide to pronunciation

This and the following chapter are intended to make you familiar with the phonetic transcription we've devised, and to help you get used to the sound of Russian.

The imitated pronunciation should be read as if it were English (based on Standard British pronunciation), except for any special rules set out below. Letters in **bold** print should be read with more stress (louder) than the others.

Pronunciation of the Russian alphabet

А а	*А а*	ah	Р р	*Р р*	ehr
Б б	*Б б*	beh	С с	*С с*	ehs
В в	*В в*	veh	Т т	*Т т*	teh
Г г	*Г г*	geh	У у	*У у*	oo
Д д	*Д д*	deh	Ф ф	*Ф ф*	ehf
Е е	*Е е*	^{y}eh	Х х	*Х х*	khah
Ё ё	*Ё ё*	^{y}o	Ц ц	*Ц ц*	tseh
Ж ж	*Ж ж*	zheh	Ч ч	*Ч ч*	ch^{y}ah
З з	*З з*	zeh	Ш ш	*Ш ш*	shah
И и	*И и*	ee	Щ щ	*Щ щ*	shch^{y}ah
Й й	*Й й*	ee **kraht**ko^{y}eh	Ъ ъ	*ъ*	**tv^{y}or**diy znahk
К к	*К к*	kah	Ы ы	*ы*	i
Л л	*Л л*	ehl	Ь ь	*ь*	m^{y}**akh**keey znahk
М м	*М м*	ehm	Э э	*Э э*	eh ahbah**rot**nah^{y}eh
Н н	*Н н*	ehn	Ю ю	*Ю ю*	^{y}oo
О о	*О о*	o	Я я	*Я я*	^{y}ah
П п	*П п*	peh			

Consonants

The pronunciation of Russian consonants can be either "hard" or "soft". Consonants are "soft" when followed by the vowels **я, е, и, ё, ю** or the "soft sign" **ь** (see p. 8). When a letter is soft, it is followed by a short **y**-sound (in our transcription, ^{y}).

Letter	Approximate pronunciation	Symbol	Example	
б	like **b** in **b**it	b	**был**	bill
в	like **v** in **v**ine	v	**ваш**	vahsh
г	like **g** in **g**o	g	**город**	**go**rraht
д	like **d** in **d**o	d	**да**	dah
ж	like **s** in plea**s**ure	zh	**жаркий**	**zhahr**keey
з	like **z** in **z**oo	z	**за**	zah
к	like **k** in **k**itten	k	**карта**	**kahr**tah
л	like **l** in **l**amp or in we**ll**	l	**лампа**	**lahm**pah
м	like **m** in **m**y	m	**масло**	**mah**slah
н	like **n** in **n**ot	n	**нет**	n^{y}eht
п	like **p** in **p**ot	p	**парк**	pahrk
р	trilled (like a Scottish r)	r	**русский**	**roos**keey
с	like **s** in **s**ee	s/ss	**слово**	**slo**vvah
т	like **t** in **t**ip	t	**там**	tahm
ф	like **f** in **f**ace	f	**ферма**	**f^{y}ehr**mah
х	like **ch** in Scottish lo**ch**	kh	**хлеб**	khl^{y}ehp
ц	like **ts** in si**ts**	ts	**цена**	tsi**nnah**
ч*	like **ch** in **ch**ip	ch^{y}	**час**	ch^{y}ahss
ш	like **sh** in **sh**ut	sh	**ваша**	**vah**shah
щ*	like **sh** followed by **ch**	shch^{y}	**щётка**	**shch^{y}ot**kah

N.B.: Voiced consonants are pronounced voiceless at the end of the word, e.g. in **зуб** – zoo**p**, **сад** – sah**t**, **друг** – droo**k**.

* These consonants are *always* pronounced "soft", i.e. followed by a short **y**-sound.

Vowels

а	between the **a** in **cat** and the **u** in **cut**	ah	**как**	kahk
е	like **ye** in **yet**	^{y}eh	**где**	gd^{y}eh
ё	like **yo** in **yonder**	^{y}o	**мёд**	m^{y}ot
и	like **ee** in **see**	ee	**синий**	**see**neey
й*	like **y** in ga**y** or bo**y**	y	**бой**	boy
о	like **o** in **hot**	o	**стол**	stoll
у	like **oo** in **boot**	oo	**улица**	**oo**leetsah
ы	a "dark" i, like the **i** in **ill**	i	**вы**	vi
э	like **e** in **met**	eh	**эта**	**eh**tah
ю	like **u** in **duke**	^{y}oo	**юг**	^{y}ook
я	like **ya** in **yard**	^{y}ah	**мясо**	**m^{y}ah**ssah

N.B. If a vowel is followed by a double consonant in our transcription, this indicates that it is short.

Other letters

ь makes the preceding consonant soft. A similar effect can be produced by pronouncing **y** as in **yet**—but very, very short—after the consonant, e.g. **плакать**—**plah**kaht^{y}.

ъ is sometimes used between two parts of a compound word, when the second part begins with **я, ю,** or **е**, to show that the pronunciation of the word should incorporate a clear separation of the two parts.

---

* **й** is a semi-vowel, i.e. always combined with a full vowel.

Diphthongs

The following stressed diphthongs exist in Russian:

ай	like **igh** in **sigh**	igh	**май**	migh
яй	like the previous sound, but preceded by the **y** in **yes**	^{y}igh	**негодяй**	neegah-**d^{y}igh**
ой	like **oy** in **boy**	oy	**вой**	voy
ей	like **ya** in **Yates**	^{y}ay	**соловей**	sahlah**v^{y}ay**
ый	like **i** in **ill** followed by the **y** in **yes**	iy	**красивый**	krah**ssee**viy
уй	like **oo** in **good** followed by the **y** in **yes**	ooy	**дуй**	dooy
юй	like the previous sound, but preceded by a short **y**-sound	^{y}ooy	**плюй**	pl^{y}ooy

Stress

Stress in Russian is irregular and must simply be learned. If a vowel or diphthong is **not** stressed, it often changes its pronunciation. This could be called a weakening of the sound.

о	unstressed, is pronounced like Russian **а**	ah	**отец**	**aht^{y}ehts**
е, я, ей, ий	unstressed, are pronounced like a short **ee** sound	ee	**теперь** **язык**	**teep^{y}ehr^{y}** **eezik**

Words may be stressed differently in the plural form; e.g. окно (window): singular окно (ahk**no**), plural окна (**ok**nah). See also GRAMMAR section.

Some basic expressions

Yes./No.	**Да./Нет.**	dah/n^{y}eht
Please.	**Пожалуйста.**	pah**zhahl**stah
Thank you.	**Спасибо.**	spahs**see**bah
Thank you very much.	**Большое спасибо.**	bahl^y**sho**^{y}eh spahs**see**bah
That's all right/ You're welcome.	**Не за что.**	**n^{y}eh**zahshtah
Excuse me/Sorry!	**Простите./Извините.**	prahs**teet**^{y}eh/ eezvee**neet**^{y}eh
May I get by, please?	**Разрешите.**	rahzree**shit**^{y}eh

Greetings *Приветствия*

Good morning.	**Доброе утро.**	**do**brah^{y}eh **oo**trah
Good afternoon.	**Добрый день.**	**do**briy d^{y}ehn^y
Good evening.	**Добрый вечер.**	**do**briy **v^{y}eh**ch^{y}eer
Good night.	**Спокойной ночи.**	spah**koy**nigh **noch**^{y}ee
Goodbye.	**До свидания.**	dah svee**dah**nee^{y}ah
Hello!	**Здравствуйте!**	**zdrahst**vooyt^{y}eh
Hi! (informal)	**Привет!**	pree**v^{y}eht**
See you later.	**До скорой встречи.**	dah **skor**righ **fstr^{y}eh**ch^{y}ee
See you! (informal)	**До скорого!/Пока!**	dah **skor**rahvah/pah**kah**
How do you do?	**Здравствуйте!**	**zdrahst**vooyt^{y}eh
What's your name?	**Как Вас зовут?**	kahk vahss zah**voot**
My name is ...	**Меня зовут ...**	meen**^{y}ah** zah**voot**
This is my husband/ my wife.	**Это мой муж/ моя жена.**	**eh**tah moy moosh/mah**^{y}ah** zhin**nah**
How are you?	**Как вы живёте?**	kahk vi zhiv**^{y}ot**^{y}eh
Very well, thanks. And you?	**Спасибо, очень хорошо. А вы?**	spahs**see**bah **och**^{y}een^y khahrah**sho**. ah vi
How's life? (informal)	**Как дела?**	kahk dee**lah**
Fine.	**Хорошо./Прекрасно.**	khahrah**sho**/pree**krahs**nah

INTRODUCTIONS, see page 92

So-so.	**Ничего./Так себе.**	neech^{y}**eevo**/tahk seeb^{y}**eh**
Bad.	**Плохо.**	**plo**khah

Questions *Вопросы*

Please …	**Будьте добры …***	**boot^{y}**tee dah**bri**
Can you tell me, please …?	**Скажите, пожалуйста …**	skah**zhit^{y}**eh pah**zhahl**stah
Where?/Where to?	**Где?/Куда?**	gd^{y}eh/koo**dah**
Where is/are …?	**Где …?**	gd^{y}eh
Where can I find/get …?	**Где мне найти/достать …?**	gd^{y}eh mn^{y}eh nigh**tee**/dah**staht^{y}**
Who?	**Кто?**	kto
Who's that?	**Кто это?**	kto **eh**tah
What?	**Что?**	shto
What's that?	**Что это?**	shto **eh**tah
What does that mean?	**Что это значит?**	shto **eh**tah **znah**ch^{y}eet
Which?	**Какой/Какая/Какое?**	kah**koy**/kah**kah^{y}**ah/kah**ko^{y}**eh
Which bus goes to …?	**Какой автобус идёт до/к …?**	kah**koy** ahf**to**bboss eed^{y}**ot** dah/k
When?	**Когда?**	kahg**dah**
When do we arrive?	**Когда мы приезжаем?**	kahg**dah** mi pree^{y}eez**zhah**eem
When does … open/close?	**Когда открывается/закрывается …?**	kahg**dah** ahtkriv**vah**eetsah/zahkriv**vah**eetsah
How?	**Как?**	kahk
What do you call that in Russian?	**Как это называется по-русски?**	kahk **eh**tah nahziv**vah**eetsah pah **roos**kee
How much/How many?	**Сколько?**	**skol^{y}**kah
How much is it?	**Сколько это стоит?**	**skol^{y}**kah **eh**tah **sto**eet
What time is it?	**Который час?**	kah**to**rriy ch^{y}ahss
How long?	**Как долго?**	kahk **dol**gah
How far?	**Как далеко?**	kahk dahlee**ko**

* Can introduce any question.

I beg your pardon?	**Простите?**	prah**steet**^{y}eh
Is that right?	**Правильно?**	**prah**veel^{y}nah
Why?	**Почему?**	pahch^{y}ee**moo**

Do you speak ...? *Вы говорите...?*

Do you speak English?	**Вы говорите по-английски?**	vi gahvah**reet**^{y}eh pah ahn**gleeys**kee
Does anyone here speak English?	**Говорит здесь кто-нибудь по-английски?**	gahvah**reet** zd^{y}ehs^{y} **kto**-neebood^{y} pah ahn**gleeys**kee
I don't speak much Russian.	**Я плохо говорю по-русски.**	^{y}ah **plo**khah gahvah**r**^{y}**oo** pah **roos**kee
Could you speak more slowly?	**Говорите, пожалуйста, медленнее.**	gahvah**reet**^{y}eh pah**zhahl**stah **m**^{y}**eh**dleennee
Could you repeat that?	**Повторите, пожалуйста.**	pahftah**reet**^{y}eh pah**zhahl**stah
Could you spell it?	**Скажите по буквам, пожалуйста.**	skah**zhit**^{y}eh pah **book**vahm pah**zhahl**stah
Could you read it?	**Читайте, пожалуйста.**	ch^{y}ee**tight**^{y}eh pah**zhahl**stah
Please write it down.	**Напишите, пожалуйста.**	nahpee**shit**^{y}eh pah**zhahl**stah
Can you translate this for me?	**Переведите мне это, пожалуйста.**	peereevee**deet**^{y}eh mn^{y}eh **eh**tah pah**zhahl**stah
Please point to the ... in the book.	**Покажите мне, пожалуйста, ... в книге.**	pahkah**zhit**^{y}eh mn^{y}eh pah**zhahl**stah ... f **kneeg**^{y}eh
word	**слово**	**slov**vah
phrase	**фразу**	**frah**zoo
sentence	**предложение**	preedlah**zheh**nee^{y}eh
Just a moment.	**Сейчас./Минуточку.**	see**ch**^{y}**ahss**/mee**noo**tahch^{y}koo
I'll see if I can find it in this book.	**Я посмотрю, могу ли я найти это в книге.**	^{y}ah pahsmah**tr**^{y}**oo** mah**goo** lee ^{y}ah nigh**tee** **eh**tah f **kneeg**^{y}eh
I (don't) understand.	**Я (не) понимаю.**	^{y}ah (nee) pahnee**mah**^{y}oo
Do you understand?	**Вы понимаете?**	vi pahnee**mah**eet^{y}eh
Do you have a dictionary/phrase-book?	**У вас есть словарь/разговорник?**	oo vahss ^{y}ehst^{y} slah**vahr**^{y}/rahzgah**vor**neek

Can I/May I . . . ? *Можно . . . ?*

I can't.	**Я не могу.**	^{y}ah nee mah**goo**
Can you tell me . . . ?	**Скажите, пожалуйста . . .**	skah**zhit**^{y}eh pah**zhahl**stah
Can you help me?	**Помогите мне, пожалуйста.**	pahmah**geet**^{y}eh mn^{y}eh pah**zhahl**stah
Can I help you?	**Можно вам помочь?**	**mozh**nah vahm pah**moch**^{y}
Can you direct me to . . . ?	**Покажите мне дорогу к/до . . .**	pahkah**zhit**^{y}eh mn^{y}eh dah**rog**goo k/dah
You can't . . .	**Нельзя . . .**	neel^{y}**z^{y}ah**

Wanting . . . *Я хочу/Я хотел бы . . .*

I'd like . . .	**Я хотел(а)* бы . . .**	^{y}ah khah**t^{y}ehl**(ah) bi
We'd like . . .	**Мы хотели бы . . .**	mi khah**t^{y}eh**lee bi
What do you want?	**Что вы хотите?**	shto vi khah**teet**^{y}eh
Could you give me . . . ?	**Дайте мне . . .**	**dight**^{y}eh mn^{y}eh
Could you bring me . . . ?	**Принесите мне . . .**	preenee**sseet**^{y}eh mn^{y}eh
I'm looking for . . .	**Я ищу . . .**	^{y}ah ee**shch**^{y}**oo**
I'm hungry.	**Мне хочется есть.**	mn^{y}eh **khoch**^{y}eetsah ^{y}ehst^{y}
I'm thirsty.	**Мне хочется пить.**	mn^{y}eh **khoch**^{y}eetsah peet^{y}
I'm tired.	**Я устал (устала)*.**	^{y}ah oo**stahl** (oo**stah**lah)
I'm lost.	**Я заблудился (заблудилась)*.**	^{y}ah zahbloo**deel**sah (zahbloo**dee**lahs^{y})
It's important.	**Это важно.**	**eh**tah **vahzh**nah
It's urgent.	**Это срочно.**	**eh**tah **sroch**^{y}nah

It is/There is . . . *Это . . . /Есть . . .*

These expressions can not be directly translated into Russian, because the verb "to be" is not used in the present tense.

It is cold.	**Холодно.**	**khol**lahdnah
Is it cold?	**Холодно?**	**khol**lahdnah
It isn't cold.	**Не холодно.**	nee **khol**lahdnah

* Feminine form: a woman would say **я хотела бы** (^{y}ah khah**t^{y}eh**lah bi), etc.

Here it is.	**Вот.**	vot
Is there a telephone?	**Здесь есть телефон?**	zd^{y}ehs^y ^{y}ehst^y tee**lee**fon
There is a telephone.	**Здесь есть телефон.**	zd^{y}ehs^y ^{y}ehst^y tee**lee**fon
Are there any newspapers?	**У вас есть газеты?**	oo vahss ^{y}ehst^y gah**z^{y}eh**ti
There aren't any newspapers.	**Газет нет.**	gah**z^{y}eht** n^{y}eht

Quality *Качество*

big/small	**большой/маленький**	bahl^y**shoy**/**mah**leen^{y}keey
quick/slow	**быстро/медленно**	**bi**strah/**m^{y}eh**dleennah
hot/cold	**горячий/холодный**	gahr^y**ah**ch^{y}eey/khah**lod**niy
full/empty	**полный/пустой**	**pol**niy/poos**toy**
easy/difficult	**лёгкий/трудный**	**l^{y}ok**hkeey/**trood**niy
heavy/light	**тяжёлый/лёгкий**	tee**zho**lliy/**l^{y}okh**keey
open/shut	**открытый/закрытый**	aht**krit**tiy/zah**krit**tiy
right/wrong	**правильный/непра-вильный**	**prah**veel^{y}niy/nee**prah**-veel^{y}niy
old/new	**старый/новый**	**stah**riy/**nov**viy
old/young	**старый/молодой**	**stah**riy/mahlah**doy**
beautiful/ugly	**красивый/некрасивый**	krah**ssee**viy/neekrah**ssee**viy
free/occupied	**свободный/занятый**	svah**bod**niy/**zah**neetiy
good/bad	**хороший/плохой**	khah**ro**shiy/plah**khoy**
well/badly	**хорошо/плохо**	khahrah**sho**/**plo**khah
better/worse	**лучше/хуже**	**looch^y**sheh/**khoo**zheh
early/late	**рано/поздно**	**rah**nah/**poz**nah
cheap/expensive	**дешёвый/дорогой**	dee**shov**viy/dahrah**goy**
clean/dirty	**чистый/грязный**	**ch^{y}ee**stiy/**gr^{y}ah**zniy
near/far	**близко/далеко**	**blee**skah/dahlee**ko**
here/there	**здесь/там**	zd^{y}ehs^y/tahm

Quantity *Количество*

a little/a lot	**мало/много**	**mah**lah/**mno**ggah
few/a few	**мало/несколько**	**mah**lah/**n^{y}eh**skahl^{y}kah
much/many	**много**	**mno**ggah
more/less (than)	**больше/меньше (чем)**	**bol^y**sheh/**m^{y}ehn^y**sheh (ch^{y}ehm)
enough/too (much)	**достаточно/слишком**	dah**stah**tahch^{y}nah/**sleesh**kahm

ADJECTIVES, see page 159

Prepositions* *Предлоги*

after lunch	**после обеда** (G)	**pos**lee ahb^{y}**eh**dah
against war	**против войны** (G)	**prot**teef vigh**ni**
apart from that	**кроме этого** (G)	**krom**^{y}eh **eh**tahvah
at the entrance	**у входа** (G)	oo **fkhod**dah
at the hospital	**в больнице** (P)	v bahl^{y}**nee**tseh
behind the door	**за дверью** (I)	zah **dv^{y}ehr**^{y}oo
for you	**для вас** (G)	dl^{y}ah vahss
from us	**от нас** (G)	aht nahss
in the street	**на улице** (P)	nah **oo**leetseh
in the water	**в воде** (P)	v vah**d^{y}eh**
in front of the church	**перед церковью** (I)	**pee**reet tsehr**kov**^{y}oo
into the water	**в воду** (A)	v **vod**doo
next to the museum	**около музея** (G)	**ok**kahlah mooz^{y}**eh**^{y}ah
on the floor	**на полу** (P)	nah pah**loo**
since when?	**с каких пор?** (G)	s kah**keekh** por
through the forest	**через лес** (A)	**ch^{y}ee**reez l^{y}ehss
to the doctor	**к врачу** (D)	k vrah**ch^{y}oo**
towards the end	**к концу** (D)	k kahn**tsoo**
under the table	**под столом** (I)	paht stah**lom**
until the morning	**до утра** (G)	dah oo**trah**
with milk	**с молоком** (I)	s mahlah**kom**
without milk	**без молока** (G)	b^{y}ehz mahlah**kah**

Some more useful words *Другие полезные слова*

already	**уже**	oo**zheh**
always	**всегда**	fseeg**dah**
and	**и**	ee
but	**но**	noh
never	**никогда**	neekahg**dah**
nobody	**никто**	neek**to**
not	**не**	nee
nothing	**ничего**	neech^{y}ee**vo**
now	**сейчас**	seech^{y}**ahss**
only	**только**	**tol**^{y}kah
or	**или**	**ee**lee
perhaps	**может быть**	**mo**zheht bit^{y}
soon	**скоро**	**skor**rah
then	**тогда**	tahg**dah**
too (also)	**тоже**	**to**zheh
very	**очень**	**och**^{y}een^{y}
yet	**ещё**	eeshch^{y}**o**

* In Russian, all prepositions are governed by one or more cases. The above prepositions are followed by a noun in the appropriate case and a letter designating it. See also GRAMMAR section.

Arrival

Passport control *Паспортный контроль*

As well as a valid passport, you will also need a tourist visa for entering Russia. (Normally, your travel agent will get it for you.) If you want to take your car, you need additional papers: an international driving licence, car registration papers, a complete itinerary, etc.

Here's my ...	**Вот...**	vot
passport	**мой паспорт**	moy **pahs**pahrt
visa	**моя виза**	mah^y**ah vee**zah
driving licence	**мои водительские права**	mah**ee** vah**deet^y**ehl^{y}skee^{y}eh prah**vah**
I'll be staying ...	**Я пробуду здесь...**	^{y}ah prah**boo**doo zd^{y}ehs^y
a few days	**несколько дней**	n^y**ehs**kahl^{y}kah dn^{y}ay
a week	**неделю**	need^y**ehl**^{y}oo
2 weeks	**две недели**	dv^{y}eh need^y**eh**lee
a month	**месяц**	m^y**eh**sseets
I don't know yet.	**Я ещё не знаю.**	^{y}ah ee**shch^{y}o** nee **znah**^{y}oo
I'm here on holiday.	**Я здесь в отпуске.**	^{y}ah zd^{y}ehs^y v **ot**poosk^{y}eh
I'm here on business.	**Я здесь по делам.**	^{y}ah zd^{y}ehs^y pah dee**lahm**
I'm just passing through.	**Я только проездом.**	^{y}ah **tol^y**kah prah^y**ehz**dahm
I've come to do a Russian course.	**Я приехал(а) на курсы русского языка.**	^{y}ah pree^y**eh**khahl(ah) nah **koor**si **roos**kahvah eezik**kah**

ТАМОЖНЯ
CUSTOMS

If things get difficult:

I'm sorry, I don't understand.	**Простите, я не понимаю.**	prah**steet^y**eh ^{y}ah nee pahnee**mah**^{y}oo
Does anyone here speak English?	**Говорит здесь кто-нибудь по-английски?**	gahvah**reet** zd^{y}ehs^y **kto-**neebood^y pah ahn**gleey**skee

CAR, see page 75

You'll have to fill in a currency and customs declaration when entering and leaving Russia. The amount of foreign currency you can take in is not limited, but it's forbidden to import and export roubles. You may bring along all articles intended for your own use, but be sure to declare valuable possessions such as photographic equipment and jewellery. Photographs and printed matter which might be considered subversive (e.g. pornography) can be confiscated.

The chart below shows what you can bring in duty-free:

Cigarettes		Cigars		Tobacco	Liquor (spirits)		Wine
250	or	250	or	250 g.	1 l.	and	2 l.

I have a ...	**У меня...**	oo **meen^{y}ah**
carton of cigarettes	**блок сигарет**	blok seegahr^{y}**eht**
bottle of whisky	**бутылка виски**	boo**til**kah **vees**kee
bottle of wine	**бутылка вина**	boo**til**kah vee**nah**
100 dollars	**100 долларов**	100 **dol**lahrahf
50 pounds	**50 фунтов**	50 **foon**tahf
May I bring this in?	**Можно это провести?**	**mozh**nah **eh**tah prahvees**tee**
It's for my personal use.	**Это для личного пользования.**	**eh**tah dl^{y}ah **leech^{y}**nahvah **pol^{y}**zahvahnee^{y}ah
This is a gift.	**Это подарок.**	**eh**tah pah**dah**rahk
I'd like a declaration form in English.	**Будьте добры, бланк декларации по-английски.**	**boot^{y}**tee dah**bri** blahnk deeklah**rah**tsi^{y}ee pah ahn**gleey**skee

Ваш паспорт, пожалуйста.	Your passport, please.
Вы хотите что-нибудь объявить?	Do you have anything to declare?
Откройте (этот) чемодан.	Please open this suitcase.
Вы должны заплатить (за это) пошлину.	You'll have to pay duty (on this).
Есть у вас ещё багаж?	Do you have any more luggage?

Baggage—Porter *Багаж – Носильщик*

Porter!	**Носильщик!**	nah**sseel**^{y}shch^{y}eek
Please take this/ my ...	**Возьмите, пожалуйста...**	vahz^y**meet**^{y}eh pah**zhahl**stah
luggage	**багаж**	bah**gahsh**
suitcase	**чемодан**	ch^{y}eemah**dahn**
(travelling) bag	**сумку**	**soom**koo
That's mine.	**Это моё.**	**eh**tah mah^y**o**
Take these things to the ...	**Отнесите эти вещи к...**	ahtnee**sseet**^{y}eh **eh**tee **v^{y}eh**shch^{y}ee k
bus	**автобусу**	ahf**tob**boossoo
left-luggage office	**камере хранения**	**kah**meeree khrah**n^{y}eh**nee^{y}ah
taxi	**такси**	tahk**see**
How much is that?	**Сколько (это) стоит?**	**skol**^{y}kah (**eh**tah) **sto**eet
There's one piece missing.	**Одного места не хватает.**	ahdnah**vo m^{y}eh**stah nee khvah**tah**^{y}eht
Are there any luggage trolleys (carts)?	**Тележки есть?**	teel^y**ehsh**kee ^{y}ehst^y

Currency exchange *Обмен валюты*

You'll find exchange facilities at airports and hotels. Remember to carry your passport and currency declaration when changing money.

Any "informal" (black-market) currency transactions are illegal.

Where can I change some money?	**Где можно обменять валюту?**	gd^{y}eh **mozh**nah ahbmeen^y**aht**^{y} vahl^y**oo**too
Can you change these traveller's cheques (checks)?	**Можете вы обменять эти дорожные чеки?**	**mo**zhit^{y}eh vi ahbmeen^y**aht**^{y} **eh**tee dah**rozh**ni^{y}eh **ch^{y}eh**kee
I'd like to change some pounds/dollars.	**Я хотел(а) бы обменять фунты/доллары.**	^{y}ah khaht^y**ehl**(ah) bi ahbmeen^y**aht**^{y} **foon**ti/**dol**lahri
Can you change this into roubles?	**Можете вы обменять это на рубли?**	**mo**zhit^{y}eh vi ahbmeen^y**aht**^{y} **eh**tah nah roo**blee**
What's the exchange rate?	**Какой валютный курс?**	kah**koy** vahl^y**oot**niy koors

BANK—CURRENCY, see page 129

Where is ...? *Где...?*

Where's the Intourist office?	**Где бюро Интуриста?**	gd^{y}eh b^{y}ooro eentoo**rees**tah
Where is ...?	**Где...?**	gd^{y}eh
newsstand	**газетный киоск**	gah**z^{y}eht**niy kee**osk**
post office	**почта**	**poch^{y}**tah
railway station	**вокзал**	vahg**zahl**
restaurant	**ресторан**	reestah**rahn**
ticket office	**билетная касса**	bee**l^{y}eht**nah^{y}ah **kah**ssah
underground (subway)	**метро**	mee**tro**
How do I get to ...?	**Как мне добраться до...?**	kahk mn^{y}eh dah**braht^{y}**sah dah
Is there a bus into town?	**Идёт ли автобус в город?**	ee**d^{y}ot** lee ahf**to**bbooss f **go**rraht
Where can I catch a taxi?	**Где мне поймать такси?**	gd^{y}eh mn^{y}eh pigh**maht^{y}** tah**ksee**
Where can I hire (rent) a car?	**Где мне взять машину напрокат?**	gd^{y}eh mn^{y}eh vz^{y}aht^{y} mah**shi**nnoo nahprah**kaht**

Hotel reservation *Заказ номера в гостинице*

You will have made arrangements for a hotel room before coming to Russia. Travellers with Intourist will be met by a representative on passing through customs.

I need hotel accommodation ...	**Мне нужен номер в гостинице.**	mn^{y}eh **noo**zhin **no**mmeer v gah**stee**neetseh
in the centre	**в центре**	f **tsehn**tr^{y}eh
near the railway station	**около вокзала**	**o**kkahlah vahg**zah**lah
I need a ... room.	**Мне нужна комната...**	mn^{y}eh noozh**nah kom**nahtah
single	**на одного**	nah ahdnah**vo**
double	**на двоих**	nah dvah**eekh**
not too expensive	**не очень дорогая**	nee **o**ch^{y}een^{y} dahrah**gah^{y}**ah
Where is the ... hotel?	**Где гостиница...?**	gd^{y}eh gah**stee**neetsah
Do you have a street map/an underground (subway) map?	**У вас есть схема города/метро?**	oo vahss ^{y}ehst^{y} **skh^{y}eh**mah **go**rrahdah/mee**tro**

HOTEL—ACCOMMODATION, see page 22

Car hire (rental) *Прокат машин*

You can either make arrangements in advance or hire a car on the spot through Intourist at airports or in certain hotels. Charges must be paid in foreign currency or with an internationally recognized credit card. An international driving licence is required. The minimum age is 21.

I'd like to hire (rent) a car.	**Я хотел(а) бы взять напрокат машину.**	^{y}ah khaht^{y}**ehl**(ah) bi vz^{y}aht^{y} nahprah**kaht** mah**shi**nnoo
a small car	**маленькую машину**	**mah**leen^{y}koo^{y}oo mah**shi**nnoo
a large car	**большую машину**	bahl^{y}**shoo**^{y}oo mah**shi**nnoo
I need it for ...	**Она мне нужна на ...**	ah**nah** mn^{y}eh noozh**nah** nah
a day/four days	**день/четыре дня**	d^{y}ehn^{y}/ch^{y}ee**ti**rree dn^{y}ah
a week/two weeks	**неделю/две недели**	need^{y}**ehl**^{y}oo/dv^{y}eh need^{y}**ehlee**
What's the charge per day?	**Сколько это стоит в день?**	**skol**^{y}kah **eh**tah **sto**eet v d^{y}ehn^{y}
What's the charge per week?	**Сколько это стоит в неделю?**	**skol**^{y}kah **eh**tah **sto**eet v need^{y}**ehl**^{y}oo
Does that include mileage?	**Включён ли в эту цену километраж?**	fkl^{y}oo**ch^{y}on** lee v **eh**too **tseh**noo keelahmee**trahsh**
Is petrol (gasoline) included in the price?	**Включён ли в эту цену бензин?**	fkl^{y}oo**ch^{y}on** lee v **eh**too **tseh**noo been**zeen**
Where can I buy petrol vouchers?	**Где мне купить талоны на бензин?**	gd^{y}eh mn^{y}eh koo**peet**^{y} tah**lo**nni nah been**zeen**
What's the charge per kilometre?*	**Сколько стоит километр?**	**skol**^{y}kah **sto**eet keelah**m^{y}eh**tr
I'd like full insurance.	**Я хотел(а) бы полное страхование.**	^{y}ah khaht^{y}**ehl**(ah) bi **pol**nah^{y}eh strahkhah**vah**nee^{y}eh
I'd like to leave the car in ...	**Я хотел(а) бы возвратить машину в ...**	^{y}ah khaht^{y}**ehl**(ah) bi vahzvrah**teet**^{y} mah**shi**nnoo v
What's the deposit?	**Какой залог?**	kah**koy** zah**lok**
I have a credit card.	**У меня есть кредитная карточка.**	oo meen^{y}**ah** ^{y}ehst^{y} kree**deet**nah^{y}ah **kahr**tahch^{y}kah
Here's my driving licence.	**Вот мои права.**	vot mah**ee** prah**vah**

* 1 kilometre = 0.62 miles

CAR, see page 75

Taxi *Такси*

You can either hail a taxi on the street or get one at a taxi rank. If the green light on the windscreen is on, this indicates the taxi is free; however, the driver may not necessarily want to take you to your destination.

You can also hail a private car, but fix the price immediately.

Where can I find a taxi?	**Где можно найти такси?**	gd^{y}eh **mozh**nah nigh**tee** tahk**see**
Please get me a taxi.	**Я хочу вызвать такси.**	^{y}ah khahch^y**oo** **vizvaht**^{y} tahk**see**
What's the fare to ...?	**Сколько стоит доехать до ...?**	**skol^{y}kah** **stoeet** dah^y**ehkhaht**^{y} dah
How far is it to ...?	**Как далеко до ...?**	kahk dah**leeko** dah
Take me to ...	**Мне нужно ...**	mn^{y}eh **noozh**nah
this address	**по этому адресу**	pah **eh**tahmoo **ahd**reessoo
the airport	**в аэропорт**	v ighrah**port**
the town centre	**в центр города**	f tsehntr **gor**rahdah
the ... Hotel	**в гостиницу ...**	v gah**stee**neetsoo
the railway station	**на вокзал**	nah vahg**zahl**
I'm in a hurry.	**Я спешу.**	^{y}ah spee**shoo**
Turn left/right at the next corner.	**Поверните налево/направо за угол.**	pahveer**neet**^{y}eh nahl^y**eh**vah/ nah**prah**vah **zahoogahl**
Go straight ahead.	**Прямо.**	pr^y**ah**mah
Please stop here.	**Остановитесь здесь, пожалуйста.**	ahstahnah**vee**tees^y zd^{y}ehs^y pah**zhahl**stah
Could you drive more slowly, please?	**Если можно, не так быстро.**	^{y}**ehs**lee **mozh**nah nee tahk **bis**trah
Could you take my luggage, please?	**Возьмите, пожалуйста, мои чемоданы.**	vahz^y**meet**^{y}eh pah**zhahl**stah mah**ee** ch^{y}eemah**dah**ni
Could you wait for me?	**Подождите меня, пожалуйста.**	pahdahzh**deet**^{y}eh meen^y**ah** pah**zhahl**stah
I'll be back in 10 minutes.	**Я вернусь через 10 минут.**	^{y}ah veer**noos**^{y} **ch^{y}ee**rees 10 mee**noot**

OTHER MEANS OF TRANSPORT, see page 72

Hotel—Other accommodation

You must make hotel arrangements before leaving your own country. Russian visas are issued only after reservations have been confirmed.

The travel bureau Intourist no longer holds a monopoly on accommodation in Russia and in major cities an increasing number of new or newly-renovated hotels are now jointly run by Western companies. These de luxe or 1st class ventures offer a new, if pricey, degree of choice of accommodation to the independent or business traveller. If you are taking an Intourist package tour though, you can state your preference of hotel but the final arrangements rest with Intourist who will let you know the decisions on arrival at the airport.

Upon arrival at the hotel, check in at reception and hand over all your documents and vouchers. The desk clerk won't give you a key to your room but a hotel pass (*пропуск* – **pro**ppoosk) that gives your name, length of stay and room number. You have to present this to the doorman every time you enter the hotel and hand it to the "floor manager" (*дежурная* – dee**zhoor**nah^{y}ah), who not only keeps the keys but an eye on the guests, too. These mostly middle-aged women will also make tea, call a taxi for you or solve any other problem.

Intourist hotels have service bureaus (*бюро обслуживания* – b^{y}oo**ro** ahps**loo**zhivvahnee^{y}ah) manned by multilingual staff who provide information, arrange outings and excursions, make reservations and give general assistance.

Apart from in the big hotels, no other accommodation is available. Sputnik, the Russian youth travel association, organizes group tours for students with accommodation in youth hostels (*молодёжная турбаза* – mahlah**d^{y}ozh**nah^{y}ah toor**bah**zah). In addition, foreigners are now allowed to stay in the home of a Russian friend or contact, but a letter of invitation is first required to accompany their visa application.

Checking in—Reception *Регистрация*

My name is ...	**Моя фамилия ...**	mah^{y}**ah** fah**mee**lee^{y}ah
I have a reservation.	**Я заказал(а) заранее.**	^{y}ah zahkah**zahl**(ah) zah**rahn**^{y}eh
We've reserved two rooms.	**Мы заказали два номера.**	mi zahkah**zah**lee dvah **no**mmeerah
Here's the confirmation.	**Вот подтверждение.**	vot pahtveerzh**d**^{y}**eh**nee^{y}eh
Do you have any vacancies?	**У вас есть свободный номер?**	oo vahss ^{y}ehst^{y} svah**bod**niy **no**mmeer
I'd like a ... room ...	**Я хотел(а) бы номер ...**	^{y}ah khaht^{y}**ehl**(ah) bi **no**mmeer
single	**на одного**	nah ahdnah**vo**
double	**на двоих**	nah dvah**eekh**
with twin beds	**с двумя кроватями**	s dvoom^{y}**ah** krah**vaht**^{y}ahmee
with a double bed	**с двуспальной кроватью**	s dvoo**spahl**^{y}nigh krah**vaht**^{y}oo
with a bath	**с ванной**	s **vahn**nigh
with a shower	**с душем**	s **doo**shehm
with a balcony	**с балконом**	s bahl**kon**nahm
with a view	**с видом**	s **vee**dahm
We'd like a room ...	**Мы хотели бы номер ...**	mi khaht^{y}**eh**lee bi **no**mmeer
at the front	**с окнами на улицу**	s **ok**nahmee nah **oo**leetsoo
at the back	**с окнами во двор**	s **ok**nahmee vah dvor
with a view of the lake/ the mountains/ the sea	**с видом на озеро/ на горы/на море**	s **vee**dahm nah **o**zeerah/ nah **go**rri/nah **mor**^{y}eh
It must be quiet.	**Номер нужен тихий.**	**no**mmeer **noo**zhehn **tee**kheey
Is there ...?	**Есть ...?**	^{y}ehst^{y}
air conditioning	**кондиционер**	kahndeetsiahn^{y}**ehr**
heating	**отопление**	ahtah**pl**^{y}**eh**nee^{y}eh
a radio/television in the room	**радио/телевизор в номере**	**rah**deeo/teelee**vee**zahr v **no**mmeer^{y}eh
a laundry service	**прачечная**	**prah**ch^{y}eech^{y}nah^{y}ah
room service	**обслуживание в номере**	ahp**sloo**zhivvahnee^{y}eh v **no**mmeer^{y}eh
hot water	**горячая вода**	gahr^{y}**ah**ch^{y}ee^{y}ah vah**dah**
a private toilet	**туалет/уборная**	tooahl^{y}**eht**/oo**bor**nah^{y}ah

CHECKING OUT, see page 31

Could you put an extra bed/a cot in the room?	**Можно поставить ещё одну кровать/детскую кровать в номер?**	**mozh**nah pah**stah**veety ee-**shchyo** ahd**noo** krah**vahty**/ **dyehts**kooyoo krah**vahty** v **no**mmeer

How much? *Сколько?*

All accommodation must be paid for in advance. The price usually includes full board.

When checking out, you'll get a pass proving that you have paid your bill.

What's the price ...?	**Сколько стоит номер ...?**	**skoly**kah **sto**eet **no**mmeer
per night	**в сутки**	f **soot**kee
per week	**в неделю**	v nee**dyeh**lyoo
for bed and breakfast	**с завтраком**	z **zahf**trahkahm
excluding meals	**без питания**	byehs pee**tah**neeyah
for full board (A.P.)	**с полным содержанием**	s **pol**nim sahdeer**zhah**neeyehm
Is everything included?	**Всё включено?**	fsyo fklyoochyee**no**
Is there any reduction for children?	**Для детей нет скидки?**	dlyah dee**tyay** nyeht **skeet**kee
Do you charge for the baby?	**За ребёнка платить особо?**	zah ree**byon**kah plah**teety** ahs**so**bbah
That's too expensive.	**Это слишком дорого.**	**eh**tah **sleesh**kahm **do**rrahgah
Don't you have anything cheaper?	**Нет ли у вас чего-нибудь подешевле?**	nyeht lee oo vahss chyee**vo**-**nee**boody pahdee**sheh**vlyeh

How long? *Сколько времени?*

We'll be staying ...	**Мы пробудем здесь ...**	mi prah**boo**deem zdyehsy
overnight only	**только сутки**	**toly**kah **soot**kee
a few days	**несколько дней**	**nyehs**kahlykah dnyay
a week (at least)	**неделю (по крайней мере)**	nee**dyeh**lyoo (pah **krigh**neey **myeh**ree)
I don't know yet.	**Я ещё не знаю.**	yah ee**shchyo** nee **znah**yoo

NUMBERS, see page 147

Decision *Решение*

May I see the room?	**Можно посмотреть номер?**	**mozh**nah pahsmah**tr**^{y}**eht**^{y} **no**mmeer
That's fine. I'll take it.	**Хорошо. Это подойдёт.**	khahrah**sho. eh**tah pahdigh**d**^{y}**ot**
No. I don't like it.	**Нет, мне не нравится.**	n^{y}eht mn^{y}eh nee **nrah**veetsah
It's too ...	**Здесь слишком ...**	zd^{y}ehs^{y} **sleesh**kahm
cold/hot dark/narrow noisy	**холодно/жарко темно/тесно шумно**	**kho**llahdnah/**zhahr**kah teem**no**/**t**^{y}**ehs**nah **shoom**nah
I asked for a room with a bath.	**Я просил(а) номер с ванной.**	^{y}ah prah**sseel**(ah) **no**mmeer s **vahn**nigh
Do you have anything ...?	**Есть ли у вас что-нибудь ...?**	^{y}ehst^{y} lee oo vahss **shto**neebood^{y}
better bigger cheaper quieter	**получше побольше подешевле потише**	pah**looch**^{y}sheh pah**bol**^{y}sheh pahdee**shehv**l^{y}eh pah**tee**sheh
Do you have a room with a better view?	**Есть ли у вас номер с лучшим видом?**	^{y}ehst^{y} lee oo vahss **no**mmeer s **looch**^{y}shim **vee**dahm

Registration *Регистрация*

Upon arrival at a hotel you'll be asked to fill in a registration form (*анкета для приезжающих* – ahn**k**^{y}**eh**tah dl^{y}ah pree^{y}eez**zhah**^{y}ooshch^{y}eekh).

Фамилия/Имя	Name/First name
Город/Улица/Номер дома	Home town/Street/Number
Гражданство/Профессия	Nationality/Occupation
День/Место рождения	Date/Place of birth
Приехавший из .../ Следующий в ...	Coming from .../ Going to ...
Номер паспорта	Passport number
Место/Число	Place/Date
Подпись	Signature

What does this mean?	**Что это значит?**	shto **eh**tah **znah**ch^{y}eet

Ваш паспорт, пожалуйста.	May I see your passport?
Будьте добры заполнить анкету.	Would you mind filling in this registration form?
Подпишитесь тут, пожалуйста.	Sign here, please.
Как долго вы здесь пробудете?	How long will you be staying?

What's my room number?	**Какой мой номер?**	kah**koy** moy **no**mmeer
Will you have our luggage sent up?	**Отправьте, пожалуйста, наш багаж в номер.**	aht**prahf^y**t^{y}eh pah**zhahl**stah nahsh bah**gahsh** v **no**mmeer
Where can I park my car?	**Где можно поставить машину?**	gd^{y}eh **mozh**nah pah**stah**veet^y mah**shi**nnoo
Does the hotel have a garage?	**Есть ли гараж в гостинице?**	^{y}ehst^y lee gah**rahsh** v gah**stee**neetseh
Can we have breakfast in our room?	**Можно получить завтрак в номер?**	**mozh**nah pahloo**ch^{y}eet^y** **zahf**trahk v **no**mmeer
I'd like to leave this in your safe.	**Я хотел(а) бы оставить это у вас в сейфе.**	^{y}ah khaht**^{y}ehl**(ah) bi ah**stah**veet^y **eh**tah oo vahss f **sayf**^{y}eh

Hotel staff *Персонал гостиницы*

hall porter	**портье, швейцар**	pahrt**^{y}eh**, shvight**sahr**
maid	**горничная**	**gor**neech^{y}nah^{y}ah
manager	**директор**	deer**^{y}ehk**tahr
porter	**носильщик**	nah**sseel^y**shch^{y}eek
receptionist	**администратор**	ahdmeenee**strah**tahr
switchboard operator	**телефонистка**	teeleefah**neest**kah
waiter	**официант**	ahfeet**siahnt**
waitress	**официантка**	ahfeet**siahnt**kah

General requirements *Общие вопросы*

The key, please.	Ключ, пожалуйста.	kl^{y}ooch^y pah**zhahl**stah
Will you wake me at 7 o'clock, please?	Разбудите меня, пожалуйста, в семь часов утра.	rahzboo**deet**^{y}eh meen^y**ah** pah**zhahl**stah f s^{y}ehm ch^y**eessof** oo**trah**
Is there a bath on this floor?	Есть ли на этаже ванная?	^{y}ehst^y lee nah ehtah**zheh** **vahn**nah^{y}ah
What's the voltage here?	Какое здесь напряжение?	kah**ko**^{y}eh zd^{y}ehs^y nahpree**zheh**nee^{y}eh
Where's the shaver socket (outlet)?	Где розетка для бритвы?	gd^{y}eh rahz^y**eht**kah dl^{y}ah **breet**vi
Can you find me a ...?	Найдите мне, пожалуйста...	nigh**deet**^{y}eh mn^{y}eh pah**zhahl**stah
babysitter	приходящую няню	preekhah**d^{y}ah**shch^{y}oo^{y}oo n^y**ahn**^{y}oo
secretary	секретаршу	seekree**tahr**shoo
typewriter	(пишущую) машинку	(**pee**shooshch^{y}oo^{y}oo) mah**shin**koo
May I have a/an/ some ...?	Есть ли у вас...?	^{y}ehst^y lee oo vahss
ashtray	пепельница	**p^{y}eh**peel^{y}neetsah
bath towel	банное полотенце	**bahn**nah^{y}eh pahlaht^y**ehn**tseh
(extra) blanket	(ещё одно) одеяло	(eesh**ch^{y}o** ahd**no**) ahdee^y**ah**lah
envelopes	конверты	kahnv^y**eh**rti
hangers	вешалки	**v^{y}eh**shahlkee
hot-water bottle	грелка	**gr^{y}ehl**kah
extra pillow	ещё одна подушка	eesh**ch^{y}o** ahd**nah** pah**doosh**kah
needle and thread	иголка с ниткой	ee**gol**kah s **neet**kigh
reading lamp	настольная лампа	nah**stol^y**nah^{y}ah **lahm**pah
soap	мыло	**mi**llah
writing paper	бумага для писем	boo**mah**gah dl^{y}ah **pee**sseem
Where's the ...?	Где...?	gd^{y}eh
dining room	столовая	stah**lov**vah^{y}ah
emergency exit	запасной выход	zahpahs**noy** **vi**khaht
hairdresser's	парикмахерская	pahreek**mah**kheerskah^{y}ah
lift (elevator)	лифт	leeft
service bureau	бюро обслуживания	b^{y}ooro ahp**sloo**zhivvahnee^{y}ah
Where are the toilets?	Где уборная?	gd^{y}eh oo**bor**nah^{y}ah

TELLING THE TIME, see page 153

Telephone – Post (Mail) *Телефон – Почта*

Can you get me Moscow 123-45-67?	**Соедините меня, пожалуйста, с Москвой, номер 123-45-67.**	sighdeeneet^{y}eh meen^{y}ah pahzhahlstah s mahskvoy nommeer 123-45-67
Do you have any stamps?	**Есть ли у вас (почтовые) марки?**	^{y}ehst^{y} lee oo vahss (pahch^{y}tovvi^{y}eh) mahrkee
Would you post this for me, please?	**Отправьте, пожалуйста.**	ahtprahf^{y}t^{y}eh pahzhahlstah
Are there any letters for me?	**Для меня писем нет?**	dl^{y}ah meen^{y}ah peesseem n^{y}eht
Are there any messages for me?	**Есть ли что-нибудь для меня?**	^{y}ehst^{y} lee shtoneebood^{y} dl^{y}ah meen^{y}ah
How much is my telephone bill?	**Сколько я должен за телефон?**	skol^{y}kah ^{y}ah dolzhin zah teeleefon

Difficulties *Трудности*

The ... doesn't work.	**...не действует/ не работает.**	... nee d^{y}aystvooeet/ nee rahbottaheet
air conditioning	**кондиционер**	kahndeetsiahn^{y}ehr
fan	**вентилятор**	veenteel^{y}ahtahr
heating	**отопление**	ahtahpl^{y}ehnee^{y}eh
radio	**радио**	rahdeeo
television	**телевизор**	teeleeveezahr
There is no light.	**Нет света.**	n^{y}eht sv^{y}ehtah
The tap (faucet) is dripping.	**Кран течёт.**	krahn teech^{y}ot
There's no hot water.	**Нет горячей воды.**	n^{y}eht gahr^{y}ahch^{y}ay vahdi
The washbasin is blocked.	**Раковина засорена.**	rahkahveenah zahssahreenah
The window/door is jammed.	**Окно/дверь не закрывается.**	ahkno/dv^{y}ehr^{y} nee zahkrivvaheetsah
The curtains are stuck.	**Занавесы не ходят.**	zahnahv^{y}ehsi nee khoddeet
The bulb is burned out.	**Лампочка перегорела.**	lahmpahch^{y}kah peereegahr^{y}ehlah

POST OFFICE AND TELEPHONE, see page 132

My room hasn't been cleaned.	**Моя комната не убрана.**	mah^y**ah kom**nahtah nee oobrahnah
The plug/switch is broken.	**Штепсель/Выключатель сломан.**	**sht^{y}ehps^{y}ehl^y/vikl^{y}oo-ch^{y}aht^{y}ehl^y slommahn**
Can you get it repaired?	**Можно починить это?**	**mozhnah pahch^{y}eeneet^y ehtah**

Laundry—Dry cleaner's *Прачечная—Химчистка*

I want these clothes ...	**Эти вещи надо ...**	**ehtee v^{y}ehshch^{y}ee nahdah**
cleaned	**почистить**	pahch^y**eesteet^y**
ironed	**погладить**	pah**glahdeet^y**
pressed	**отутюжить**	ahtoot^y**oozhit^y**
washed	**выстирать**	**visteeraht^y**
When will they be ready?	**Когда будет готово?**	kahg**dah boo**deet gah**tovvah**
I need them ...	**Мне нужно ...**	mn^{y}eh **noozh**nah
today	**сегодня**	seevodn^{y}ah
tonight	**сегодня вечером**	seevodn^{y}ah v^{y}ehch^{y}eerahm
tomorrow	**завтра**	**zahf**trah
before Friday	**до пятницы**	dah p^y**aht**neetsi
Can you ... this?	**Можно ли это ...?**	**mozh**nah lee **eh**tah
mend	**заштопать**	zah**shtoppaht^y**
patch	**залатать**	zahlah**taht^y**
stitch	**зашить**	zah**shit^y**
Can you sew on this button?	**Пришейте, пожалуйста, пуговицу.**	**preeshayt^{y}eh pahzhahlstah poogahveetsoo**
Can you get this stain out?	**Можно вывести это пятно?**	**mozhnah vivveestee ehtah peetno**
Is my laundry ready?	**Моё бельё готово?**	mah^{y}o beel^{y}o gahtovvah
This isn't mine.	**Это не моё.**	**eh**tah nee mah^{y}o
There's something missing.	**Чего-то не хватает.**	ch^{y}ee**vo**ttah nee khvah**tah**eet
There's a hole in this.	**Тут дырка.**	toot **dir**kah

Hairdresser—Barber *Парикмахерская*

Is there a hairdresser/ beauty salon in the hotel?	**Есть ли парикмахерская/косметический кабинет в гостинице?**	^{y}ehst^y lee pahreek**mah**kheerskah^{y}ah/kahsm^{y}eh**teech**^{y}eeskeey kahbee**n^{y}eht** v gah**stee**neetseh
Can I make an appointment for Thursday?	**Можно записаться на четверг?**	**mozh**nah zahpee**saht^y**sah nah ch^{y}eet**v^{y}ehrk**
I'd like a haircut, please.	**Я хочу постричься.**	^{y}ah khah**ch^{y}oo** pah**streech^y**sah
bleach	**обесцвечивание**	ahb^{y}ehs**tsv^{y}eh**ch^{y}eevahnee^{y}eh
blow-dry	**сушить феном**	soo**shit^y f^{y}eh**nahm
colour rinse	**оттеночное полоскание**	ahtt**^{y}eh**nahch^{y}nah^{y}eh pahlah**skah**nee^{y}eh
dye	**окраска**	ah**krah**skah
face pack	**косметическая маска**	kahsm^{y}eh**teech**^{y}eeskah^{y}ah **mah**skah
haircut	**стрижка**	**streesh**kah
hairstyle	**причёска**	preech**^{y}o**skah
manicure	**маникюр**	mahneek**^{y}oor**
parting (part)	**пробор**	prah**bor**
permanent wave	**перманент**	p^{y}ehrmah**n^{y}ehnt**
setting lotion	**фиксатор (для волос)**	feek**sah**tahr (dl^{y}ah vah**loss**)
shampoo and set	**мытье головы с укладкой**	**mit**^{y}eh gahlah**vi** s oo**klaht**kigh
with a fringe (bangs)	**с чёлкой**	s **ch^{y}ol**kigh
I'd like a shampoo for ... hair.	**Я хотел(а) бы шампунь для ... волос.**	^{y}ah khah**t^{y}ehl**(ah) bi shahm**poon^y** dl^{y}ah ... vah**loss**
normal/dry/ greasy (oily)	**нормальных/сухих/ жирных**	nahr**mahl^y**nikh/soo**kheekh**/ **zhir**nikh
Do you have a colour chart?	**Есть ли у вас таблица цветов?**	^{y}ehst^y lee oo vahss tah**blee**tsah tsvee**tof**
Don't cut it too short.	**Не очень коротко.**	nee **och^y**een^y **ko**rrahtkah
A little more off the ...	**Чуть побольше ...**	ch^{y}oot^y pah**bol^y**sheh
back	**на затылке**	nah zah**tilk**^{y}eh
neck	**на шее**	nah **sheh**^{y}eh
sides	**по бокам**	pah bah**kahm**
top	**сверху**	**sv^{y}ehr**khoo
I don't want any hairspray.	**Лака не нужно.**	**lah**kah nee **noozh**nah

DAYS OF THE WEEK, see page 151

I'd like a shave.	**Я хочу побриться.**	yah khah**chyoo** pah**breetysah**
Would you trim my . . ., please?	**Подправьте, пожалуйста, . . .**	paht**prahvytyeh** pah**zhahl**stah
beard	**бороду**	**bor**rahdoo
moustache	**усы**	oo**ssi**
sideboards (sideburns)	**бакенбарды**	bahkyehn**bahr**di

Checking out *Отъезд*

Please have my bill ready.	**Приготовьте мне счёт, пожалуйста.**	preegah**tovytyeh** mnyeh shchyot pah**zhahl**stah
I'm leaving early in the morning.	**Я уезжаю рано утром.**	yah ooyeez**zhahyoo** **rah**nah **oo**trahm
We'll be checking out around noon.	**Мы уезжаем около двенадцати.**	mi ooyeez**zhahyehm** **ok**kahlah dvee**naht**sahtee
I must leave at once.	**Я должен (должна) немедленно уехать.**	yah **dol**zhehn (dahlzh**nah**) neem**yehd**leennah oo**yeh**khahty
Is everything included?	**Всё включено?**	fsyo fklyoochyee**no**
Can I pay by credit card?	**Можно платить кредитной карточкой?**	**mozh**nah plah**teety** kree**deet**nigh **kahr**tahchykigh
I think there's a mistake.	**Вы не ошиблись?**	vi nee ah**shib**leesy
Can you get us a taxi?	**Закажите для нас такси, пожалуйста.**	zahkah**zhityeh** dlyah nahss tahk**see** pah**zhahl**stah
Would you send someone to bring down our luggage?	**Пришлите, пожалуйста, кого-нибудь вынести наш багаж.**	pree**shleetyeh** pah**zhahl**stah kah**vo**nneeboody **vin**neestee nahsh bah**gahsh**
Here's the forwarding address.	**Вот следующий адрес.**	vot **slyeh**dooyooshchyeey **ah**dreess
You have my home address.	**У вас есть мой домашний адрес.**	oo vahss yehsty moy dah**mahsh**neey **ah**dreess
It's been a very enjoyable stay.	**Всё было очень хорошо.**	fsyo **bil**lah **ochyeeny** khahrah**sho**

Camping *Кемпинг*

During the brief summer season – June to August and, in some areas, part of September – authorized camp sites are operated near many cities. Campers may park a car and pitch a tent for a fixed rate that includes amenities, from showers to cooking facilities, plus a guided tour of nearby attractions. Arrangements must be made in advance through travel agents outside Russia.

Is there a camp site near here?	**Есть ли здесь недалеко кемпинг?**	^{y}ehst^y lee zd^{y}ehs^y needahlee**ko** **kehm**peeng
Can we camp here?	**Можно здесь устроить стоянку?**	**mozh**nah zd^{y}ehs^y oos**tro**eet^y stah^y**ahn**koo
Do you have room for a tent/caravan (trailer)?	**Есть ли место для палатки/каравана?**	^{y}ehst^y lee **m^{y}ehs**tah dl^{y}ah pah**laht**kee/kahrah**vah**nah
What's the charge ...?	**Сколько стоит ...?**	**skol^y**kah **sto**eet
per day	**на день**	nah d^{y}ehn^y
per person	**на человека**	nah ch^{y}eelahv^y**eh**kah
for a car	**на машину**	nah mah**shi**nnoo
for a tent	**на палатку**	nah pah**laht**koo
for a caravan (trailer)	**на караван**	nah kahrah**vahn**
What are the facilities?	**Какие здесь удобства?**	kah**kee^y**eh zd^{y}ehs^y oo**dopst**vah
Is there ...?	**Есть ли ...?**	^{y}ehst^y lee
drinking water	**питьевая вода**	peetee**vah^y**ah vah**dah**
electricity	**электричество**	ehleek**treech^y**ehstvah
playground	**площадка для игр**	plah**shch^{y}aht**kah dl^{y}ah eegr
restaurant	**ресторан**	reestah**rahn**
shop	**магазин**	mahgah**zeen**
swimming pool	**бассейн**	bah**ss^{y}ayn**
Where are the showers/toilets?	**Где душ/уборная?**	gd^{y}eh **doosh**/oo**bor**nah^{y}ah
Where can I get butane gas?	**Где мне достать газ в баллонах?**	gd^{y}eh mn^{y}eh dahs**taht^y** gahs v bah**lon**nahkh
May we light a fire?	**Можно разжечь костёр?**	**mozh**nah rahz**zhehch^y** kahst^y**or**
May we use the electric stove?	**Можно пользоваться электроплиткой?**	**mozh**nah **pol^y**zahvaht^{y}sah ehl^{y}ehktrah**pleet**kigh

CAMPING EQUIPMENT, see page 106

Eating out

Бар (bahr)
Bar, usually found in hotels (you'll have to pay in foreign currency).

Блинная (**bleen**nah^{Y}ah)
Serves *блины* (blee**ni**), Russian pancakes, with various toppings, sweet and savoury.

Буфет (boof^{Y}**eht**)
Snack bar, in hotels, theatres, at the station, etc., good for light meals. You can buy food and drink by the gram or litre and eat it at one of the nearby tables (or take it with you).

Закусочная (zah**koo**ssahch^{Y}nah^{Y}ah)
Kind of snack bar.

Кафе (kah**feh**)
Despite its name, a Russian "café" is the equivalent of a Western restaurant. Many close by 9 p.m., 11 p.m. at the latest.

Кафе-кондитерская (kah**feh**-kahn**deet**^{Y}ehr-skah^{Y}ah)
Also called simply *Кондитерская*; serves coffee and cakes.

Кафе-мороженое (kah**feh**-mah**ro**zheh-nah^{Y}eh)
Ice-cream parlour serving ice cream, drinks and cocktails.

Кафетерий (kahfeet^{Y}**eh**reey)
Cafeteria; usually no seats. Small dishes, snacks and salads.

Кооперативное кафе (kahp^{Y}ehra**teev**nah^{Y}eh kah**feh**)
Privately-run restaurant.

Пельменная (peel^{Y}**m**^{Y}**ehn**nah^{Y}ah)
Small restaurants serving mainly *пельмени* (peel^{Y}**m**^{Y}**eh**nee, a kind of meat dumpling).

Пивной бар (peev**noy** bahr)
Serves beer and appetizers, always crowded.

Пирожковая (peerahsh**kov**vah^{Y}ah)
Snack bar selling only *пирожки* (peerahsh**kee**) savoury pastries with various fillings (meat, cabbage, rice, jam, etc.).

Ресторан (reestah**rahn**)	Restaurant; in most cases it is a place where you go not just for a meal but for a whole evening's entertainment, with music and dancing. It is advisable to reserve a table in advance (by telephone). If you have the chance, don't restrict yourself to Russian food, but try restaurants where they serve Georgian, Armenian, Azerbaijani or Uzbek specialities. All restaurants close by midnight. Many restaurants close at 5 p.m. to re-open at 7 p.m.
Столовая (stah**lov**vah^{y}ah)	Cafeteria or canteen (public establishment); self-service, low prices, no alcohol.
Чайная (**ch^{y}igh**nah^{y}ah)	tearoom or small café
Шашлычная (shahsh**lich^y**nah^{y}ah)	Serves *шашлык* (shahsh**lik**), pieces of lamb grilled on skewers, as well as other typical dishes from the Caucasus and Central Asia.

Meal times

Breakfast (*завтрак* —**zahf**trahk): from 7 a.m. to 10 a.m.

Lunch (*обед* —ah**b^{y}eht**): from about 11 a.m. to 4 p.m.

Dinner (*ужин*—**oo**zhin): from about 6 p.m. to 10 or 10.30 p.m. As restaurants close at 11 p.m. (midnight at the latest), Russians usually arrive early.

Eating habits

Dinner is traditionally the main meal of the day, consisting of several courses. Eating plays an important part in Russian social life and it is at table that you'll find Russians at their most hospitable. Over a good meal with a little vodka to raise the spirits, you'll see Russian character and philosophy blossom. Don't forget to wish your friends a hearty appetite— *"Приятного аппетита!"* (pree^y**aht**nahvah ahpee**tee**tah).

Russian cuisine *Русская кухня*

An old Russian proverb says: *Щи да каша — пища наша* ("our food is *shch^{y}ee* and *kahshah*"); but there is more to Russian cuisine than just cabbage soup and cereals. The country's geographical, climatic and ethnic variety is reflected in a rich and varied cuisine. Here are some typical dishes: As a starter, try caviar (served with bread and butter), smoked and salted fish or meat, a salad or *bleeni.* Typical Russian soups are *borshch^y* and *shch^{y}ee,* or—in summer—*ahkroshkah* (served chilled). Fish dishes are usually prepared with sturgeon, sterlet, pike-perch or salmon. Poultry dishes like *Chicken Kiev* or *Chicken tabaka* (originally Georgian) are popular. A Caucasian speciality made with lamb is *shashlik*.

Many excellent dairy products are used in Russian cuisine, especially *smeetahnah,* sour cream, which is used both in soups and sauces, as well as desserts (or as a topping for *bleeni*). You'll find desserts and pastries galore, as well as excellent ice cream.

As for drinks, the most famous are probably vodka and tea. Also very popular is *kvahss,* a drink fermented from black bread.

Слушаю вас.	Yes, please?
Вы уже выбрали?	Have you made your choice?
Советую взять…	I recommend …
Что будете пить?	What would you like to drink?
У нас нет…	We don't have …

Are you hungry? *Вы хотите есть?*

I'm hungry/I'm thirsty.	**Я хочу есть/ Я хочу пить.**	^{y}ah khah**ch^{y}oo** ^{y}ehst^y/ ^{y}ah khah**ch^{y}oo** peet^y
Is there a good restaurant around here?	**Есть ли поблизости хороший ресторан?**	^{y}ehst^y lee pah**blee**zahstee khah**ro**shiy reestah**rahn**

Can you recommend a good restaurant?	**Можете ли вы посоветовать хороший ресторан?**	**mo**zhit^{y}eh lee vi pahsah**v^{y}eh**tahvaht^y khah**ro**shiy reestah**rahn**
I'd like to reserve a table for 4.	**Я хотел(а) бы заказать столик на четверых.**	^{y}ah khaht**^{y}ehl**(ah) bi zahkah**zaht^y sto**leek nah ch^{y}eet-vee**rikh**
We'll come at 8.	**Мы будем в восемь.**	mi **boo**deem v **vo**sseem^y
Is this table free?	**Этот столик свободен?**	**eh**taht **sto**leek svah**bo**ddeen
Could we have a table ...?	**Дайте нам, пожалуйста, столик...**	**dight**^{y}eh nahm pah**zhahl**stah **sto**leek
in the corner	**в углу**	v oog**loo**
by the window	**у окна**	oo ahk**nah**
outside	**снаружи**	snah**roo**zhi
on the terrace	**на террасе**	nah teer**rah**s^{y}eh

At the restaurant *В ресторане*

Waiter/Waitress!	**Официант/Девушка!**	ahfeet**siahnt/d^{y}eh**vooshkah
I'd like something to eat/drink.	**Я хотел(а) бы съесть/выпить что-нибудь.**	^{y}ah khaht**^{y}ehl**(ah) bi s^{y}ehst^y/**vi**ppeet^y **shto**-neebood^y
May I have the menu, please?	**Принесите, пожалуйста, меню.**	preenee**sseet**^{y}eh pah**zhahl**stah meen**^{y}oo**
Do you have local dishes?	**У вас есть национальные блюда?**	oo vahss ^{y}ehst^y nahtsiah**nahl**^{y}ni^{y}eh **bl^{y}oo**dah
What do you recommend ...?	**Что вы посоветуете...?**	shto vi pahsah**v^{y}eh**tooeet^{y}eh
I'll have ...	**Я возьму...**	^{y}ah vahz^y**moo**
as a starter	**на закуску**	nah zah**koos**koo
as a first course	**на первое**	nah **p^{y}ehr**vah^{y}eh
as a second course	**на второе**	nah ftah**ro**^{y}eh
for dessert	**на десерт**	nah dees**^{y}ehrt**
Could you bring us ..., please?	**Принесите нам, пожалуйста...**	preenee**sseet**^{y}eh nahm pah**zhahl**stah
ashtray	**пепельницу**	**p^{y}eh**peel^{y}neetsoo
cup	**чашку**	**ch^{y}ahsh**koo
fork	**вилку**	**veel**koo
glass	**стакан**	stah**kahn**
knife	**нож**	nosh
napkin (serviette)	**салфетку**	sahlf**^{y}eht**koo

plate	**тарелку**	tahr^y**ehl**koo
spoon	**ложку**	**losh**koo
bread	**хлеб**	khl^{y}ehp
butter	**масло**	**mahs**lah
lemon	**лимон**	lee**mon**
mustard	**горчицу**	gahr**ch^{y}ee**tsoo
oil	**(растительное) масло**	(rahs**tee**teel^{y}nah^{y}eh) **mahs**lah
pepper	**перец**	**p^{y}eh**reets
salt	**соль**	sol^y
sugar	**сахар**	**sah**khahr
vinegar	**уксус**	**ook**soos
Do you have vegetarian dishes?	**У вас есть вегетарианские блюда?**	oo vahss ^{y}ehst^y veegeetahree**ahn**skee^{y}eh **bl^{y}oo**dah
Do you have a children's menu?	**Есть ли у вас детское меню?**	^{y}ehst^y lee oo vahss **d^{y}ehts**kah^{y}eh meen**^{y}oo**
Can I have some more ...?	**Принесите ещё немного...**	preenee**sseet**^{y}eh ee**shch^{y}o** neem**no**ggah
Just a small portion.	**Только маленькую порцию.**	**tol^y**kah **mah**leen^{y}koo^{y}oo **por**tsi^{y}oo
Nothing more, thanks.	**Больше ничего, спасибо.**	**bol^y**sheh neech^{y}ee**vo** spahs**see**bah

Diet *Диета*

You'll find dietetic meals at "dietetic canteens", *диетическая столовая* (dee^{y}eh**tee**ch^{y}eeskah^{y}ah stah**lo**vvah^{y}ah).

I'm on a special diet.	**Я на особой диете.**	^{y}ah nah ahs**so**bigh dee**^{y}eh**t^{y}eh
I mustn't eat food containing ...	**Мне нельзя есть блюда, содержащие...**	mn^{y}eh neel^y**z^{y}ah** ^{y}ehst^y **bl^{y}oo**dah sahdeer**zhah**shch^{y}ee^{y}eh
alcohol	**алкоголь**	ahlkah**gol^y**
fat/flour	**жир/муку**	zhirr/**moo**koo
salt/sugar	**соль/сахар**	sol^y/**sah**khahr
Do you have ... for diabetics?	**Есть ли у вас... для диабетиков?**	^{y}ehst^y lee oo vahss ... dl^{y}ah deeah**b^{y}eh**teekahf
dessert	**десерт/сладкие блюда**	dees**^{y}ehrt**/**slaht**kee^{y}eh **bl^{y}oo**dah
fruit juice	**фруктовый сок**	frook**to**vviy sok
special menu	**особое меню**	ahs**so**bah^{y}eh meen**^{y}oo**
Can I have an artificial sweetener?	**Принесите, пожалуйста, сахарин.**	preenee**sseet**^{y}eh pah**zhahl**stah sahkhah**reen**

Breakfast *Завтрак*

A Russian breakfast can be quite hearty. You can either have tea or coffee with bread, butter and jam, or—if your appetite allows—try ham, eggs, cheese, hot cereals and sausages.

When is breakfast served?	**Во сколько завтрак?**	vah **skol^{y}**kah **zahf**trahk
I'd like to have breakfast.	**Я хотел(а) бы позавтракать.**	^{y}ah khaht^{y}**ehl**(ah) bi pahz**ahf**trahkaht^{y}
I'll have ...	**Принесите мне ...**	preenee**sseet**^{y}eh mn^{y}eh
cocoa	**какао**	kah**kaho**
coffee	**кофе**	**ko**fee
black	**чёрный**	**ch^{y}or**niy
with milk	**с молоком**	s mahlah**kom**
big/small	**большой/маленький**	bahl^{y}**shoy/mah**leen^{y}keey
fruit juice	**сок**	sok
milk	**молоко**	mahlah**ko**
hot/cold	**горячее/холодное**	gahr^{y}**ah**ch^{y}ee^{y}eh/khah**lod**nah^{y}eh
tea	**чай**	ch^{y}igh
with lemon	**с лимоном**	s lee**mon**nahm
with milk	**с молоком**	s mahlah**kom**
May I have some ...?	**Дайте мне ...**	**dight**^{y}eh mn^{y}eh
bread	**хлеб**	khl^{y}ehp
black	**чёрный**	**ch^{y}or**niy
white	**белый**	**b^{y}eh**liy
butter	**масло**	**mahs**lah
cheese	**сыр**	sirr
eggs	**яйца**	^{y}**igh**tsah
boiled egg	**варёное яйцо**	vahr^{y}**o**nah^{y}eh ^{y}ee**ytso**
fried	**яичницу**	^{y}ee**eesh**neetsoo
scrambled	**яичницу-болтунью**	^{y}ee**eesh**neetsoo-bahl**toon**^{y}oo
ham and eggs	**яичницу с ветчиной**	^{y}ee**eesh**neetsoo s veetch^{y}ee**noy**
honey	**мёд**	m^{y}ot
hot cereal	**кашу**	**kah**shoo
jam	**джем, варенье**	dzhehm, vahr^{y}**ehn**^{y}eh
marmalade	**варенье**	vahr^{y}**ehn**^{y}eh
roll	**булочку**	**boo**lahch^{y}koo
salt/pepper	**соль/перец**	sol^{y}/p^{y}ehreets
sausages	**сосиски**	sah**sees**kee
sugar	**сахар**	**sah**khahr

What's on the menu? *Что в меню?*

Restaurants in Russia don't usually display the menu outside. It is probably best to ask the waiter's advice.

Under the headings below you'll find alphabetical lists of dishes that might be offered on a Russian menu, with their English equivalents. You can simply show the book to the waiter. If you want some fruit, for instance, let *him* point to what's available on the appropriate list. Use pages 36 and 37 for ordering in general.

	page	
Starters (Appetizers)	41	**Закуски**
Pancakes	42	**Блины**
Salads	42	**Салаты**
Cheese and dairy products	43	**Сыр и молочные продукты**
Soups	44	**Супы**
Fish and seafood	45	**Рыба и дары моря**
Meat	47	**Мясо**
Game and poultry	49	**Дичь и птица**
Vegetables	50	**Овощи**
Cereals, rice, potatoes	51	**Каша, рис, картофель**
Fruit	52	**Фрукты**
Dessert	53	**Десерт/Сладкие блюда**
Drinks	55	**Напитки**
Wine	55	**Вино**
Beer	56	**Пиво**
Vodka	57	**Водка**
Other alcoholic drinks	58	**Другие спиртные напитки**
Tea	59	**Чай**
Kvass	59	**Квас**
Coffee	54	**Кофе**
Other beverages	60	**Другие напитки**
Snacks—Picnic	62	**Лёгкая еда – Пикник**

The menu *Меню*

Гарнир	Side dish
На заказ	Made to order
Национальные блюда	Local dishes
Шеф-повар рекомендует . . .	The chef recommends . . .

блюда из яиц	**bl^{y}oo**dah eez ^{y}ee**eets**	egg dishes
вино	vee**no**	wine
дары моря	**dah**ri mor^{y}ah	seafood
десерт	dees^{y}**ehrt**	dessert
дичь	deech^{y}	game
закуски	zah**koos**kee	starters, snacks, savouries
холодные	khah**lod**ni^{y}eh	cold
горячие	gahr^{y}**ah**ch^{y}ee^{y}eh	hot
картофель	kahr**to**feel^{y}	potatoes
кофе	**ko**fee	coffee
лапша	lahp**shah**	pasta
макароны	mahkah**ro**nni	pasta
молочные блюда	mah**loch^{y}**ni^{y}eh **bl^{y}oo**dah	dairy products
мясо	**m^{y}ah**ssah	meat
напитки	nah**peet**kee	drinks
овощи	**o**vvahshch^{y}ee	vegetables
пиво	**pee**vah	beer
птица	p**tee**tsah	poultry
рис	reess	rice
рыба	**ri**bbah	fish
салаты	sah**lah**ti	salads
сладкие блюда	**slaht**kee^{y}eh **bl^{y}oo**dah	dessert
соки и воды	**so**kkee ee vah**di**	soft drinks
соусы	**so**oossi	sauces
супы	**soo**pi	soups
сыр	sirr	cheese
фрукты	**frook**ti	fruit
чай	ch^{y}igh	tea
шампанское	shahm**pahns**kah^{y}eh	champagne (sparkling wine)

Starters (Appetizers) *Закуски*

These are often divided into "cold" and "hot". When ordering a starter, just say "*На закуску...*" (nah zah**koo**skoo) and the name of the dish you have chosen.

What do you recommend?	**Что вы мне посоветуете взять?**	shto vi mn^{y}eh pahsah**v^{y}eh**tooeet^{y}eh vz^{y}aht^{y}

The most famous of Russian appetizers is certainly caviar, *икра* (ee**krah**). When available, it's generally served with white bread, butter and a slice of lemon. Black caviar comes from sturgeon, red (the cheaper sort) from salmon.

ассорти мясное	ahsahr**tee** meesno^{y}eh	assorted meats
ассорти рыбное	ahsahr**tee** **rib**nah^{y}eh	assorted fish
буженина с гарниром	boozheh**nee**nah z gahr**nee**rahm	cold boiled pork with vegetables
ветчина	veetch^{y}ee**nah**	ham
гренки	green**kee**	toast
грибы	gree**bi**	mushrooms
маринованные	mahree**nov**vahnni^{y}eh	pickled
солёные	sahl^{y}oni^{y}eh	salted
в сметане	f smee**tah**nee	with sour cream
жульен грибной	zhool^{y}**ehn** greeb**noy**	sliced mushrooms, fried with onions and sour cream
жульен куриный	zhool^{y}**ehn** koo**ree**niy	sliced chicken, fried and served with sour cream
заливное из мяса	zahleev**no**^{y}eh eez **m^{y}ah**ssah	meat in aspic
заливное из рыбы	zahleev**no**^{y}eh eez **rib**bi	fish in aspic
икра	ee**krah**	caviar
зернистая	zeer**nees**tah^{y}ah	fresh black
кетовая	**k^{y}eh**tahvah^{y}ah	red
паюсная	**pah**^{y}oosnah^{y}ah	pressed black
кильки	**keel**^{y}kee	spiced sprats
колбаса	kahlbah**ssah**	sausage (mortadella)
копчёная колбаса	kahp**ch^{y}o**nah^{y}ah kahlbah**ssah**	salami
креветки	kreev^{y}**eht**kee	prawns (shrimp)
маслины	mahs**lee**ni	olives
осетрина	ahssee**tree**nah	sturgeon
заливная	zahleev**nah**^{y}ah	in aspic
с гарниром	z gahr**nee**rahm	with vegetables
под майонезом	paht mah^{y}ah**neh**zahm	in mayonnaise

паштет	pahsht^y**eht**	pâté (mostly liver)
редиски	ree**dees**kee	radishes
селёдка, сельдь	seel^y**o**tkah, s^{y}ehl^{y}d^y	herring
сыр	sirr	cheese
шпроты	**shpro**tti	sprats
яйца	^{y}**igh**tsah	eggs
яйца с икрой	^{y}**igh**tsah s ee**kroy**	hard-boiled eggs with caviar
крутые яйца с хреном	kroo**ti**^{y}eh ^{y}**igh**tsah s **khr^{y}eh**nahm	hard-boiled eggs with horseradish

Pancakes *Блины*

Russian pancakes are usually made with yeast and served with different fillings. When invited to a Russian home, you may get a whole "pancake-meal", starting with savoury pancakes (filled with caviar or fish) and ending with sweet ones (filled with jam). Both savoury and sweet pancakes are topped with sour cream *(сметана)* and/or butter.

блины с икрой	blee**ni** s ee**kroy**	pancakes with caviar
блины с сёмгой	blee**ni** s **s^{y}om**gigh	pancakes with salmon
блины со сметаной	blee**ni** sah smee**tah**nigh	pancakes with sour cream
блины с вареньем	blee**ni** s vahr^y**eh**n^{y}ehm	pancakes with jam

Salads *Салаты*

винегрет	veeneegr^y**eht**	salad made of beets and other vegetables
зелёный салат	zeel^y**o**nniy sah**laht**	lettuce salad
салат	sah**laht**	salad
из крабов	ees **krah**bahf	crabmeat
из лука	eez **loo**kah	onion
из огурцов	eez ahgoor**tsof**	cucumber
из помидоров	ees pahmee**do**rahf	tomato
из редиски	eez ree**dees**kee	radish
из свежей капусты	ees **sv^{y}eh**zhay kah**poo**sti	raw cabbage
картофельный	kahr**to**feel^{y}niy	potato
с сельдью	s **s^{y}ehl^y**d^{y}oo	herring
«Столичный»	stah**leech**^{y}niy	with beef or poultry, potatoes, eggs, carrots, apples, mayonnaise, sour cream

SNACKS—PICNIC, see page 62

Cheese and dairy products *Сыр и молочные продукты*

Cheese is generally eaten as an appetizer, at breakfast or as a light snack. There is a wide variety of excellent dairy products.

брынза (**brin**zah)	cheese made from sheep's milk, strong and salty
кефир (kee**feer**)	kefir (sour milk)
простокваша (prahstah**kvah**shah)	yoghourt
ряженка (r^y**ah**zhinkah)	baked sour milk, usually served chilled
сливки (**sleef**kee)	cream
сметана (smee**tah**nah)	sour cream, an integral part of Russian cuisine. It's used in soups, salads, vegetable and meat dishes as well as on desserts.

сыр	sirr	cheese
закусочный	zah**koo**sahch^{y}niy	snack-cheese
латвийский	laht**veey**skeey	Latvian
пошехонский	pahshee**khon**skeey	"Poshekhonye"
российский	rah**sseey**skeey	"Russian"

сырок (sir**rok**)	fresh white cheese (or spread)
творог (tvor**rahk**)	white cheese similar to cottage cheese. This extremely popular soft cheese is the main ingredient in a number of dishes.
топлёное молоко (tah**pl^{y}o**nah^{y}eh mahlah**ko**)	baked milk, served chilled

Some popular dishes:

вареники (vahr^y**eh**neekee)	Ukrainian dumplings filled with white cheese
ватрушка (vah**troosh**kah)	cheese pastry (made from white cheese); when savoury, it is served with soups, when sweet, it is served with tea, milk, etc.
сырники со сметаной (**sirr**neekee sah smee**tah**nigh)	white cheese fritters served with sour cream

Soups *Супы*

*Borshch^y^* and *shch^y^ee* are the best known Russian soups abroad. A little sour cream is usually added to vegetable soups.

борщ	borshch^y^	made from beef, vegetables (mainly beetroot), sour cream
московский	mahs**kofs**keey	red borshch (plus bacon)
украинский	ookrah**eens**keey	ukrainian (with garlic)
холодный	khah**lod**niy	cold borshch
бульон	bool^y^**on**	broth or consommé
из курицы	ees **koo**reetsi	chicken consommé
с лапшой	s lahp**shoy**	with noodles
с пирожками	s peerahsh**kah**mee	with savoury pastries
с рисом	s **rees**sahm	with rice
с фрикадельками	s freekah**d^y^ehl^y^**kahmee	with meat dumplings
с яйцом	s eey**tsom**	with egg
окрошка	ah**krosh**kah	summer soup (cold) based on *kvahss* *, with cucumber, eggs, onions and sour cream
солянка	sah**l^y^ahn**kah	with salted cucumbers and olives
мясная	mees**nah^y^**ah	with meat
рыбная	**rib**nah^y^ah	with fish
свекольник	svee**kol^y^**neek	vegetable soup (mainly beetroot); usually cold
суп	soop	soup
гороховый	gah**ro**khahviy	pea soup
грибной	greeb**noy**	mushroom soup
из фасоли	ees fah**so**lee	bean soup
из цветной капусты	ees tsveet**noy** kah**poos**ti	cauliflower soup
картофельный	kahr**to**feel^y^niy	potato soup
овощной	ahvahshch^y^**noy**	vegetable soup
уха	oo**khah**	fish soup
харчо	khahr**ch^y^o**	Georgian, spicy mutton and rice soup
шурпа	shoor**pah**	Uzbek mutton soup with bacon and tomatoes

* see page 59

щи	shch^{y}ee	made from fresh cabbage or sauerkraut
зелёные с яйцом	zeel^{y}onni^{y}eh s eey**tsom**	sorrel soup thickened with a beaten egg
кислые	**kees**li^{y}eh	with sauerkraut
свежие	**sv^{y}eh**zhi^{y}eh	with fresh cabbage

Fish and seafood *Рыба и дары моря*

With its thousands of miles of coastline on the Atlantic and Pacific Oceans, as well as those on the Black Sea and Baltic Sea, the Soviet Union ranks among the world's leading fishing nations.

I'll have fish as a first/second course.	**На первое/второе я возьму рыбу.**	nah **p^{y}ehr**vah^{y}eh/ftah**ro**^{y}eh ^{y}ah vahz^y**moo rib**boo
камбала	**kahm**bahlah	flounder/plaice
карп	kahrp	carp
кета	kee**tah**	Siberian salmon
краб	krahp	crab
креветки	kreev**^{y}eht**kee	prawns
лещь	l^{y}ehshch^y	bream
лососина	lahsah**see**nah	salmon
макрель	mah**kr^{y}ehl^y**	mackerel
минога	mee**no**ggah	lamprey
налим	nah**leem**	burbot
окунь	**o**koon^y	perch
омар	ah**mahr**	lobster
осетрина	ahssee**tree**nah	sturgeon
палтус	**pahl**toos	halibut/turbot
раки	**rah**kee	crayfish
сельдь, селёдка	s^{y}ehl^{y}d^y, seel^y**ot**kah	herring
сёмга	**s^{y}om**gah	salmon
скумбрия	**skoom**bree^{y}ah	mackerel/scomber
сом	som	sheatfish (large catfish)
стерлядь	**st^{y}ehr**l^{y}ahd^y	sterlet
судак	soo**dahk**	pike perch
треска	trees**kah**	cod
тунец	toon**^{y}ehts**	tunny, tuna
угорь	**oo**gahr^y	eel
устрицы	**oo**streetsi	oysters
форель	fahr**^{y}ehl^y**	trout
шпроты	**shpro**tti	sprats (in oil)
щука	**shch^{y}oo**kah	pike

baked	**печёный**	pee**ch^{y}o**niy
fried	**жареный**	**zhah**reeniy
grilled	**жареный на рашпере (вертеле)**	**zhah**reeniy nah **rahsh**-peer^{y}eh (**v^{y}ehr**teel^{y}eh)
marinated	**маринованный**	mahree**no**vvahnniy
poached	**отварной**	ahtvahr**noy**
raw	**сырой**	sir**roy**
smoked	**копчёный**	kahp**ch^{y}o**niy
steamed	**паровой**	pahrah**voy**
stewed	**тушёный**	too**sho**niy

Fish dishes *Рыбные блюда*

осетрина в томате	ahssee**tree**nah f tah**mah**tee	sturgeon in tomato sauce
осетрина под белым соусом	ahssee**tree**nah pahd **b^{y}eh**lim **soo**osahm	sturgeon in white sauce
осетрина под маринадом	ahssee**tree**nah pahd mahree**nah**dahm	pickled sturgeon
осетрина на вертеле	ahssee**tree**nah nah **v^{y}ehr**teel^{y}eh	spit-grilled sturgeon
осетрина паровая	ahssee**tree**nah pahrah-**vah**^{y}ah	steamed sturgeon served with a light sauce
осетрина по-русски	ahssee**tree**nah pah **roo**skee	poached sturgeon with tomato sauce and vegetables
осетрина «фри»	ahssee**tree**nah free	fried sturgeon
палтус жареный	**pahl**toos **zhah**reeniy	fried halibut
рыбные котлеты	**rib**ni^{y}eh kaht**l^{y}eh**ti	fish croquettes
стерлядь паровая	**st^{y}ehr**l^{y}ahd^y pahrah-**vah**^{y}ah	steamed sterlet
судак в томатном соусе	soo**dahk** f tah**maht**nahm **so**oos^{y}eh	sautéed pike-perch served in tomato sauce
судак жареный в тесте	soo**dahk** **zhah**reeniy f **t^{y}eh**stee	pike-perch fried in batter
судак отварной, соус яичный	soo**dahk** ahtvahr**noy** **so**oos ^{y}ee**eesh**niy	poached pike-perch in egg sauce

Meat *Мясо*

What kind of meat do you have?	**Какое у вас мясо?**	kah**ko**^{y}eh oo vahss **m^{y}ah**ssah
beef	**говядина**	gahv^{y}**ah**deenah
lamb	**молодая баранина**	mahlah**dah**^{y}ah bah**rah**neenah
mutton	**баранина**	bah**rah**neenah
pork	**свинина**	svee**nee**nah
veal	**телятина**	teel^{y}**ah**teenah

антрекот	ahntree**kot**	rib steak
баранина жареная	bah**rah**neenah **zhah**reenah^{y}ah	mutton roast
бараньи отбивные	bah**rah**nee ahtbeev**ni**^{y}eh	mutton chops
бекон	b^{y}eh**kon**	bacon
биточки	bee**toch**^{y}kee	meat patties
бифштекс	beef**shtehks**	beefsteak
ветчина	veetch^{y}**eenah**	ham
говядина тушёная	gahv^{y}**ah**deenah too**sho**nah^{y}ah	pot roast
говядина отварная	gahv^{y}**ah**deenah ahtvahr**nah**^{y}ah	boiled beef
грудинка баранья	groo**deen**kah bah**rahn**^{y}ah	breast of mutton
грудинка телячья	groo**deen**kah teel^{y}**ah**ch^{y}ah	breast of veal
жаркое	zhahr**ko**^{y}eh	roast
котлета отбивная	kahtl^{y}**eh**tah ahtbeev**nah**^{y}ah	cutlet, chop
котлета рубленая	kahtl^{y}**eh**tah **roo**bleenah^{y}ah	meat patties
ножки свиные	**nosh**kee svee**ni**^{y}eh	pig's knuckles
печёнка	peech^{y}**on**kah	liver
поросёнок жареный	pahrahs^{y}**o**nahk **zhah**reeniy	roasted sucking-pig
почки	**poch**^{y}kee	kidneys
рагу	rah**goo**	meat stew
ромштекс	rahm**shtehks**	rumpsteak
ростбиф	**rost**beef	roast beef
рулет мясной	rool^{y}**eht** mees**noy**	meat loaf
свиные отбивные	svee**ni**^{y}eh ahtbeev**ni**^{y}eh	pork chops
сосиски	sah**see**skee	sausages (frankfurters)
тефтели	teeft^{y}**eh**lee	meat balls
филе	feel^{y}**eh**	fillet
фрикадельки	freekahd^{y}**ehl**^{y}kee	meat quenelles
шницель по-венски	**shnee**tsehl^{y} pah v^{y}**ehn**skee	escalope breaded pork escalope
эскалоп	ehskah**lop**	tenderloin steak
язык	ee**zik**	tongue

baked	**печёный**	peech^{y}oniy
boiled	**варёный**	vahr^{y}oniy
braised	**тушёный**	too**sho**niy
fried	**жареный**	**zhah**reeniy
grilled	**жареный на рашпере (вертеле)**	**zhah**reeniy nah **rahsh**peer^{y}eh (**v^{y}ehr**teel^{y}eh)
roasted	**жареный**	**zhah**reeniy
stewed	**тушёный**	too**sho**niy
stuffed	**фаршированный**	fahrshi**rov**vahnniy

Russian meat dishes *Русские мясные блюда*

азу	ah**zoo**	chopped meat in a savoury sauce
бефстроганов, картофель «фри»	beef**stro**gahnahf kahr**to**feel^{y} free	beef Stroganoff with chips (french fries)
бифштекс натуральный	beef**shtehks** nahtoo**rahl^{y}**niy	grilled beefsteak
говядина тушёная с кореньями	gah**v^{y}ah**deenah too**sho**nah^{y}ah s kahr**^{y}eh**neemee	beef braised with aromatic vegetables
голубцы	gahloop**tsi**	cabbage, stuffed with meat and rice
гуляш	gool**^{y}ahsh**	goulash
жаркое из свинины со сливами	zhahr**ko**^{y}eh ees svee**nee**ni sah **slee**vahmee	roast pork with plums
котлеты натуральные из баранины	kahtl**^{y}eh**ti nahtoo**rahl^{y}**ni^{y}eh eez bah**rah**neeni	grilled mutton chops
люля-кебаб	**l^{y}**ool^{y}ah-kee**bahp**	long beef or mutton meatballs (Azerbaidjan)
плов из баранины	plof eez bah**rah**neeni	mutton pilaw: rice with minced mutton
ростбиф с гарниром	**rost**beef s gahr**nee**rahm	roast beef with vegetables
поджарка	pahd**zhahr**kah	roasted pieces of meat served with a sauce
шашлык	shahsh**lik**	Shashlik, pieces of lamb grilled on skewers (Caucasus)

Game and poultry *Дичь и птица*

бекас	bee**kahss**	snipe
вальдшнеп	**vahl^{y}d**shnehp	woodcock
гусь	goos^{y}	goose
заяц	**zah**eets	hare
индейка	eend^{y}**ay**kah	turkey
кролик	**kro**leek	rabbit
курица	**koo**reetsah	chicken
куропатка	koorah**paht**kah	partridge
перепел	**p^{y}eh**reep^{y}ehl	quail
рябчик	**r^{y}ahb**ch^{y}eek	hazel-grouse
тетерев	**t^{y}eh**teer^{y}ehf	black grouse
утка	**oot**kah	duck
цыплёнок	tsip**l^{y}o**nahk	chicken
котлеты из кур пожарские	kaht**l^{y}eh**ti ees koor pah**zhahr**skee^{y}eh	minced chicken patties *Pozharsky* style
котлеты по-киевски	kaht**l^{y}eh**ti pah **kee**^{y}ehfskee	Chicken Kiev: chicken breasts stuffed with butter
курица отварная с рисом	**koo**reetsah ahtvahr**nah**^{y}ah s **ree**ssahm	boiled chicken with rice
куропатка жареная с вареньем	koorah**paht**kah **zhah**reenah^{y}ah s vah**r^{y}eh**n^{y}ehm	roast partridge with jam
рябчики жареные с вареньем	**r^{y}ahb**ch^{y}eekee **zhah**reeni^{y}eh s vah**r^{y}eh**n^{y}ehm	grilled hazel-hen with jam
утка с тушёной капустой	**oot**kah s too**sho**nigh kah**poos**tigh	roast duck with stewed cabbage
утка с яблоками	**oot**kah s **^{y}ah**blahkahmee	duck stuffed with apples
филе из кур фаршированное грибами	feel**^{y}eh** ees koor fahrshi**ro**vahnnah^{y}eh gree**bah**mee	minced chicken patties with mushroom filling
цыплёнок жареный с картофелем	tsip**l^{y}o**nahk **zhah**reeniy s kahr**to**feel^{y}ehm	grilled chicken with potatoes
цыплята «табака»	tsip**l^{y}ah**tah tah**bah**kah	Georgian fried chicken
цыплята жареные в сметане	tsip**l^{y}ah**tah **zhah**reeni^{y}eh f smee**tah**n^{y}eh	roast chicken in sour cream
чахохбили из кур	ch^{y}ahkhokh**bee**lee ees koor	Caucasian chicken casserole, served with tomatoes and a lot of onions

Vegetables *Овощи*

The most commonly-found vegetables are cabbage, beetroot, cucumbers, tomatoes and potatoes. Mushrooms are gathered in autumn, salted and marinated.

What vegetables do you have?	**Какие у вас есть овощи?**	kah**kee**^{y}eh oo vahss ^{y}**ehst**^{y} **ovvahshch**^{y}**ee**
баклажаны	bahklah**zhah**ni	aubergines (eggplant)
бобы	bah**bi**	broad beans
горох	gah**rokh**	peas
грибы	gree**bi**	mushrooms
кабачки	kahbahch^y**kee**	marrow, courgette (zucchini)
картофель	kahr**to**feel^y	potatoes
капуста	kah**poo**stah	cabbage
красная капуста	**krahs**nah^{y}ah kah**poo**stah	red cabbage
кукуруза	kookoo**roo**zah	corn
лук	look	onion(s)
зелёный лук	zeel^y**o**nniy look	spring onion(s)
лук-порей	look pahr^y**ay**	leeks
морковь	mahr**kov**^{y}	carrot(s)
огурец	ahgoor^y**ehts**	cucumber
перец (сладкий)	**p**^{y}**eh**reets (**slaht**keey)	green pepper
перец горький	**p**^{y}**eh**reets **gor**^{y}keey	pimento
петрушка	pee**troosh**kah	parsley
помидоры	pahmee**do**ri	tomatoes
редиска	ree**dees**kah	radishes
репа	**r**^{y}**eh**pah	turnip
свёкла	**sv**^{y}**o**klah	beetroot
сельдерей	seel^{y}deer^y**ay**	celery
фасоль	fah**sol**^{y}	french beans (green beans)
хрен	khr^y**eh**n	horseradish
цветная капуста	tsveet**nah**^{y}ah kah**poo**stah	cauliflower
шпинат	shpee**naht**	spinach
чеснок	ch^{y}ees**nok**	garlic

baked	**печёный**	pee**ch**^{y}**o**niy
boiled	**варёный**	vahr^y**o**niy
braised	**тушёный**	too**sho**niy
marinated, pickled	**маринованный**	mahree**no**vvahnniy
stuffed	**фаршированный**	fahrshi**ro**vvahnniy
in butter	**в масле**	v **mahs**l^{y}eh

Cereals, rice, potatoes *Каша, рис, картофель*

Kahshah is a type of gruel usually made from buckwheat and served as a side dish with meat or poultry. (It can also be served at breakfast as a hot cereal, like porridge.) Rice replaces *kahshah* in the Caucasus and Central Asia, where it is prepared as *plov* (similar to the Turkish *pilav*).

вермишель	v^{Y}ehrmee**shehl^{Y}**	pasta or vermicelli
картофель	kahr**to**feel^{Y}	potatoes
жареный	**zhah**reeniy	fried
картофель фри	kahr**to**feel^{Y} free	french fries
отварной	ahtvahr**noy**	boiled
каша	**kah**shah	gruel
гречневая	**gr^{Y}ehch^{Y}**neevah^{Y}ah	buckwheat
манная	**mahn**nah^{Y}ah	semolina
пшённая	**pshon**nah^{Y}ah	millet
лапша	lahp**shah**	soup noodles
макароны	mahkah**ro**nni	pasta, macaroni
плов	plof	pilaw (rice dish prepared with lamb, chicken or veal and vegetables)
рис	reess	rice
рисовая каша	**ree**ssahvah^{Y}ah **kah**shah	rice gruel

Other specialities:

пельмени (peel^{Y}**m^{Y}eh**nee)	stuffed dumplings (usually called "Siberian" *peel^{Y}m^{Y}ehnee,* because they were very popular in Siberia)
пирог (pee**rok**)	large pie filled with meat, cabbage, mushrooms, fish, etc. and topped with pastry
пирожок (peerah**zhok**)	small pies with various fillings: meat, cabbage, mushrooms, onions, jam, etc.
хачапури (khahch^{Y}ah**poo**ree)	a Georgian speciality: a sort of hot pancake filled with cheese (a popular snack)

Sauces *Соусы*

белый соус (**b^{Y}eh**liy **soo**oss)	white sauce
сметанный соус (smee**tahn**niy **soo**oss)	sour cream sauce (sometimes with mushrooms)

Fruit *Фрукты*

You probably won't be able to get fresh fruit in restaurants, but you can try at markets. In shops, you'll find marinated fruit in jars.

абрикос	ahbree**koss**	apricot
айва	igh**vah**	quince
ананас	ahnah**nahss**	pineapple
апельсин	ahpeel^{y}**seen**	orange
арбуз	ahr**boos**	watermelon
банан	bah**nahn**	banana
брусника*	broos**nee**kah	cranberries
виноград*	veenah**graht**	grapes
вишня	**veesh**n^{y}ah	sour cherry
гранат	grah**naht**	pomegranate
грейпфрут	**grayp**froot	grapefruit
груша	**groo**shah	pear
дыня	**din**^{y}ah	melon
ежевика*	eezhee**vee**kah	blackberries
земляника*	zeemlee**nee**kah	(wild) strawberries
изюм	eez^{y}**oom**	raisins
инжир	een**zhirr**	fig
клубника*	kloob**nee**kah	(garden) strawberries
клюква*	**kl^{y}ook**vah	red berries (kind of cranberries)
лимон	lee**mon**	lemon
малина*	mah**lee**nah	raspberries
мандарин	mahndah**reen**	tangerine
миндаль	meen**dahl^{y}**	almonds
орех	**ahr^{y}ehkh**	nut
грецкий	**gr^{y}ehts**keey	walnut
земляной	zeemlee**noy**	peanut
лесной	lees**noy**	hazelnut
персик	**p^{y}ehr**seek	peach
ревень	reev^{y}**ehn^{y}**	rhubarb
слива	**slee**vah	plum
смородина*	smah**ro**deenah	currants
чёрная	**ch^{y}or**nah^{y}ah	black currants
финик	**fee**neek	date
черешня	ch^{y}eer^{y}**ehsh**n^{y}ah	cherry
яблоко	^{y}**ah**blahkah	apple
ягоды	^{y}**ah**gahdi	berries

* Words with singular form but plural meaning

Dessert *Десерт – Сладкие блюда*

If you didn't have a sweet tooth before going to Russia, you are likely to develop one during your stay.

What is there for dessert?	**Что у вас есть на десерт?**	shto oo vahss ^{y}ehst^y nah dees^y**ehrt**
Please bring me ...	**Принесите мне ..., пожалуйста.**	preenees**seet**^{y}eh mn^{y}eh ... pah**zhahl**stah
Something light, please.	**Что-нибудь лёгкое, пожалуйста.**	**shto**-neebood^y **l^{y}okh**kah^{y}eh pah**zhahl**stah
Nothing more, thank you.	**Больше ничего, спасибо.**	**bol**^{y}sheh neech^{y}ee**vo** spahs**see**bah

The desserts listed below may not all be available in a restaurant, but you might find them in coffee shops, at "buffets" (snack bars) or at ice-cream parlours and stalls in the street. In any case, try the famous Russian ice cream!

блинчики с вареньем	**bleen**ch^{y}eekee s vahr^y**ehn**^{y}ehm	pancakes (small *bleeni*) with jam
ватрушка	vah**troosh**kah	cottage cheese tart
картошка	kahr**tosh**kah	"potato", a pastry made from marzipan
кекс	k^{y}ehks	sponge cake
кисель	kees^y**ehl**^{y}	fruit jelly, topped with sugar, milk or cream
компот	kahm**pot**	fruit compote
мороженое	mah**ro**zhehnah^{y}eh	ice cream
ванильное	vah**neel**^{y}nah^{y}eh	vanilla
фруктовое	frook**tov**vah^{y}eh	fruit
шоколадное	shahkah**lahd**nah^{y}eh	chocolate
эскимо	ehskee**mo**	on a stick
наполеон	nahpahlee**on**	cream slice (mille-feuille)
оладьи	ah**lah**dee	small pancakes
с яблоками	s **^{y}ahb**lahkahmee	apple puffs
печенье	pee**ch^{y}ehn**^{y}eh	cookies, biscuits
пирог	pee**rok**	pie, cake or tart
с лимоном	s lee**mon**nahm	lemon tart
с творогом	s **tvor**rahgahm	cottage cheese tart
с фруктами	s **frook**tahmee	fruit tart
пирожное	pee**rozh**nah^{y}eh	cake
миндальное	meen**dahl**^{y}nah^{y}eh	with almonds
ореховое	ahr^y**eh**khahvah^{y}eh	with nuts
пончики	**ponch**^{y}eekee	kind of doughnut

пряники	pr^y**ah**neekee	honey cakes
рисовый пудинг с киселём	**ree**ssahviy **poo**deeng s keeseel^y**om**	rice pudding with starchy fruit jelly
ромовая баба	rahmah**vah**^{y}ah **bah**bah	rum baba
рулет	rool^y**eht**	sponge roll
торт	tort	a rich cake
бисквитный	bees**kveet**niy	sponge cake
песочный	pee**soch**^{y}niy	shortcake
сливочный	**slee**vahch^{y}niy	with cream
слоёный	slah^y**o**niy	puff pastry
халва	khahl**vah**	halva (kind of nougat)
шоколад	shahkah**laht**	chocolate
шоколадный бисквит	shahkah**lahd**niy bees**kveet**	chocolate sponge cake
эклер	ehk**l**^{y}**ehr**	éclair
яблоко в тесте	^{y}**ah**blahkah f **t**^{y}**ehs**t^{y}eh	apple baked in pastry
яблочный пирог	^{y}**ah**blahch^{y}niy pee**rok**	apple pie

Cakes and tarts are often topped with cream:

сливки	**sleef**kee	cream
взбитые сливки	**vzbee**ti^{y}eh **sleef**kee	whipped cream

Coffee *Кофе*

Coffee does not belong to the Russian tradition. If you want strong coffee, ask for "eastern-style coffee"— *кофе по-восточному* (**ko**fee pah vahs**toch**^{y}nahmoo), similar to Turkish coffee. If you order coffee with milk, you'll often get a glass of very sweet coffee (with condensed milk).

I'd like (a/some) ...	**Дайте мне, пожалуйста...**	**dight**^{y}eh mn^{y}eh pah**zhahl**stah
coffee	**кофе**	**ko**fee
big/small cup	**большую/маленькую чашку**	bahl^y**shoo**^{y}oo/**mah**leen^{y}koo-^{y}oo **ch**^{y}**ahsh**koo
black coffee	**чёрный**	**ch**^{y}**or**niy
Turkish coffee	**по-восточному**	pah vahs**toch**^{y}nahmoo
with/without milk	**с молоком/без молока**	s mahlah**kom**/beez mahlah**kah**
with/without sugar	**с сахаром/без сахара**	s **sah**khahrahm/bees **sah**khahrah

Drinks *Напитки*

I'd like something to drink.	**Я хотел(а) бы выпить что-нибудь.**	^{y}ah khaht^{y}**ehl**(ah) bi **vi**ppeet^{y} **shto**-neebood^{y}
I'd like some ...	**Я хотел(а) бы ...**	^{y}ah khaht^{y}**ehl**(ah) bi
beer	**пиво**	**pee**vah
champagne	**шампанское**	shahm**pahns**kah^{y}eh
mineral water	**минеральную воду**	meenee**rahl^{y}**noo^{y}oo **vo**ddoo
wine	**вино**	vee**no**
Please bring me ...	**Принесите, пожалуйста ...**	preenee**sseet**^{y}eh pah**zhahl**stah
a cup of ...	**чашку ...**	**ch^{y}ahsh**koo
a glass of ...	**стакан .../ кружку ...**	stah**kahn**/ **kroosh**koo
a small glass of ...	**рюмку ...**	**r^{y}oom**koo
a bottle of ...	**бутылку ...**	boo**ti**lkoo
half a bottle of ...	**полбутылки ...**	polboo**ti**lkee

Wine *Вино*

The best Russian wines come from Georgia (two examples: *Tsinandali*, a dry white wine, and *Mukuzani*, a red table wine) and Crimea, but Ukraine, as well as some regions of Central Asia, also produce good wines.

"Soviet champagne" or sparkling wine (*шампанское*—shahm**pahns**kah^{y}eh) is a popular drink. Dry, it can accompany almost any meal; sweet, it is usually enjoyed after meals or with dessert.

May I have the wine list, please?	**Дайте мне, пожалуйста, прейскурант вин.**	**dight**^{y}eh mn^{y}eh pah**zhahl**stah prayskoo**rahnt** veen
Which wine would you recommend?	**Какое вино вы нам посоветуете?**	kah**ko**^{y}eh vee**no** vi nahm pahsah**v^{y}eh**tooeet^{y}eh
How much is a bottle of ...?	**Сколько стоит бутылка ...?**	**skol^{y}**kah **sto**eet boo**ti**lkah
I'd like a bottle of ...	**Я хотел(а) бы бутылку ...**	^{y}ah khaht^{y}**ehl**(ah) bi boo**ti**lkoo
red wine	**красного вина**	**krahs**nahvah vee**nah**
white wine	**белого вина**	**b^{y}eh**lahvah vee**nah**
champagne	**шампанского**	shahm**pahns**kahvah

red	**красное**	**krahs**nah^{y}eh
white	**белое**	**b^{y}eh**lah^{y}eh
rosé	**розовое**	**ro**zahvah^{y}eh
dry	**сухое**	soo**kho**^{y}eh
semi-dry	**полусухое**	pahloosoo**kho**^{y}eh
sparkling	**шипучее**	shi**poo**ch^{y}ee^{y}eh
sweet	**сладкое**	**slaht**kah^{y}eh
semi-sweet	**полусладкое**	pahloo**slaht**kah^{y}eh
chilled	**холодное**	khah**lod**nah^{y}eh
with ice	**со льдом**	sah l^{y}**dom**

What's the name of this wine?	**Как называется это вино?**	kahk nahzi**vvah**eetsah **eh**tah vee**no**
Where does this wine come from?	**Откуда это вино?**	aht**koo**dah **eh**tah vee**no**
Please bring me another ...	**Пожалуйста, ещё...**	pah**zhahl**stah eesh**ch^{y}o**
bottle	**одну бутылку**	ahd**noo** boo**til**koo
carafe	**один графин**	ah**deen** grah**feen**
glass	**один стакан**	ah**deen** stah**kahn**

Beer *Пиво*

Both imported beer (like pilsener) and Russian brews are available, although the latter may taste a little weak to the Western palate.

An inexpensive brand of Russian beer is *Zhigulevskoye*, but when dining out in elegant places you're likely to be offered one of these brands (lager-type beers):

рижское	**rish**skah^{y}eh	Rizhskoye
московское	mah**skof**skah^{y}eh	Moskovskoye

Bring me a bottle of beer, please.	**Принесите мне, пожалуйста, бутылку пива.**	preenee**sseet**^{y}eh mn^{y}eh pah**zhahl**stah boo**til**koo **pee**vah
Lager, please.	**Светлого пива, пожалуйста.**	**sv^{y}eht**lahvah **pee**vah pah**zhahl**stah
Do you have dark beer?	**Есть ли у вас тёмное пиво?**	^{y}ehst^{y} lee oo vahss **t^{y}om**nah^{y}eh **pee**vah

Vodka *Водка*

Vodka is a spirit made from wheat that looks like water (the word "vodka" is a diminutive form of "water", *вода*—vah**dah**).

It is traditionally taken with the starter, but can also accompany the other courses.

Vodka is served chilled and always neat in small glasses. The etiquette of vodka drinking is as follows: drain the glass in one go, then chase it down with a morsel of food (usually a piece of black bread or salted cucumber).

The smallest measure of vodka you can order is 50 grams (equal to a single or a shot glass), the next measure being 100 grams (like a double or double shot). On the other hand, you may order a glass of wine which usually equals 200 grams. A bottle of vodka normally contains about a pint, and a bottle of wine about a pint and a half. With this in mind, you can say:

I'd like 50 grams of vodka, please.	**Дайте мне, пожалуйста, 50 грамм водки.**	**dight**^{y}eh mn^{y}eh pah**zhahl**stah 50 grahm **vot**kee
I'd like 150 grams of the same, please.	**Пожалуйста, 150 того же самого.**	pah**zhahl**stah 150 tah**vo** zheh **sah**mahvah

It is common to propose a toast when raising your glass. One phrase you will certainly hear very often and learn quickly is "*За ваше здоровье!*" (zah **vah**sheh zdah**rov**^{y}eh), meaning "Cheers!", or, literally, "To your health!".

Here are a few more ideas:

Here's to our host/hostess!	**За здоровье хозяина/хозяики!**	zah zdah**rov**^{y}eh khah**z**^{y}**igh**nah/khah**z**^{y}**igh**kee
Health and happiness!	**За ваше здоровье и благополучие!**	zah **vah**sheh zdah**rov**^{y}eh ee blahgahpah**looch**^{y}ee^{y}eh
Here's to future co-operation between our organizations!	**За наше будущее сотрудничество!**	zah **nah**sheh **boo**dooshch^{y}eh^{y}eh sahtrood**neech**^{y}eestvah

Other alcoholic drinks *Другие спиртные напитки*

Brandy (called *коньяк* —kah**n^{y}ahk**)—the best ones come from Armenia – comes a close second to vodka in popularity in Russia.

Don't expect to find exotic drinks in small cafés. For these you'll have to go to the more sophisticated bars and restaurants. Here's what you may want to order:

aperitif	**аперитив**	ahpeeree**teef**
beer	**пиво**	**pee**vah
brandy	**брэнди**	"brandy"
cognac	**коньяк**	kah**n^{y}ahk**
gin	**джин**	dzhin
gin-fizz	**джин-физ**	dzhin-feez
gin and tonic	**джин с тоником**	dzhin s **to**neekahm
liqueur	**ликёр**	leek^y**or**
port	**портвейн**	pahrtv^y**ayn**
rum	**ром**	rom
sherry	**херес**	**kh^{y}ehr**^{y}ehss
vermouth	**вермут**	**v^{y}ehr**moot
vodka	**водка**	**vot**kah
screwdriver	**водка с апельсиновым соком**	**vot**kah s ahpeel^y**see**nahvim **so**kahm
whisky	**виски**	**vees**kee
neat (straight)	**натуральное**	nahtoo**rahl^y**nah^{y}eh
on the rocks	**со льдом**	sah l^{y}dom
whisky and soda	**виски с содовой**	**vees**kee s **so**dahvigh

But you should also try ...

коньяк «Енисели»	kah**n^{y}ahk** ^{y}ehnees^y**eh**lee	brandy, of exceptional quality
коньяк «ОС»	kah**n^{y}ahk** o ehss	brandy, well aged
Мускат крымский	moos**kaht krim**skeey	Crimean red muscat wine
Салхино	**sahl**kheeno	red dessert wine
Чёрные глаза	**ch^{y}or**ni^{y}eh glah**zah**	"Dark Eyes", red dessert wine

I'd like to try some Pertsovka*, please.	**Я хотел(а) бы попробовать перцовки.**	^{y}ah khaht^y**ehl**(ah) bi pah**pro**bahvaht^y peer**tsof**kee

* a pepper-flavoured vodka

Tea *Чай*

Tea is the most popular Russian beverage. When invited to a Russian home, you may get to see one of the traditional *samovars* (*самовар*—sahmah**vahr**). "Samovar" can be translated by "self-boiler"; it holds the hot water which is used to dilute the strong tea prepared in a separate tea pot. Formerly, samovars were fuelled by charcoal which has now been replaced, more prosaically, by electricity.

You might consider buying one as a souvenir, but if you're lucky enough to find a charcoal-burning samovar, do check that it is not pre-1917. If it is, make sure you fill in the appropriate forms for customs.

Tea is sometimes served in glasses and is often sweetened by jam or honey rather than sugar.

A glass of tea, please.	**Стакан чая, пожалуйста.**	stah**kahn ch^{y}igh^{y}ah** pah**zhahl**stah
with lemon	**с лимоном**	s lee**mon**nahm
with milk	**с молоком**	s mahlah**kom**
with honey	**с мёдом**	s **m^{y}o**dahm
with jam	**с вареньем**	s vahr^{y}**eh**n^{y}ehm

ЧАЙНАЯ
TEAROOM

Kvass *Квас*

A popular soft drink and a good thirst-quencher in summer, when it is sold from small stalls in the streets. *Kvass* looks like dark beer, is made from black bread and yeast, and is used as an ingredient in some Russian dishes, such as the cold soup *ahkroshkah* (see page 44).

A small glass, please.	**Маленькую кружку, пожалуйста.**	**mah**leen^{y}koo^{y}oo **kroosh**koo pah**zhahl**stah
A big one, please.	**Большую, пожалуйста.**	bahl^{y}**shoo**^{y}oo pah**zhahl**stah

Other beverages *Другие напитки*

Nowadays, you get typical Western soft drinks like Coca Cola, Pepsi Cola or Fanta in Russia, generally sold for street kiosks. (By the way, there is a Russian "Coke" as well, called "*байкал*"—bigh**kahl**.)

Instead of these, you might like to try some of the fruit juices and mineral water sold at stands in the streets. The most famous brands of mineral water are *Narzan (Нарзан)* and *Borzhom (Боржом)*.

The drink called "cocktail" (*коктейль*) is not what you might expect: it's a soft drink made from fruit juice or lemonade, to which ice cream and sometimes whipped cream are added, similar to an American soda.

I'd like a/some ...	**Я хотел(а) бы...**	ʸah khahtʸ**ehl**(ah) bi
cocoa	**какао**	kah**kaho**
coffee	**кофе**	**ko**fee
juice	**сок**	sok
apple	**яблочный**	ʸ**ah**blahchʸniy
apricot	**абрикосовый**	ahbree**ko**ssahviy
birch-tree	**берёзовый**	beerʸ**o**zahviy
cherry	**вишнёвый**	veesh**n**ʸ**o**viy
grape	**виноградный**	veenah**grahd**niy
grapefruit	**грейпфрутовый**	**grayp**frootahviy
orange	**апельсиновый**	ahpeelʸ**see**nahviy
pineapple	**ананасовый**	ahnah**nah**ssahviy
pomegranate	**гранатовый**	grah**nah**tahviy
plum	**сливовый**	slee**vo**viy
raspberry	**малиновый**	mah**lee**nahviy
tangerine	**мандариновый**	mahndah**ree**nahviy
tomato	**томатный**	tah**maht**niy
lemonade	**лимонад**	leemah**naht**
milk	**молоко**	mahlah**ko**
sour milk	**кефир**	kee**feer**
mineral water	**минеральную воду**	meeneer**ahl**ʸnooʸoo **vo**ddoo
tea	**чай**	chʸigh

СОКИ И ВОДЫ

FRUIT JUICES AND MINERAL WATER

COFFEE, see also page 54

Complaints *Жалобы*

Could you give us another table?	**Дайте нам, пожалуйста, другой столик.**	**dight**^{y}eh nahm pah**zhahl**stah droo**goy** sto**leek**
There is a plate/glass missing.	**У нас не хватает тарелки/стакана.**	oo nahss nee khvah**tah**eet tahr^{y}**ehl**kee/stah**kah**nah
I don't have a knife/fork/spoon.	**У меня нет ножа/вилки/ложки.**	oo meen^{y}**ah** n^{y}eht nah**zhah**/**veel**kee/**losh**kee
That's not what I ordered.	**Этого я не заказывал(а).**	**eh**tahvah ^{y}ah nee zah**kah**zivvahl(ah)
I asked for ...	**Я заказал(а) ...**	^{y}ah zahkah**zahl**(ah)
I think there's a mistake.	**Вы, наверно, ошиблись.**	vi nah**v**^{y}**ehr**nah ah**shib**lees^{y}
May I change this?	**Я могу поменять это?**	^{y}ah mah**goo** pahmeen^{y}**aht**^{y} **eh**tah
I asked for a small portion (for the child).	**Я заказал(а) маленькую порцию (для ребёнка).**	^{y}ah zahkah**zahl**(ah) **mah**leen^{y}koo^{y}oo **por**tsi^{y}oo (dl^{y}ah reeb^{y}**on**kah)
The meat is ...	**Мясо ...**	**m**^{y}**ah**ssah
overdone	**пережарено**	peeree**zhah**reenah
underdone	**недожарено**	needah**zhah**reenah
too rare	**сырое**	sir**ro**^{y}eh
too tough	**жёсткое**	**zhost**kah^{y}eh
This is too ...	**Это (слишком) ...**	**eh**tah (**sleesh**kahm)
bitter	**горько**	**gor**^{y}kah
salty	**пересолено**	peeree**so**leenah
sour	**кисло**	**kees**lah
sweet	**сладко**	**slaht**kah
I don't like this.	**Это мне не нравится.**	**eh**tah mn^{y}eh nee **nrah**veetsah
The food is cold.	**Еда холодная.**	ee**dah** khah**lod**nah^{y}ah
This isn't fresh.	**Это не свежее.**	**eh**tah nee **sv**^{y}**eh**zheh^{y}eh
Have you forgotten our drinks?	**Вы не забыли про наши напитки?**	vi nee zah**bi**lee prah **nah**shi nah**peet**kee
This isn't clean.	**Это плохо вымыто.**	**eh**tah **plo**khah **vim**mitah
Would you ask the head waiter to come over?	**Позовите, пожалуйста, мэтр д'отеля.**	pahzah**veet**^{y}eh pah**zhahl**stah mehtrdo**tehl**^{y}ah

The bill (check) *Счёт*

I'd like to pay.	**Пожалуйста, счёт.**	pah**zhahl**stah shch^{y}ot
We'd like to pay separately.	**Мы хотели бы платить отдельно.**	mi khaht^y**eh**lee bi plah**teet^y** ahtd^y**ehl^y**nah
I think there's a mistake in this bill.	**Вы не ошиблись?**	vi nee ah**shiblees^y**
What is this amount for?	**Что входит в эту сумму?**	shto **fkho**deet v **eh**too **soom**moo
Is service included?	**Обслуживание включено?**	ahp**sloo**zhivvahnee^{y}eh fkl^{y}ooch^y**eeno**
Is everything included?	**Всё включено?**	fs^{y}o fkl^{y}ooch^y**eeno**
Do you accept traveller's cheques?	**Вы берёте дорожные чеки?**	vi beer^y**o**t^{y}eh dah**rohzhni^{y}eh** **ch^{y}eh**kee
Do you accept Intourist meal vouchers?	**Вы берёте обеденные талоны Интуриста?**	vi beer^y**o**t^{y}eh ahb^y**eh**deenni^{y}eh tah**lo**nni eentoo**ree**stah
Can I pay with this credit card?	**Я могу платить кредитной карточкой?**	^{y}ah mah**goo** plah**teet^y** kree**deet**nigh **kahr**tahch^y-kigh
Thank you, this is for you.	**Спасибо, это вам.**	spah**ssee**bah **eh**tah vahm
Keep the change.	**Оставьте себе сдачу.**	ah**stahf^y**t^{y}eh seeb^y**eh** **zdah**ch^{y}oo
That was delicious.	**Было очень вкусно.**	billah och^{y}een^y **fkoos**nah
We enjoyed it, thank you.	**Нам очень понравилось, спасибо.**	nahm **och^{y}een^y** pahn**rah**vee-lahs^y spah**ssee**bah

Snacks—Picnic *Лёгкая еда – Пикник*

The following phrases and words will come in handy if you want a quick snack. See pages 33 and 120 for further information and more phrases.

I'll have one of those, please.	**Дайте мне один такой, пожалуйста.**	**dight^y**eh mn^{y}eh ah**deen** tah**koy** pah**zhahl**stah
to the left/right	**слева/справа**	**sl^{y}eh**vah/**sprah**vah
above/below	**наверху/внизу**	nahveer**khoo**/vnee**zoo**

TIPPING, see inside back cover/NUMBERS, see page 147

Give me two of those and one of those.	**Дайте мне, пожалуйста, два таких и один такой.**	**dight**^{y}eh mn^{y}eh pah**zhahl**stah dvah tah**keekh** ee ah**deen** tah**koy**
I'd like ...	**Я хотел(а) бы...**	^{y}ah khaht^{y}**ehl**(ah) bi
pancakes	**блины**	blee**ni**
pastries (savoury)	**пирожки**	**peerahshkee**
roast chicken	**жареную курицу**	**zhah**reenoo^{y}oo **koo**reetsoo
sandwich	**бутерброд**	booteer**brod**
caviar	**с икрой**	s eek**roy**
cheese	**с сыром**	s **si**rrahm
ham	**с ветчиной**	s veetch^{y}ee**noy**
salmon	**с сёмгой**	s **s**^{y}**om**gigh

Here's a basic list of food and drink that might come in useful when shopping for a picnic.

I'd like a/an/some ... please.	**Я хотел(а) бы...**	^{y}ah khaht^{y}**ehl**(ah) bi
apples	**яблоки**	^{y}**ah**blahkee
bananas	**бананы**	bah**nah**ni
biscuits (Br.)	**печенье**	pee**ch**^{y}**ehn**^{y}eh
bread	**хлеб**	khl^{y}ehp
butter	**масло**	**mahs**lah
cheese	**сыр**	sirr
chocolate	**шоколад**	shahkah**laht**
bar	**плитку**	**pleet**koo
chocolates	**шоколадные конфеты**	shahkah**lahd**ni^{y}eh kahn**f**^{y}**eh**ti
coffee	**кофе**	**ko**fee
cookies	**печенье**	pee**ch**^{y}**ehn**^{y}eh
cottage cheese	**творог**	**tvo**rrahk
cucumbers	**огурцы**	ahgoor**tsi**
drink	**напиток**	nah**pee**tahk
eggs	**яйца**	^{y}**igh**tsah
fruit	**фрукты**	**frook**ti
fruit juice	**фруктовый сок**	frook**to**vviy sok
ham	**ветчину**	veetch^{y}ee**noo**
ice cream	**мороженое**	mah**ro**zhehnah^{y}eh
lemonade	**лимонад**	leemah**naht**
lemons	**лимоны**	lee**mo**nni
kefir (sour milk drink)	**кефир**	kee**feer**
milk	**молоко**	mahlah**ko**
mineral water	**минеральную воду**	meenee**rahl**^{y}noo^{y}oo **vo**ddoo
mustard	**горчицу**	gahr**ch**^{y}**ee**tsoo
oranges	**апельсины**	ahpeel^{y}**see**ni

pepper	**перец**	p^y**eh**reets
pickles	**маринованные огурцы**	mahreenovahnni^yeh ahgoortsi
raisins	**изюм**	eez^y**oom**
rolls	**булочки**	**boo**lahch^ykee
salt	**соль**	sol^y
sausage	**колбасу**	kahlbah**ssoo**
frankfurters	**сосиски**	sah**see**skee
liver sausage	**ливерную колбасу**	**lee**veernoo^yoo kahlbah**ssoo**
sugar	**сахар**	**sah**khahr
sweets (candy)	**конфеты/карамель**	kahnf^y**eh**ti/kahrahm^y**ehl**^y
tea	**чай**	ch^yigh
tomatoes	**помидоры**	pahmee**do**ri
yoghurt	**простоквашу/ йогурт**	prahstah**kvah**shoo/ ^y**o**goort

Bread *Хлеб*

There is a rich variety of black and white bread; besides, every region has its own special sorts and forms of bread.

Here is a choice of the most common sorts:

хлеб	khl^y**eh**p	bread
белый	b^y**eh**liy	white
ржаной	rzhah**noy**	rye
чёрный	ch^y**o**rniy	black
булочка	**boo**lahch^ykah	roll
сдобная булочка	**zdob**nah^yah **boo**lahch^ykah	sweet roll, bun

... and forms:

батон	bah**ton**	long loaf
буханка	boo**khahn**kah	loaf
булка, булочка	**bool**kah, **boo**lahch^ykah	roll

Here are different sorts of black bread you may want to try: *бородинский* (bahrah**deen**skeey), *рижский* (**reesh**skeey), *заварной* (zahvahr**noy**), *обдирный* (ahb**deer**niy), *орловский* (ahr**lof**skeey).

Хала (**khah**lah) is a plaited loaf, sometimes with poppy seeds.

Travelling around

Plane *Самолёт*

Is there a flight to St. Petersburg?	**Есть ли рейс на Санкт Петербург?**	^{Y}ehst^{Y} lee rayss nah sahnkt **peh**teerboorg
Is it a direct flight?	**Это прямой полёт?**	**eh**tah pree**moy** pahl^{Y}**ot**
When's the next flight to Kiev?	**Когда вылетает следующий самолёт в Киев?**	kahg**dah** villee**tah**eet **sl^{Y}eh**doo^{Y}ooshch^{Y}eey sahmahl^{Y}**ot** f **kee**^{Y}ehf
Is there a connection to Baku?	**Есть ли пересадка на Баку?**	^{Y}ehst^{Y} lee peeree**saht**kah nah bah**koo**
I'd like a ticket to Tashkent.	**Дайте мне, пожалуйста, билет до Ташкента.**	**dight**^{Y}eh mn^{Y}eh pah**zhahl**stah beel^{Y}**eht** dah tahshk^{Y}**ehn**tah
single (one-way)	**в один конец**	v ah**deen** kahn^{Y}**ehts**
return (roundtrip)	**туда и обратно**	too**dah** ee ah**braht**nah
What time should I check in?	**Во сколько надо регистрировать багаж?**	vah **skol**^{Y}kah **nah**dah reegee**streer**ahvaht^{Y} bah**gahsh**
Is there a bus to the airport?	**Есть ли автобус до аэропорта?**	^{Y}ehst^{Y} lee ahf**to**bbooss dah ighrah**por**tah
How do I get to the air terminal?	**Как мне проехать к аэровокзалу?**	kahk mn^{Y}eh prah^{Y}**eh**khaht^{Y} k ighrahvahg**zah**loo
What's the flight number?	**Какой номер рейса?**	kah**koy** **no**mmeer **ray**ssah
What time do we arrive?	**Когда мы прилетаем?**	kahg**dah** mi preelee**tah**eem
I'd like to ... my flight.	**Я хотел(а) бы ... рейс.**	^{Y}ah khaht^{Y}**ehl**(ah) bi ... rayss
change	**поменять**	pahmeen^{Y}**aht**^{Y}
confirm	**подтвердить**	pahttveer**deet**^{Y}
I'd like to cancel my flight.	**Я хотел(а) бы отказаться от билета.**	^{Y}ah khaht^{Y}**ehl**(ah) bi ahtkah**zaht**^{Y}sah aht beel^{Y}**eh**tah

ПРИБЫТИЕ
ARRIVAL

ВЫЛЕТ
DEPARTURE

Train *Поезд*

Unless you have a great deal of time at your disposal, the train is unlikely to be your sole method of transport within Russia. However it cannot be beaten if you want time to soak in the atmosphere, meet people and practise your linguistic skills. Railway stations are always animated and exciting places where you can glimpse the diversity of the peoples of the former Soviet Union. On long journeys, your reservations will normally be made in advance. For short trips out to the suburbs, check with your Intourist representative beforehand on any travel limits that must be observed.

Экспресс (ehk**sprehss**)	Long-distance express with luxury coaches; stops only at main stations; fare is higher
Скорый поезд (**skor**riy **po**eezd)	Standard long-distance train; stopping at main stations; fare is higher
Пассажирский поезд (pahssah**zhirs**keey **po**eezd)	Inter-city train; doesn't stop at very small stations; regular fare. This type of train is seldom available for tourist travel.
Электричка (ehleek**treech**ʸkah)	Local train stopping at almost every station
Международный вагон (meezhdoonah**rod**niy vah**gon**)	Sleeper with individual compartments (usually double) and washing facilities
Купированный вагон (koo**pee**rahvahnniy vah**gon**)	Car with compartments for four persons; berths with blankets and pillows. You can choose between "soft" and "hard", which correspond to our first and second class:
Мягкий вагон (**m**ʸ**ahkh**keey vah**gon**)	"soft" (1st class); individual compartments for two or four persons
Жёсткий вагон (**zhost**keey vah**gon**)	"hard" (2nd class)
Плацкартный вагон (plahts**kahrt**niy vah**gon**)	2nd class only; no individual compartments, but with sleeping places (4 persons and 2 persons aside)

ДЛЯ КУРЯЩИХ SMOKER	ДЛЯ НЕКУРЯЩИХ NONSMOKER

To the railway station *На вокзал*

Where's the railway station?	**Где вокзал?**	gd^{y}eh vahg**zahl**
Is there ...?	**Есть ...?**	^{y}ehst^{y}
bus	**автобус**	ahf**to**bbooss
tram (streetcar)	**трамвай**	trahm**vigh**
underground (subway)	**метро**	mee**tro**
Taxi!	**Такси!**	tahk**see**
Take me to Leningrad Railway Station.	**Пожалуйста, на Ленинградский вокзал.**	pah**zhahl**stah nah leeneen**grahts**keey vahg**zahl**

ВХОД	ENTRANCE
ВЫХОД	EXIT
БИЛЕТНЫЕ КАССЫ	TICKETS

Information *Справки*

Where's the ...?	**Где ...?**	gd^{y}eh
booking office	**предварительная продажа билетов**	preedvah**ree**teel^{y}nah^{y}ah prah**dah**zhah beel^{y}**eh**tahf
left-luggage office (baggage check)	**камера хранения**	**kah**meerah khrah**n^{y}eh**nee^{y}ah
lost property (lost and found) office	**бюро находок**	b^{y}oo**ro** nah**kho**ddahk
newsstand	**газетный киоск**	gahz^{y}**eh**tniy kee**osk**
platform 7	**платформа 7**	plaht**for**mah 7
reservations office	**предварительная продажа билетов**	preedvah**ree**teel^{y}nah^{y}ah prah**dah**zhah beel^{y}**eh**tahf
snack bar	**буфет**	boof^{y}**eht**
ticket office	**билетные кассы**	beel^{y}**eh**tni^{y}eh **kah**ssi
track 3	**путь 3**	poot^{y} 3
waiting room	**зал ожидания**	zahl ahzhi**ddah**nee^{y}ah
Where are the toilets?	**Где туалет?**	gd^{y}eh tooahl^{y}**eht**

ПРИГОРОДНЫЕ ПОЕЗДА	SUBURBAN LINES
ПОЕЗДА ДАЛЬНЕГО СЛЕДОВАНИЯ	LONG-DISTANCE LINES

TAXI, see page 21

When is the ... train to Volgograd?	**Когда... поезд на Волгоград?**	kahg**dah** ... **po**eezd nah volgah**graht**
first/last/next	**первый/последний/ следующий**	**p^{y}ehr**viy/pah**sl^{y}ehd**neey **sl^{y}eh**doo^{y}ooshch^{y}eey
What time does the train to Zagorsk leave?	**Во сколько отходит поезд в Загорск?**	vah **skol^{y}**kah aht**kho**ddeet **po**eezd v zah**gorsk**
What's the fare to Odessa?	**Сколько стоит билет до Одессы?**	**skol^{y}**kah **sto**eet beel**^{y}eht** dah ah**dehs**si
Is it a through train?	**Это прямой поезд?**	**eh**tah pree**moy po**eezd
Is there a connection to ...?	**Есть ли пересадка на...?**	^{y}ehst^{y} lee peeree**saht**kah nah
Do I have to change trains?	**Мне надо делать пересадку?**	mn^{y}eh **nah**dah **d^{y}eh**laht^{y} peeree**saht**koo
Is the train running on time?	**Поезд отходит вовремя?**	**po**eezd aht**kho**ddeet **vo**vr^{y}ehm^{y}ah
What time does the train arrive in Kiev?	**Во сколько поезд приходит в Киев?**	vah **skol^{y}**kah **po**eezd pree**kho**ddeet f **kee**^{y}ehf
Where is the dining car/sleeping car?	**Где вагон-ресторан/ спальный вагон?**	gd^{y}eh vah**gon**-reestah**rahn**/ **spahl^{y}**niy vah**gon**
Does this train stop in Minsk?	**Останавливается ли этот поезд в Минске?**	ahstah**nah**vleevaheetsah lee **eh**taht **po**eezd v **meen**sk^{y}eh
Which platform does the train to St. Petersburg leave from?	**С какой платформы отходит поезд на Санкт Петербург?**	s kah**koy** plaht**for**mi aht**kho**ddeet poeezd nah sahnkt **peh**teerboorg
Which platform does the train from Riga arrive at?	**На какую платформу приходит поезд из Риги?**	nah kah**koo**^{y}oo plaht**for**moo pree**kho**ddeet **po**eezd eez **ree**gee
I'd like (to buy) a timetable.	**Я хотел(а) бы (купить) расписание поездов.**	^{y}ah khaht**^{y}ehl**(ah) bi (koo**peet^{y}**) rahspee**sah**-nee^{y}eh paheez**dof**

РАСПИСАНИЕ ПОЕЗДОВ	TIMETABLE
К ПОЕЗДАМ	TO THE TRAINS
НА ПЛАТФОРМЫ 5–6	TO PLATFORMS 5–6

Это прямой поезд.	It's a direct train.
Пересадка в...	You have to change at ...
В...вы должны пересесть на местный поезд.	Change at ... and get a local train.
Платформа номер 7...	Platform 7 is ...
там/внизу слева/справа	over there/downstairs on the left/right
Поезд на Смоленск отходит с платформы номер 5.	The train to Smolensk will leave from platform 5.
Поезд на Брест опаздывает на 30 минут.	The train to Brest will be 30 minutes late.

Tickets *Билеты*

You can get tickets through your guide or the Service Bureau at your hotel. If you want to buy them yourself at the railway station, it'll cost you more in time and nerves.

One ticket to Moscow, please.	**Один билет до пожалуйста.**	ah**deen** beel^{y}**eht** dah mahsk**vi** pah**zhahl**stah
single (one-way)	**в один конец**	v ah**deen** kahn^{y}**ehts**
return (roundtrip)	**туда и обратно**	too**dah** ee ah**braht**nah
"soft" (1st)	**мягкий вагон**	**m^{y}ahkh**keey vah**gon**
"hard" (2nd)	**жёсткий вагон**	**zhost**keey vah**gon**
for today	**на сегодня**	nah see**vo**dn^{y}ah
for the 5th of November	**на пятое ноября**	nah **p^{y}ah**tah^{y}eh nahee**br^{y}ah**
How much does it cost?	**Сколько стоит?**	**skol^{y}**kah **sto**eet
half price	**полцены**	poltseh**ni**
full fare	**полная цена**	**pol**nah^{y}ah tsin**nah**
supplement	**доплата**	dah**plah**tah
I'd like to reserve a seat.	**Мне нужна плац-карта.**	mn^{y}eh noozh**nah** plahts-**kahr**tah
I'd like a ticket for the sleeping car.	**Билет в спальный вагон, пожалуйста.**	beel^{y}**eht** f **spahl^{y}**niy vah**gon** pah**zhahl**stah

DATES, see page 151 / NUMBERS, see page 147

All aboard! *Занимайте места!*

Is this the right platform for the train to Kharkov?	**Поезд на Харьков отходит с этой платформы?**	**po**eezd nah **khahr^y**kahf aht**khod**deet s **eh**tigh plaht**for**mi
Is this the train to Yaroslavl?	**Это поезд на Ярославль?**	**eh**tah **po**eezd nah ^{y}ahrah**slahvl^y**
Where is carriage no ...?	**Где вагон номер ...?**	gd^{y}eh vah**gon** **no**mmeer
May I get past?	**Разрешите, пожалуйста.**	rahzree**shit^y**eh pah**zhahl**stah
Is this seat taken?	**Это место занято?**	**eh**tah **m^{y}ehs**tah **zah**neetah

On the train *В поезде*

The attendant (*проводник* – prahvahd**neek**) will check your ticket, bring you tea and try to solve any problems.

There is usually a dining car on long-distance trains, but it's always a good idea to bring a picnic along.

I think that's my seat.	**Мне кажется, это моё место.**	mn^{y}eh **kah**zhehtsah **eh**tah mah**^{y}o m^{y}ehs**tah
Here's my reservation.	**Вот моя плацкарта.**	vot mah**^{y}ah** plahts**kahr**tah
Would you let me know before we get to Rostov?	**Скажите мне, пожалуйста, когда мы будем подъезжать к Ростову.**	skah**zhit^y**eh mn^{y}eh pah**zhahl**stah kahg**dah** mi **boo**deem pahd^{y}eez**zhaht^y** k rahs**to**vvoo
What town is this?	**Какой это город?**	kah**koy** **eh**tah **go**rraht
How long does the train stop here?	**Сколько поезд стоит здесь?**	**skol^y**kah **po**eezd stah**eet** zd^{y}ehs^y
When do we get to Moscow?	**Во сколько мы будем в Москве?**	vah **skol^y**kah mi **boo**deem v mahsk**v^{y}eh**
May I open/close the window?	**Можно открыть/закрыть окно?**	**mozh**nah aht**krit^y**/zah**krit^y** ahk**no**
Would you mind if we change places?	**Можем мы поменяться местами?**	**mo**zhehm mi pahmee**n^{y}aht^y**sah mees**tah**mee
Where's the dining car/snack bar?	**Где вагон-ресторан/буфет?**	gd^{y}eh vah**gon**-reestah**rahn**/boof**^{y}eht**

In the sleeping car *В спальном вагоне*

You'll have to book your berth in advance.

Where is compartment no. ...?	**Где купе номер ...?**	gd^{y}eh koo**peh no**mmeer
Where's my berth?	**Где моя полка?**	gd^{y}eh mah^y**ah pol**kah
I'd like a lower/upper berth.	**Я хотел(а) бы нижнюю/верхнюю полку.**	^{y}ah khaht^y**ehl**(ah) bi **neezh**n^{y}oo^{y}oo/**v^{y}ehrkh**n^{y}oo-^{y}oo **pol**koo
Would you wake me at 7 o'clock?	**Разбудите меня, пожалуйста, в семь часов утра.**	rahzboo**deet**^{y}eh meen**^{y}ah** pah**zhahl**stah f s^{y}ehm^y ch^{y}ee**ssof** oo**trah**
Could you bring us some tea?	**Можете ли вы принести нам чай?**	**mo**zhit^{y}eh lee vi preenees**tee** nahm ch^{y}igh
3 glasses, please.	**Три стакана, пожалуйста.**	tree stah**kah**nah pah**zhahl**stah
May I turn out/turn on the light?	**Можно выключить/включить свет?**	**mozh**nah vikl^{y}ooch^{y}eet^y/fkl^{y}oo**ch^{y}eet^y** sv^{y}eht

Baggage and porters *Багаж и носильщики*

Porter!	**Носильщик!**	nah**sseel^y**shch^{y}eek
Can you take my luggage, please?	**Возьмите, пожалуйста, мой багаж.**	vahz^y**meet**^{y}eh pah**zhahl**stah moy bah**gahsh**
Put it down here, please.	**Поставьте его сюда, пожалуйста.**	pah**stahv^y**t^{y}eh ee**vo** s^{y}oo**dah** pah**zhahl**stah
Where's the left-luggage office (baggage check)?	**Где камера хранения?**	gd^{y}eh **kah**meerah khrah**n^{y}eh**nee^{y}ah
I'd like to leave my luggage, please.	**Я хочу сдать багаж в камеру хранения.**	^{y}ah khah**ch^{y}oo** zdaht^y bah**gahsh** f **kah**meeroo khrah**n^{y}eh**nee^{y}ah
I'd like to register (check) my luggage.	**Я хочу отправить этот багаж.**	^{y}ah khah**ch^{y}oo** aht**prah**veet^y **eh**taht bah**gahsh**

ПРИЁМ БАГАЖА

REGISTERING (CHECKING) BAGGAGE

PORTERS, see also page 18

Public transport *Общественный транспорт*

Underground (Subway) *Метро*

The "metro" is the fastest and most convenient way of getting around in town. There are good networks in Moscow, St. Petersburg, Kiev and some other major cities. Moscow has the most extensive underground, which is worth a visit for its fabulous décor alone. It runs from 6 a.m. to 1 a.m., and the fare is standard, regardless of the distance. You'll need to buy some tokens (*жетоны*—zheh**to**nee) at the counter, and drop one in the automat to enter the metro. If you're planning to get around Moscow a lot though, you may decide to buy a pass (*единый билет*—^{y}e**dee**nee beel^{y}**eht**), valid for 8 days, 16 days or monthly for travel on the metro, bus, trolleybus and tram.

Where's the nearest underground (subway) station?	**Где ближайшая станция метро?**	gd^{y}eh blee**zhigh**shah^{y}ah **stahn**tsi^{y}ah mee**tro**
Does this train go to ...?	**Этот поезд идёт до ...?**	**eh**taht **po**eezd eed^{y}**ot** dah
Where do I have to change?	**Где мне надо делать пересадку?**	gd^{y}eh mn^{y}eh **nah**dah **d^{y}eh**laht^{y} peeree**saht**koo
Could you tell me which is the next station, please?	**Скажите, пожалуйста, какая следующая станция?**	skah**zhit**^{y}eh pah**zhahl**stah kah**kah**^{y}ah **sl^{y}eh**doo^{y}oosh-ch^{y}ah^{y}ah **stahn**tsi^{y}ah

ОСТОРОЖНО, ДВЕРИ ЗАКРЫВАЮТСЯ!	MIND THE DOORS!
СЛЕДУЮЩАЯ СТАНЦИЯ...	NEXT STATION ...

Which line should I take to ...?	**По какой линии мне доехать до ...?**	pah kah**koy lee**nee mn^{y}eh dah^{y}**eh**khaht^{y} dah
Can you tell me when to get off?	**Вы мне скажете, когда надо сходить?**	vi mn^{y}eh **skah**zhit^{y}eh kahg**dah nah**dah skhah**deet**^{y}

ВХОД	ENTRANCE
ВЫХОД	EXIT
ПЕРЕХОД	FOR CHANGING (to another line)

Bus – Tram (Streetcar) *Автобус – Трамвай*

Buses are not as fast as the underground and run less frequently; on the other hand, you see more of the city. The fare is standard, regardless of the distance (but you can't change buses on the same ticket). It is a good idea to buy a booklet of tickets at a newsstand or metro station, although you can also get one in the bus, from the driver. Tickets have to be cancelled on the bus.

I'd like a booklet of tickets.	**Дайте мне, пожалуйста, книжечку.**	**dight**^{y}eh mn^{y}eh pah**zhahl**stah **knee**zhehch^{y}koo
Which tram (streetcar) goes to the centre?	**Какой трамвай идёт в центр?**	kah**koy** trahm**vigh** eed^{y}**ot** f tsehntr
Which bus goes to Moscow State University?	**Какой автобус идёт к МГУ?**	kah**koy** ahf**to**bbooss eed^{y}**ot** k ehm geh oo
Which bus do I take for the ... Hotel?	**На каком автобусе я могу доехать до гостиницы ...?**	nah kah**kom** ahf**to**bbooss^{y}eh ^{y}ah mah**goo** dah^{y}**eh**khaht^{y} dah gah**stee**neetsi
Where's the ...?	**Где ...?**	gd^{y}eh
bus stop	**остановка автобуса**	ahstah**nof**kah ahf**to**bboossah
terminus	**конечная остановка**	kahn^{y}**eh**ch^{y}nah^{y}ah ahstah**nof**kah
When's the next bus?	**Когда идёт следующий автобус?**	kahg**dah** eed^{y}**ot** **sl^{y}eh**doo^{y}ooshch^{y}eey ahf**to**bbooss
Do I have to change buses?	**Мне надо делать пересадку?**	mn^{y}eh **nah**dah **d^{y}eh**laht^{y} peeree**saht**koo
How many bus stops are there to ...?	**Сколько остановок до ...?**	**skol**^{y}kah ahstah**no**vvahk dah
Can you tell me when to get off?	**Вы мне скажете, когда надо сходить?**	vi mn^{y}eh **skah**zhit^{y}eh kahg**dah nah**dah skhah**deet**^{y}
Are you getting off now/at the next stop?	**Вы сейчас/на следующей сходите?**	vi see**ch^{y}ahss**/nah **sl^{y}eh**doo^{y}ooshch^{y}eey **skho**deet^{y}eh
Excuse me. Does this bus/trolleybus go to the Red Square?	**Будьте добры. Этот автобус/троллейбус идёт до Красной площади?**	**boot**^{y}tee dah**bri. eh**taht ahf**to**bbooss/trahl^{y}**ay**booss eed^{y}**ot** dah **krahs**nigh **plo**shch^{y}ahdee

Ship *Пароход*

When does the next ship for ... leave?	**Когда отходит следующий пароход в ...?**	kahg**dah** aht**khod**deet **sl^{y}eh**doo^{y}ooshch^{y}eey pahrah**khot v**
Where's the embarkation point?	**Где пристань?**	gd^{y}eh **pree**stahn^{y}
Where can I get tickets for a ...?	**Где можно купить билеты ...?**	gd^{y}eh **mozh**nah koo**peet^{y}** beel**^{y}eh**ti
crossing	**на переправу**	nah peeree**prah**voo
cruise	**в круиз**	f kroo**ees**
tour of the harbour	**на экскурсию по гавани**	nah ehks**koor**see^{y}oo pah **gah**vahnee
Volga trip	**в круиз по Волге**	f kroo**ees** pah **vol**g^{y}eh
How long does the journey (trip) take?	**Сколько времени длится путешествие?**	**skol^{y}**kah **vr^{y}eh**meenee **dleet**sah pootee**shehst**vee^{y}eh
Which ports do we stop at?	**В какие порты мы будем заходить?**	f kah**kee**^{y}eh pahr**ti** mi **boo**deem zahkhah**deet^{y}**
boat	**лодка**	**lot**kah
cabin	**каюта**	kah**^{y}oo**tah
single	**отдельная**	ahtd**^{y}ehl^{y}**nah^{y}ah
double	**двухместная**	dvookh**m^{y}ehst**nah^{y}ah
deck	**палуба**	**pah**loobah
ferry	**паром**	pah**rom**
hydrofoil	**судно на подводных крыльях**	**sood**nah nah pahd**vod**nikh **kril**^{y}ahkh
life belt	**спасательный круг**	spah**sah**teel^{y}niy krook
life boat	**спасательная лодка**	spah**sah**teel^{y}nah^{y}ah **lot**kah
motor boat	**моторная лодка**	mah**tor**nah^{y}ah **lot**kah
motor ship	**теплоход**	teeplah**khot**
ship	**корабль, судно**	kah**rahbl^{y}**, **sood**nah
steamboat	**пароход**	pahrah**khot**

Other means of transport *Другие способы передвижения*

One method of transport you may want to try in town is the *маршрутное такси* (mahrsh**root**nah^{y}eh tahk**see**), which has space for 11 persons and follows fixed routes indicated on the outside.

bicycle	**велосипед**	veelahsee**p^{y}eht**
helicopter	**вертолёт**	veertah**l^{y}ot**
motor cycle	**мотоцикл**	mahtah**tsikl**
motorbike/scooter	**мотороллер**	mahtah**rol^{y}**ehr

Car *Машина*

The following documents are required: International Driving Licence, car registration papers and a declaration certifying that you'll be taking your car out of Russia. When entering the country, you'll have to pay road tax. Foreign tourists are not allowed to deviate from their itinerary which has to be organised and approved in advance.

Petrol is sold in units of 10 litres and is paid for with coupons (vouchers), which can be bought from Intourist (at the border). Petrol stations are rather scarce.

Observe speed limits. The use of seatbelts is compulsory.

Where's the nearest filling station?	**Где ближайшая заправочная станция?**	gd^{y}eh blee**zhigh**shah^{y}ah zah**prah**vahch^{y}nah^{y}ah **stahn**tsi^{y}ah
Full tank, please.	**Полный бак, пожалуйста.**	**pol**niy bahk pah**zhahl**stah
Give me 20 litres of ...	**Дайте мне двадцать литров ...**	**dight**^{y}eh mn^{y}eh 20 **lee**trahf
super (premium)	**бензина 98**	been**zee**nah 98
extra (95-octane)	**бензина 95**	been**zee**nah 95
regular	**бензина 93**	been**zee**nah 93
diesel	**дизельного топлива**	**dee**zeel^{y}nahvah **to**pleevah
Please check the ...	**Проверьте, пожалуйста ...**	prah**v^{y}ehr^{y}**t^{y}eh pah**zhahl**stah
battery	**аккумулятор**	ahkoomoo**l^{y}ah**tahr
brake fluid	**тормозную жидкость**	tahrmahz**noo**^{y}oo **zhit**kahst^{y}
oil/water	**масло/воду**	**mah**slah/**vo**ddoo
Would you check the tyre pressure?	**Проверьте, пожалуйста, давление в шинах.**	prah**v^{y}ehr^{y}**t^{y}eh pah**zhahl**stah dah**vl^{y}eh**nee^{y}eh f **shin**nahkh
Please check the spare tyre, too.	**Проверьте и запасное колесо, пожалуйста.**	prah**v^{y}ehr^{y}**t^{y}eh ee zahpahs**no**^{y}eh kahlee**sso** pah**zhahl**stah
Can you mend this puncture (fix this flat)?	**Можно заделать этот прокол?**	**mozh**nah zah**d^{y}eh**laht^{y} **eh**taht prah**kol**
Would you change the ..., please?	**Замените, пожалуйста ...**	zahmee**neet**^{y}eh pah**zhahl**stah
fan belt	**клиновидный ремень**	kleenah**veed**niy reem**^{y}ehn^{y}**

CAR HIRE, see page 20

spark(ing) plugs	**свечи**	**sv^{y}eh**ch^{y}ee
tyre	**шину**	**shi**nnoo
wipers	**стеклоочистители**	steeklahahch^{y}ees**tee**teelee
Would you clean the windscreen (windshield)?	**Помойте, пожалуйста, ветровое стекло.**	pah**moy**t^{y}eh pah**zhahl**stah veetrah**vo**^{y}eh steek**lo**
Where can I get my car washed?	**Где можно вымыть машину?**	gd^{y}eh **mozh**nah **vi**mmit^{y} mah**shi**nnoo
Is there a car wash?	**Есть ли здесь автомойка?**	^{y}ehst^{y} lee zd^{y}ehs^{y} ahftah**moy**kah

Asking the way *Как пройти/проехать... ?*

Can you tell me the way to ...?	**Как проехать до ... ?**	kahk prah**^{y}eh**khaht^{y} dah
How do I get to ...?	**Как доехать до ... ?**	kahk dah**^{y}eh**khaht^{y} dah
Is this the road to ...?	**Это дорога в/на ... ?**	**eh**tah dah**ro**ggah v/nah
How far is the next village?	**Как далеко/Сколько километров до ближайшей деревни?**	kahk dahlee**ko**/**skol^{y}**kah keelah**m^{y}eh**trahf dah blee**zhigh**shay deer**^{y}eh**vnee
How far is it to ... from here?	**Как далеко до ... отсюда?**	kahk dahlee**ko** dah ... ahts**^{y}oo**dah
Is there a motorway (expressway)?	**Есть ли автомагистраль?**	^{y}ehst^{y} lee ahftah-mahgees**trahl^{y}**
How long does it take by car/on foot?	**Сколько времени ехать на машине/идти пешком?**	**skol^{y}**kah **vr^{y}eh**meenee **^{y}eh**khaht^{y} nah mah**shin**^{y}eh/eet**tee** peesh**kom**
Can I drive to the centre of town?	**Можно доехать до центра города?**	**mozh**nah dah**^{y}eh**khaht^{y} dah **tsehn**trah **go**rrahdah
Can you tell me where ... is?	**Будьте добры! Скажите пожалуйста, где ...**	**boot**^{y}tee dah**bri**. skah-**zhit**^{y}eh pah**zhahl**stah gd^{y}eh
How can I find this place/address?	**Как мне найти это место/этот адрес?**	kahk mn^{y}eh nigh**tee** **eh**tah **m^{y}eh**stah/**eh**taht **ah**dreess
Where's this?	**Где это находится?**	gd^{y}eh **eh**tah nah**kho**ddeetsah
Can you show me on the map where I am?	**Покажите, пожалуйста, на карте, где я нахожусь.**	pahkah**zhit**^{y}eh pah**zhahl**stah nah **kahrt**^{y}eh gd^{y}eh ^{y}ah nahkhah**zhoos^{y}**

Это не та дорога.	You've taken the wrong road.
Поезжайте прямо.	Go straight ahead.
Это там, налево/направо.	It's down there on the left/right.
напротив/позади ... около/после ...	opposite/behind ... next to/after ...
север/юг восток/запад	north/south east/west
Поезжайте до первого/ второго перекрёстка.	Go to the first/second crossroad (intersection).
У светофора сверните налево.	Turn left at the traffic lights.
На углу сверните направо.	Turn right at the next corner.
Поезжайте по этой/той дороге.	Take this/that road.
Это улица одностороннего движения.	It's a one-way street.
Вам надо вернуться в .../ ехать назад в ...	You have to go back to ...
Следуйте за дорожными знаками ...	Follow signs for ...

Parking *Стоянка*

Where can I park?	**Где можно поставить машину?**	gd^{y}eh **mozh**nah pah**stah**veet^{y} mah**shi**nnoo
Is there a ... nearby?	**Есть ли здесь поблизости ... ?**	^{y}ehst^{y} lee zd^{y}ehs^{y} pah**blee**zahstee
car park multistorey car park	**автостоянка крытая стоянка**	ahftahstah^{y}**ahn**kah **kri**ttah^{y}ah stah^{y}**ahn**kah
May I park here?	**Можно здесь поставить машину/парковаться?**	**mozh**nah zd^{y}ehs^{y} pah**stah**veet^{y} mah**shi**nnoo/ pahrkah**vaht^{y}**sah
How long can I park here?	**Сколько времени можно здесь стоять/ парковаться?**	**skol^{y}**kah **vr^{y}eh**meenee **mozh**nah zd^{y}ehs^{y} stah^{y}**aht^{y}**/ pahrkah**vaht^{y}**sah
What's the charge per hour?	**Сколько стоит час?**	**skol^{y}**kah **sto**eet ch^{y}ahss
Is there a parking attendant?	**Это охраняемая стоянка?**	**eh**tah ahkhrahn^{y}**ah**eemah^{y}ah stah^{y}**ahn**kah

Breakdown – Road assistance *Авария – ГАИ*

The *ГАИ* (short for *Госавтоинспекция*, the state vehicle inspection authority) patrols the traffic on highways and gives road assistance.

My car has broken down.	**У меня авария.**	oo meen^y**ah** ahv**ah**ree^{y}ah
Excuse me, please!	**Будьте добры!**	**boot**^{y}tee dah**bri**
Can you help me?	**Можете ли вы мне помочь?**	**mo**zhit^{y}eh lee vi mn^{y}eh pah**moch**^{y}
Where can I make a phone call?	**Где можно позвонить?**	gd^{y}eh **mozh**nah pahzvah**neet**^{y}
Where's the nearest garage?	**Где ближайшая станция обслуживания?**	gd^{y}eh blee**zhigh**shah^{y}ah **stahn**tsi^{y}ah ahps**loo**zhivvahnee^{y}ah
Can you send a mechanic/a breakdown van (tow truck)?	**Можете прислать механика/буксирный автомобиль?**	**mo**zhit^{y}eh pree**slaht**^{y} mee**khah**neekah/book**seer**niy ahftahmah**beel**^{y}
My car won't start.	**Двигатель не заводится.**	**dvee**gahteel^y nee zah**vo**ddeetsah
The battery is dead.	**Аккумулятор разрядился.**	ahkoomool^y**ah**tahr rahzree**deel**sah
I have a flat tyre.	**У меня проколота шина.**	oo meen^y**ah** prah**ko**llahtah **shin**nah
There is something wrong with the …	**… не в порядке/не работает.**	… nee f pahr^y**aht**k^{y}eh/nee rah**bo**ttah^{y}eht
brake/brakes	**тормоз/тормоза**	**tor**mahs/tahrmah**zah**
brake lights	**стоп-сигнал**	stop-see**gnahl**
carburettor	**карбюратор**	kahrb^{y}oo**rah**tahr
clutch	**сцепление**	stsehpl^y**eh**nee^{y}eh
exhaust pipe	**выхлоп**	**vi**khlahp
gears	**передачи**	peeree**dah**ch^{y}ee
headlights	**фары**	**fah**ri
motor	**двигатель/мотор**	**dvee**gahteel^y/mah**tor**
radiator	**радиатор**	rahdee**ah**tahr
wheel	**колесо**	kahlee**sso**
Can you lend me …?	**Вы мне можете одолжить …?**	vi mn^{y}eh **mo**zhit^{y}eh ahdahl**zhit**^{y}
jack	**домкрат**	dahm**kraht**
spanner	**гаечный ключ**	**gah**eech^{y}niy kl^{y}ooch^y
tools	**инструменты**	eenstroom^y**eh**nti

Do you have any spare parts?	**Есть ли у вас запчасти?**	^{y}ehst^{y} lee oo vahss zahp**ch^{y}ahs**tee

Repair *Ремонт*

Can you repair my car?	**Можете ли вы от-ремонтировать машину?**	**mo**zhit^{y}eh lee vi ahtreemahn**tee**rahvaht^{y} mah**shi**nnoo
How long will it take?	**Сколько времени займёт ремонт?**	**skol^{y}**kah **vr^{y}eh**meenee zigh**m^{y}ot** ree**mont**
How much will it cost?	**Сколько это будет стоить?**	**skol^{y}**kah **eh**tah **boo**deet **sto**eet^{y}

Accident *Несчастный случай*

Please call the police/ road assistance.	**Вызовите милицию/ ГАИ, пожалуйста.**	vizzah**veet**^{y}eh mee**lee**tsi^{y}oo/ **gah**ee pah**zhahl**stah
There's been an accident. It's about 2 km from ...	**Несчастный случай. Примерно в двух километрах от ...**	nee**shch^{y}ahst**niy **sloo**ch^{y}igh. pree**m^{y}ehr**nah v dvookh keelah**m^{y}eh**trahkh aht
There are people injured.	**Есть раненые.**	^{y}ehst^{y} **rah**neeni^{y}eh
Call a doctor/an ambulance quickly.	**Вызовите врача/ скорую помощь.**	vizzah**veet**^{y}eh vrah**ch^{y}ah**/ **sko**rroo^{y}oo **po**mmahshch^{y}
What's your name and address?	**Как ваша фамилия и адрес?**	kahk **vah**shah fah**mee**lee^{y}ah ee **ah**dreess

N.B. Insurance is not obligatory, but it is advisable to take out a policy with the state insurance agency Ingosstrakh (*Ингосстрах*).

Road signs *Дорожные знаки*

ОБГОН ЗАПРЕЩЁН	no overtaking (passing)
ОБЪЕЗД	diversion (detour)
ОГРАНИЧЕНИЕ СКОРОСТИ	reduce speed
ОДНОСТОРОННЕЕ ДВИЖЕНИЕ	one-way traffic
ОПАСНЫЙ ПОВОРОТ	dangerous bend (curve)
ПРОЕЗД ЗАПРЕЩЁН	no through road
СТОП	stop
СТОЯНКА ЗАПРЕЩЕНА	no parking

EMERGENCY, see page 155

Sightseeing

Is there an Intourist office?	**Есть ли здесь бюро Интуриста?**	^{y}ehst^y lee zd^{y}ehs^y b^y**ooro** eentoo**ree**stah
What are the main points of interest?	**Какие здесь главные достопримечательности?**	kah**kee**yeh zd^{y}ehs^y **glahv**-ni^{y}eh dahstahpreemee-**ch^{y}aht**^{y}ehl^{y}nahstee
We're only here for …	**Мы здесь только на…**	mi zd^{y}ehs^y **tol^y**kah nah
a few hours	**несколько часов**	**n^{y}ehs**kahl^{y}kah ch^{y}ee**ssof**
a day	**день**	d^{y}ehn^y
a week	**неделю**	nee**d^{y}ehl**^{y}oo
Can you recommend a sightseeing tour/ an excursion?	**Какую экскурсию вы можете нам посоветовать?**	kah**koo**^{y}oo ehks**koor**see^{y}oo vi **mo**zhit^{y}eh nahm pah-sah**v^{y}eh**tahvaht^y
I'd like to sign up for this tour.	**Я хочу записаться на эту экскурсию.**	^{y}ah khah**ch^{y}oo** zahpee-**ssaht**^{y}sah nah **eh**too ehks**koor**see^{y}oo
Where is the bus stop?	**Где остановка автобуса?**	gd^{y}eh ahstah**nof**kah ahf**to**bboossah
Will someone pick us up from the hotel?	**Заедут ли за нами в гостиницу?**	zah**^{y}eh**doot lee zah **nah**mee v gahs**tee**neetsoo
How much does the tour cost?	**Сколько стоит экскурсия?**	**skol^y**kah **stoeet** ehks**koor**see^{y}ah
What time does it start?	**Во сколько начинается?**	vah **skol^y**kah nahch^{y}ee-**nah**eetsah
Is lunch included in the price of the tour?	**Включён ли обед в цену экскурсии?**	fkl^{y}oo**ch^{y}on** lee ah**b^{y}eht** f **tseh**noo ehks**koor**see
What time do we get back?	**Когда мы вернёмся?**	kahg**dah** mi veern**^{y}om**sah
Do we have free time in …?	**Будет ли у нас свободное время в…?**	**boo**deet lee oo nahss svah-**bod**nah^{y}eh **vr^{y}ehm**^{y}ah v
Is there an English-speaking guide?	**Есть ли гид, говорящий по-английски?**	^{y}ehst^y lee geet gahvah**r^{y}ah**-shch^{y}eey pah ahn**gleey**skee

Where is/Where are the ...?	**Где находится/находятся ...?**	gd^{y}eh nah**kho**ddeetsah/ nah**khod**^{y}ahtsah
art gallery	**картинная галерея**	kahr**tee**nah^{y}ah gahleer^y**eh**^{y}ah
avenue	**проспект**	prahsp^y**ehkt**
Botanical gardens	**ботанический сад**	bahtah**nee**ch^{y}eeskeey saht
boulevard	**бульвар**	bool^y**vahr**
building	**здание**	**zdah**nee^{y}eh
castle	**замок**	**zah**mahk
cathedral	**собор**	sah**bor**
cave	**пещера**	pee**shch^{y}eh**rah
cemetery	**кладбище**	**klahd**beeshch^{y}eh
chapel	**часовня**	ch^{y}ah**ssov**n^{y}ah
church	**церковь**	**tsehr**kahf^y
city centre	**центр города**	tsehntr **go**rrahdah
concert hall	**концертный зал**	kahn**tsehrt**niy zahl
convent	**монастырь**	mahnah**stir**^{y}
department store	**универмаг**	ooneev^{y}ehr**mahk**
docks	**пристань**	**pree**stahn^y
downtown area	**центр города**	tsehntr **go**rrahdah
exhibition	**выставка**	**vi**stahfkah
factory	**завод, фабрика**	zah**vot**, **fah**breekah
fair	**ярмарка-выставка**	^{y}**ahr**mahrkah-**vi**stahfkah
fortress	**крепость**	kr^y**eh**pahst^y
fountain	**фонтан**	fahn**tahn**
gardens	**сад**	saht
harbour	**гавань, порт**	**gah**vahn^y, port
Kremlin*	**Кремль**	kr^{y}ehml^y
lake	**озеро**	**o**zeerah
law courts	**суд**	soot
library	**библиотека**	beebleeaht^y**eh**kah
market	**рынок**	**ri**nnahk
covered market	**крытый рынок**	**kri**ttiy **ri**nnahk
memorial	**памятник, мемориал**	**pah**meetneek, meemahree**ahl**
monastery	**монастырь**	mahnah**stir**^{y}
monument	**памятник**	**pah**meetneek
museum	**музей**	mooz^y**ay**
observatory	**обсерватория**	ahps^{y}ehrvah**to**rree^{y}ah
old town	**старая часть города**	**stah**rah^{y}ah ch^{y}ahst^y **go**rrahdah
opera house	**оперный театр**	**o**ppeerniy tee**ahtr**
palace	**дворец**	dvahr^y**ehts**
park	**парк**	pahrk
planetarium	**планетарий**	plahnee**tah**reey

* The Moscow Kremlin is certainly the most famous, but other ancient cities have "Kremlins" as well ("Kremlin" means fortress).

Red Square	**Красная Площадь**	**krahs**nah^{y}ah **plo**shch^{y}eed^{y}
ruins	**развалины**	rahz**vah**leeni
square	**площадь**	**plo**shch^{y}eed^{y}
stadium	**стадион**	stahdee**on**
statue	**статуя**	**stah**too^{y}ah
street	**улица**	**oo**leetsah
temple	**храм**	khrahm
theatre	**театр**	tee**ahtr**
tomb	**могила, усыпальница**	mah**gee**lah, oosi**pahl^{y}**neetsah
tower	**башня**	**bahsh**n^{y}ah
town centre	**центр города**	tsehntr **go**rrahdah
town hall	**горсовет**	gorsah**v^{y}eht**
university	**университет**	ooneev^{y}ehrsee**t^{y}eht**
zoo	**зоопарк**	zah**pahrk**

Admission *Вход*

Is ... open on Sundays?	**Открыт ли ... по воскресеньям?**	aht**krit** lee ... pah vahskree**s^{y}eh**n^{y}ahm
When does it open/ close?	**Когда открывается/ закрывается?**	kahg**dah** ahtkri**vvah**eetsah/ zahkri**vvah**eetsah
What is the entrance fee?	**Сколько стоит билет?**	**skol^{y}**kah **sto**eet bee**l^{y}eht**
Is there any reduction for ...?	**Есть ли скидка для ...?**	^{y}ehst^{y} lee **skeet**kah dl^{y}ah
children	**детей**	dee**t^{y}ay**
disabled	**инвалидов**	eenvah**lee**dahf
groups	**групп**	groop
pensioners	**пенсионеров**	p^{y}ehns^{y}ah**n^{y}eh**rahf
students	**студентов**	stoo**d^{y}ehn**tahf
Do you have a guide-book (in English)?	**Есть ли у вас путеводитель (на английском языке)?**	^{y}ehst^{y} lee oo vahss pootee-vah**dee**teel^{y} (nah ahn**gleey**skahm eezi**k^{y}eh**)
Can I buy a catalogue?	**Я хотел(а) бы купить каталог.**	^{y}ah khah**t^{y}ehl**(ah) bi koo**pee**t^{y} kahtah**lok**
Is it all right to take pictures?	**Можно снимать?**	**mozh**nah snee**maht^{y}**

ВХОД БЕСПЛАТНЫЙ	ADMISSION FREE
ФОТОГРАФИРОВАТЬ ВОСПРЕЩАЕТСЯ	NO CAMERAS ALLOWED

Who—What—When? *Кто – Что – Когда?*

What's that building?	Что это за здание?	shto **eh**tah zah **zdah**nee^{Y}eh
Who was the ...?	Кто был ...?	kto bill
architect	архитектор	ahrkheet^{Y}**ehk**tahr
artist	художник	khoo**dozh**neek
painter	живописец/художник	zhivvah**pee**sseets/khoo**dozh**neek
sculptor	скульптор	**skool^{Y}p**tahr
Who built it?	Кто его построил?	kto ee**vo** pah**stro**eel
Who painted that picture?	Кто написал эту картину?	kto nahpee**ssahl eh**too kahr**tee**noo
When did he/she live?	Когда он жил/ она жила?	kahg**dah** onn zhill/ ah**nah** zhi**llah**
When was it built?	Когда было построено?	kahg**dah bi**llah pah**stro**^{Y}ehnah
Where's the house where ... lived?	Где дом, в котором жил/жила ...?	gd^{Y}eh dom f kah**to**rrahm zhill/zhi**llah**
I'm/We're interested in ...	Меня/Нас интересует ...	meen^{Y}**ah**/nahss eenteeree**ssoo**eet
antiques	антиквариат	ahnteekvahree**aht**
archaeology	археология	ahrkheeah**lo**ggee^{Y}ah
architecture	архитектура	ahrkheeteek**too**rah
art	искусство	ees**koost**vah
botany	ботаника	bah**tah**neekah
ceramics	керамика	kee**rah**meekah
coins	нумизматика	noomeez**mah**teekah
fine arts	изобразительное искусство	eezahbrah**zee**teel^{Y}nah^{Y}eh ees**koost**vah
furniture	мебель	**m^{Y}eh**b^{Y}ehl^{Y}
geology	геология	geeah**lo**ggee^{Y}ah
handicrafts	ремёсла	reem^{Y}**o**slah
history	история	ees**to**rree^{Y}ah
icons	иконы	ee**ko**nni
literature	литература	leeteerah**too**rah
medicine	медицина	meedee**tsi**nnah
music	музыка	**moo**zikkah
natural history	естествознание	eest^{Y}ehstvah**znah**nee^{Y}eh
ornithology	орнитология	ahrneetah**lo**ggee^{Y}ah
painting	живопись	**zhi**vvahpees^{Y}
pottery	керамика	kee**rah**meekah
sculpture	скульптура	skool^{Y}p**too**rah
zoology	зоология	zah**lo**ggee^{Y}ah

It's …	**Это …**	**eh**tah
amazing	**поразительно**	pahrah**zeet**^{y}ehl^{y}nah
awful	**ужасно**	oo**zhahs**nah
beautiful	**красиво/прекрасно**	krah**ssee**vah/pree**krahs**nah
impressive	**впечатляюще**	fpeech^{y}eet**l^{y}ah**^{y}ooshch^{y}eh
interesting	**интересно**	eenteer**^{y}ehs**nah
magnificent	**великолепно**	veeleekah**l^{y}ehp**nah
pretty	**мило**	**mee**lah
sinister	**жутко**	**zhoot**kah
strange	**странно**	**strahn**nah
stupendous	**изумительно**	eezoo**meet**^{y}ehl^{y}nah
superb	**великолепно**	veeleekah**l^{y}ehp**nah
terrible	**страшно/ужасно**	**strahsh**nah/oo**zhahs**nah
ugly	**безобразно**	b^{y}ehzah**brahz**nah

Religious services *Богослужения*

Most churches are open to the public during services only. When entering a church, visitors should be dressed decently. Protestant and Catholic church services are held at embassies.

Is there a/an … near here?	**Есть ли тут поблизости …?**	^{y}**ehst**^{y} lee toot pah**blee**zahstee
Baptist church	**баптистский молитвенный дом**	bahp**teests**keey mah**leet**veenniy dom
Catholic church	**католическая церковь**	kahtah**lee**ch^{y}ehskah^{y}ah **tsehr**kahf^{y}
Orthodox church	**православная церковь**	prahvah**slahv**nah^{y}ah **tsehr**kahf^{y}
Protestant church	**протестантская церковь**	praht^{y}eh**stahnts**kah^{y}ah **tsehr**kahf^{y}
mosque	**мечеть**	mee**ch^{y}eht^{y}**
synagogue	**синагога**	seenah**go**ggah
What time is mass?	**Когда служба?**	kahg**dah** **sloozh**bah
Where can I find a clergyman who speaks English?	**Где найти священника, который говорит по-английски?**	gd^{y}eh nigh**tee** sveeshch^{y}**eh**neekah kah**to**rriy gahvah**reet** pah ahn**gleey**skee
I'd like to visit the church/cathedral.	**Я хотел(а) бы осмотреть церковь/собор.**	^{y}ah khaht**^{y}ehl**(ah) bi ahsmahtr^{y}**eht**^{y} **tsehr**kahf^{y}/sah**bor**
May I take a picture?	**Можно фотографировать?**	**mozh**nah fahtahgrah**fee**rahvaht^{y}

In the countryside *В деревне*

Is there a scenic route to ...?	**Есть ли живописная дорога до ...?**	^{y}ehst^y lee zhivvah**pees**nah^{y}ah dah**ro**ggah dah
How far is it to ...?	**Как далеко до ...?**	kahk dahlee**ko** dah
Can we get there on foot?	**Можно дойти пешком?**	**mozh**nah digh**tee** peesh**kom**
How high is that mountain?	**Какой высоты эта гора?**	kah**koy** vissah**ti** **eh**tah gah**rah**
What kind of ... is that?	**Что это за ...?**	shto **eh**tah zah
animal/bird	**животное/птица**	zhi**vvot**nah^{y}eh/**ptee**tsah
flower/tree	**цветок/дерево**	tsvee**tok**/**d^{y}ehr**^{y}ehvah

bridge	**мост**	most
canal	**канал**	kah**nahl**
cliff	**обрыв**	ah**brif**
collective farm (kolkhoz)	**колхоз**	kahl**khos**
cottage	**дача**	**dah**ch^{y}ah
farm	**ферма**	**f^{y}ehr**mah
field	**поле**	**pol**^{y}eh
forest	**лес**	l^{y}ehss
garden	**сад**	saht
hill	**холм**	kholm
lake	**озеро**	**o**zeerah
marsh	**болото**	bah**lo**ttah
meadow	**луг**	look
(mountain) pass	**перевал**	peeree**vahl**
path	**тропинка**	trah**peen**kah
peak	**пик**	peek
pond	**пруд**	proot
river	**река**	ree**kah**
road	**дорога**	dah**ro**ggah
sea	**море**	**mor**^{y}eh
spring	**источник**	ees**toch^y**neek
steppe	**степь**	st^{y}ehp^y
taiga	**тайга**	tigh**gah**
valley	**долина**	dah**lee**nah
village	**село/деревня**	see**lo**/deer**^{y}ehv**n^{y}ah
vineyard	**виноградник**	veenah**grahd**neek
wall	**стена**	stee**nah**
waterfall	**водопад**	vahdah**paht**
wood	**лес**	l^{y}ehss

Relaxing

Do you have an entertainment guide?	**Есть ли у вас программа культурных мероприятий?**	yehsty lee oo vahss prah**grahm**mah koolytoornikh myehrahpreey**ah**teey
When does ... start?	**Когда начинается ...?**	kahg**dah** nahchy**ee**nah**h**eetsah
concert	**концерт**	kahn**tsehrt**
film	**фильм**	feelym
performance	**спектакль**	speek**tahkly**
show	**представление**	preetstah**vlyeh**neeyeh

Cinema – Theatre *Кино – Театр*

What's on at the cinema tonight?	**Что идёт сегодня вечером в кино?**	shto eed**yot** see**vo**dnyah **vyeh**chyeerahm f kee**no**
What's playing at the ... theatre?	**Что идёт в театре ...?**	shto eed**yot** f tee**ah**tryeh
What sort of play is it?	**Что это за пьеса?**	shto **eh**tah zah **pyeh**ssah
Who's it by?	**Кто её написал?**	kto ee**yo** nahpee**ssahl**
Can you recommend a ...?	**Можете ли вы мне порекомендовать ...?**	**mo**zhityeh lee vi mnyeh pahreekahmeendah**vahty**
good film	**хороший фильм**	khah**ro**shiy feelym
comedy	**комедию**	kah**myeh**deeyoo
musical	**музыкальное ревю**	moozi**kahly**nahyeh reev**yoo**
documentary	**документальный фильм**	dahkoomeen**tahly**niy feelym
Who are the actors?	**Какие там актёры?**	kah**kee**yeh tahm ahkt**yo**ri
Who's playing the lead?	**Кто играет главную роль?**	kto ee**grah**yeht **glahv**nooyoo roly
Who's the director?	**Кто режиссёр?**	kto reezhiss**yor**

Circus *Цирк*

Try and get tickets to the circus (especially the Moscow Circus) or the Circus on Ice.

I'd like to go to the circus/Circus on Ice.	**Я хотел(а) бы пойти в цирк/в Цирк на льду.**	^{y}ah khaht^y**ehl**(ah) bi pigh**tee** f tsirk/f tsirk nah l^{y}doo

Opera – Ballet – Concert *Опера – Балет – Концерт*

Can you recommend a ...?	**Можете ли вы мне порекомендовать ...?**	**mo**zhit^{y}eh lee vi mn^{y}eh pahreekahmeendah**vaht^y**
ballet	**балет**	bahl^y**eht**
concert	**концерт**	kahn**tsehrt**
opera	**оперу**	**o**ppeeroo
operette	**оперетту**	ahpeer^y**eht**too
Where's the opera house/the concert hall?	**Где оперный театр/концертный зал?**	gd^{y}eh **o**ppeerniy tee**ahtr**/kahn**tsehrt**niy zahl
What's on at the opera tonight?	**Что сегодня в опере?**	shto see**vo**dn^{y}ah v **o**ppeer^{y}eh
Who's singing/dancing?	**Кто поёт/танцует?**	kto pah^y**ot**/tahn**tsoo**^{y}eht
Which orchestra is playing?	**Какой оркестр играет?**	kah**koy** ahr**k^{y}ehstr** ee**grah**^{y}eht
What are they playing?	**Что они играют?**	shto ah**nee** ee**grah**^{y}oot
Who's the conductor/soloist?	**Кто дирижёр/солист/солистка?**	kto deeree**zhor**/sah**leest**/sah**leest**kah

Tickets *Билеты*

Are there any tickets left for tonight?	**У вас ещё остались билеты на сегодня?**	oo vahss ee**shch^{y}o** ahstah-lees^y beel^y**eh**ti nah see**vo**dn^{y}ah
How much are the seats?	**Сколько стоят билеты?**	**skol**^{y}kah **sto**eet bee-l^y**eh**ti
What time does it begin?	**Во сколько начало?**	vah **skol**^{y}kah nahch^y**ah**lah

I'd like to reserve 2 seats for ...	**Я хотел(а) бы заказать два билета на ...**	^{y}ah khaht^y**ehl**(ah) bi zahkah**zaht^y** dvah beel^y**eh**tah nah
Friday (evening)	**пятницу (вечером)**	p^y**aht**neetsoo (**v^{y}eh**ch^{y}eerahm)
the matinée (on Tuesday)	**дневной спектакль (во вторник)**	dneev**noy** speek**tahkl^y** (vah **ftor**neek)
I'd like a seat in the ...	**Я хотел(а) бы место ...**	^{y}ah khaht^y**ehl**(ah) bi **m^{y}ehs**tah
stalls (orchestra)	**в партере**	f pahr**t^{y}ehr**^{y}eh
dress circle	**в бельэтаже**	v b^{y}ehl^{y}eh**tah**zheh
upper circle	**на балконе**	nah bahl**kon**^{y}eh
in a box	**в ложе**	v **lo**zheh
Somewhere in the middle.	**Где-нибудь в середине.**	**gd^{y}eh**-neebood^y f seeree**deen**^{y}eh
May I have a programme, please?	**Дайте, пожалуйста, программу.**	**dight**^{y}eh pah**zhahl**stah prah**grahm**moo
Where's the cloakroom?	**Где гардероб?**	gd^{y}eh gahrdee**rop**

Извините, всё распродано.	I'm sorry, we're sold out.
Осталось только несколько мест на балконе.	There are only a few seats left in the upper circle.
Ваш билет, пожалуйста.	Your ticket, please.
Вот ваше место.	This is your seat.

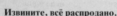

Nightclubs—Discos *Ночной клуб – Дискотека*

You'll find nightclubs and discos mainly in hotels. And you can join in with locals enjoying a dinner-and-dance at most restaurants.

Is there a ...?	**Здесь есть ...?**	zd^{y}ehs^y ^{y}ehst^y
discotheque	**дискотека**	deeskaht^y**eh**kah
nightclub	**ночной клуб**	nahch^y**noy** kloop
Where can we go dancing?	**Где можно танцевать?**	gd^{y}eh **mozh**nah tahntseh**vaht^y**
Would you like to dance?	**Не хотите потанцевать?**	nee khah**teet**^{y}eh pahtahntseh**vaht^y**

Sports *Спорт*

Most of the sports common in the West are also played in Russia. You'll probably find sports a good topic of conversation.

The most popular sports are: ice hockey, skiing and skating, in winter; football, volleyball, riding, in summer. Water sports, especially swimming, are very popular all year round, as well as hunting and fishing. A typical Russian tradition and very relaxing for both body and spirits: the "baths" *(баня*—**bah**n^{y}ah*)*.

Are there any sporting events going on?	**Есть ли какие-нибудь спортивные мероприятия?**	^{y}ehst^y lee kah**kee**^{y}ehnee-**bood**^{y} spahr**teev**ni^{y}eh m^{y}ehrahpree^y**ah**tee^{y}ah

athletics	**лёгкая атлетика**	l^y**okh**kah^{y}ah ahtl^y**eh**teekah
basketball	**баскетбол**	bahskeet**bol**
boxing	**бокс**	boks
car racing	**(автомобильные) гонки**	(ahftahmah**beel**^{y}ni^{y}eh) **gon**kee
cycle racing	**велогонки**	veelah**gon**kee
football (soccer)	**футбол**	foot**bol**
(ice-)hockey	**хоккей**	khahk**k^{y}ay**
field hockey	**хоккей на траве**	khahk**k^{y}ay** nah trah**v^{y}eh**
(horse) racing	**бега/скачки**	bee**gah/skahch**^{y}kee
rowing	**гребля**	**gr^{y}eh**bl^{y}ah
tennis	**теннис**	**t^{y}eh**nnees
volleyball	**волейбол**	vahleey**bol**

Is there a football (soccer) match this weekend?	**В конце недели будет футбольный матч?**	f kahn**tseh** need^y**eh**lee **boo**deet foot**bol**^{y}niy mahtch^y
Which teams are playing?	**Какие команды играют?**	kah**kee**^{y}eh kah**mahn**di ee**grah**^{y}oot
Can you get me a ticket?	**Вы можете достать мне билет?**	vi **mo**zhit^{y}eh dah**staht**^{y} mn^{y}eh beel**^{y}eht**
I'd like to see a boxing match.	**Я хотел(а) бы посмотреть соревнование по боксу.**	^{y}ah khaht**^{y}ehl**(ah) bi pahsmah**tr^{y}eht**^{y} sahreevnah**vah**nee^{y}eh pah **bok**soo
What's the admission charge?	**Сколько стоит билет?**	**skol**^{y}kah **sto**eet beel**^{y}eht**

… and if you don't just want to watch:

Are there any tennis courts?	**Здесь есть теннисные корты?**	zd^{y}ehs^y ^{y}ehst^y **tyehn**neesni^{y}eh **korti**
I'd like to play tennis.	**Я хотел(а) бы (по-) играть в теннис.**	^{y}ah khaht^y**ehl**(ah) bi (pah-) ee**graht^y** f t^y**ehn**nees
What's the charge per …?	**Сколько стоит …?**	**skol^y**kah **sto**eet
day/round/hour	**день/игра/час**	d^{y}ehn^y/ee**grah**/ch^{y}ahss
Can I hire rackets?	**Можно взять напрокат ракетки?**	**mozh**nah vz^{y}aht^y nahprah**kaht** rahk^y**eht**kee

cycling	**велоспорт**	veelah**sport**
mountaineering	**альпинизм**	ahl^{y}pee**neezm**
riding	**верховая езда**	veerkhah**vah**^{y}ah eez**dah**
sailing	**парусный спорт**	**pah**roosniy sport
swimming	**плавание**	**plah**vahnee^{y}eh

Is there any good fishing?	**Где здесь можно ловить рыбу?**	gd^{y}eh zd^{y}ehs^y **mozh**nah lah**veet^y** **rib**boo
Is there any good hunting?	**Куда хорошо пойти на охоту?**	koo**dah** khahrah**sho** pigh**tee** nah ah**khot**too
Do I need a fishing licence?	**Надо иметь разрешение на рыбную ловлю?**	**nah**dah eem^y**eht^y** rahzree**sheh**nee^{y}eh nah **rib**noo^{y}oo **lov**l^{y}oo
Can one swim in the lake/river?	**В этом озере/в этой реке можно плавать?**	v **eh**tahm oz**eer**^{y}eh/v **eh**tigh reek^y**eh** **mozh**nah **plah**vaht^y
Is there a swimming pool here?	**Есть ли здесь бассейн?**	^{y}ehst^y lee zd^{y}ehs^y bahss^y**ayn**
Is it open-air or indoors?	**Он на открытом воздухе или крытый?**	on nah aht**krit**tahm **voz**dookh^{y}eh **ee**lee **krit**tiy
Is it heated?	**Вода подогревается?**	vah**dah** pahdahgree**vah**eetsah
What's the temperature of the water?	**Какая температура воды?**	kah**kah**^{y}ah teempeerah**too**rah vah**di**

On the beach *На пляже*

Is the beach sandy or stony?	**На пляже песок или галька?**	nah **pl^{y}ah**zheh pee**ssok** **ee**lee **gahl^y**kah

Is it safe to swim here?	**Здесь не опасно плавать?**	zd^{y}ehs^{y} nee ah**pahss**nah **plah**vaht^{y}
Is there a lifeguard?	**Есть ли здесь спасательная команда?**	^{y}ehst^{y} lee zd^{y}ehs^{y} spah**sah**teel^{y}nah^{y}ah kah**mahn**dah
Is the water deep?	**Здесь глубоко?**	zd^{y}ehs^{y} gloobah**ko**
There are some big waves today.	**Сегодня большие волны.**	see**vodn**^{y}ah bahl^{y}**shi**^{y}eh **vol**ni
I'd like to hire ...	**Я хотел(а) бы взять напрокат ...**	^{y}ah khaht^{y}**ehl**(ah) bi vz^{y}aht^{y} nahprah**kaht**
deck chair	**шезлонг**	shehz**long**
motor boat	**моторную лодку**	mah**tor**noo^{y}oo **lot**koo
rowing-boat	**лодку**	**lot**koo
sailing-boat	**парусную лодку**	**pah**roosnoo^{y}oo **lot**koo
skin-diving equipment	**снаряжение аквалангиста**	snahree**zheh**nee^{y}eh ahkvahlahn**gees**tah
sunshade (umbrella)	**зонтик**	**zon**teek
water-skis	**водные лыжи**	**vod**ni^{y}eh **li**zhi

КУПАТЬСЯ ВОСПРЕЩАЕТСЯ NO SWIMMING

Winter sports *Зимний спорт*

I'd like to ski.	**Я хотел(а) бы (по-) ходить на лыжах.**	^{y}ah khaht^{y}**ehl**(ah) bi (pah-) khah**deet**^{y} nah **li**zhahkh
I'd like to skate.	**Я хотел(а) бы (по-) кататься на коньках.**	^{y}ah khaht^{y}**ehl**(ah) bi (pah-) kah**taht**^{y}sah nah kahn^{y}**kahkh**
Is there a skating rink near here?	**Здесь есть поблизости каток?**	zd^{y}ehs^{y} ^{y}ehst^{y} pah**blee**zahstee kah**tok**
I'd like to do some cross-country skiing.	**Я хотел(а) бы пойти в лыжный поход.**	^{y}ah khaht^{y}**ehl**(ah) bi pigh**tee** v **lizh**niy pah**khot**
I'd like to hire (rent) ...	**Я хотел(а) бы взять напрокат ...**	^{y}ah khaht^{y}**ehl**(ah) bi vz^{y}aht^{y} nahprah**kaht**
poles	**лыжные палки**	**lizh**ni^{y}eh **pahl**kee
skates	**коньки**	kahn^{y}**kee**
skiing equipment	**лыжное снаряжение**	**lizh**nah^{y}eh snahree**zheh**nee^{y}eh
skis	**лыжи**	**li**zhi
sled	**санки**	**sahn**kee

Making friends

Introductions *Знакомство*

There is no equivalent of Mr., Mrs. or Miss in Russian. The only forms foreigners can use are *господин* (gahspah**deen,** Mr.) and *госпожа* (gahspah**zhah,** Mrs. and Miss), although these forms are not used anymore in Russia.

It is polite to address people you know by their first name and patronymic, derived from the father's name. (E.g. Nikolay, whose father's name is Ivan, would be called *Nikolay Ivanovich;* Natalia, whose father's name is Peter—*Пётр*—, would be addressed as *Natalia Petrovna.*)

May I introduce ...?	**Разрешите познакомить вас...**	rahzree**shit**^{y}eh pahznah**ko**meet^y vahss
my husband	**с моим мужем**	s mah**eem moo**zhehm
my wife	**с моей женой**	s mah^y**ay** zheh**noy**
My name is ...	**Меня зовут...**	meen^y**ah** zah**voot**
What's your name?	**Как вас зовут?**	kahk vahss zah**voot**
How do you do?	**Здравствуйте!**	**zdrahst**vooyt^{y}eh
Pleased to meet you.	**Очень приятно.**	och^{y}een^y pree^y**aht**nah
How are you?	**Как вы поживаете?**	kahk vi pahzhiv**vah**eet^{y}eh

Follow-up *Более близкое знакомство*

How long have you been here?	**Сколько вы уже здесь пробыли?**	**skol**^{y}kah vi oo**zheh** zd^{y}ehs^y prah**bi**llee
We've been here a week.	**Мы тут уже неделю.**	mi toot oo**zheh** need^y**ehl**^{y}oo
Are you enjoying your stay?	**Вам тут нравится?**	vahm toot **nrah**veetsah
Yes, I like it very much.	**Да, мне очень нравится.**	dah mn^{y}eh **och**^{y}een^y **nrah**veetsah
What do you think of the country/people?	**Что вы думаете о стране/людях?**	shto vi **doo**maheet^{y}eh ah strahn^y**eh**/**l**^{y}**ood**^{y}ahkh
Where are you from?	**Вы откуда?**	vi aht**koo**dah

COUNTRIES, see page 146

I'm ...	**Я...**	^{y}ah
American	**американец/американка**	ahmeeree**kah**neets/ahmeeree**kahn**kah
British/English	**англичанин/англичанка**	ahnglee**ch^{y}ah**neen/ahnglee**ch^{y}ahn**kah
Canadian	**канадец/канадка**	kah**nah**deets/kah**naht**kah
Irish	**ирландец/ирландка**	eer**lahn**deets/eer**laht**kah
Where are you staying?	**Где вы остановились?**	gd^{y}eh vi ahstahnah**vee**lees^{y}
Are you on your own?	**Вы здесь один (одна)?**	vi zd^{y}ehs^{y} ah**deen** (ahd**nah**)
I'm with ...	**Я с...**	^{y}ah s
my wife	**женой**	zheh**noy**
my husband	**мужем**	**moo**zhehm
my family	**семьёй**	seem**^{y}oy**
my parents	**родителями**	rah**dee**teel^{y}ahmee
my boyfriend	**другом**	**droo**gahm
my girlfriend	**подругой**	pah**droo**gigh

grandfather/grandmother	**дедушка/бабушка**	**d^{y}eh**dooshkah/**bah**booshkah
father/mother	**отец/мать**	aht**^{y}ehts**/maht^{y}
son/daughter	**сын/дочь**	sinn/doch^{y}
brother/sister	**брат/сестра**	braht/sees**trah**
uncle/aunt	**дядя/тётя**	**d^{y}ah**d^{y}ah/**t^{y}o**t^{y}ah
nephew/niece	**племянник/племянница**	pleem**^{y}ahn**neek/plee**m^{y}ahn**neetsah

Are you married? (man)	**Вы женаты?**	vi zheh**nah**ti
Are you married? (woman)	**Вы замужем?**	vi **zah**moozhehm
Do you have children?	**У вас есть дети?**	oo vahss ^{y}ehst^{y} **d^{y}eh**tee
What do you do?	**Кто вы по профессии?**	kto vi pah prah**f^{y}eh**ssee
Where do you work?	**Где вы работаете?**	gd^{y}eh vi rah**bo**ttaheet^{y}eh
I'm a student.	**Я студент (студентка).**	^{y}ah stoo**d^{y}ehnt** (stoo**d^{y}ehnt**kah)
What are you studying?	**Что вы изучаете?**	shto vi eezoo**ch^{y}ah**eet^{y}eh
Where are you studying?	**Где вы учитесь?**	gd^{y}eh vi **oo**ch^{y}eet^{y}ehs^{y}

The weather *Погода*

What a lovely day!	**Какой прекрасный день!**	kah**koy** pree**krahs**niy d^{y}ehn^y
What awful weather!	**Какая ужасная погода!**	kah**kah**^{y}ah oo**zhahs**nah^{y}ah pah**go**ddah
It is cold/hot today.	**Сегодня холодно/ жарко.**	see**vo**dn^{y}ah **kho**llahdnah/ **zhahr**kah
Is it usually as warm as this?	**Здесь всегда так тепло?**	zd^{y}ehs^y fseeg**dah** tahk tee**plo**
The sun is shining.	**Светит солнце.**	**sv^{y}eh**teet **son**tseh
It's raining.	**Идёт дождь.**	eed**^{y}ot** doshch^y
Do you think it's going to ... tomorrow?	**Как вы думаете, завтра ...?**	kahk vi **doo**might^{y}eh **zahf**trah
be a nice day	**будет хороший день**	**boo**deet khah**ro**shiy d^{y}ehn^y
rain	**будет дождь**	**boo**deet doshch^y
snow	**будет снег**	**boo**deet sn^{y}ehk
What is the weather forecast?	**Какой прогноз погоды?**	kah**koy** prahg**nos** pah**go**ddi

cloud	**облако**	**o**blahkah
fog	**туман**	too**mahn**
frost	**мороз**	mah**ros**
ice	**лёд**	l^{y}ot
lightning	**молния**	**mol**nee^{y}ah
moon	**луна**	loo**nah**
rain	**дождь**	doshch^y
sky	**небо**	**n^{y}eh**bah
snow	**снег**	sn^{y}ehk
star	**звезда**	zveez**dah**
storm	**буря**	**boo**r^{y}ah
sun	**солнце**	**son**tseh
thunder	**гром**	grom
thunderstorm	**гроза**	grah**zah**
wind	**ветер**	**v^{y}eh**teer

Invitations *Приглашения*

May we invite you to have dinner with us on ...?	**Мы хотели бы пригласить вас на ужин в ...**	mi khaht**^{y}eh**lee bi preeglah**seet^y** vahss nah **oo**zhin v

DAYS OF THE WEEK, see page 151

May I invite you to lunch?	**Можно пригласить вас на обед?**	**mozh**nah preeglah**seet**^{y} vahss nah ah**b**^{y}**eht**
Why don't you come round this evening?	**Заходите к нам сегодня вечером.**	zahkhah**deet**^{y}eh k nahm see**vod**n^{y}ah **v**^{y}**eh**ch^{y}eerahm
We're giving a party. Are you coming?	**У нас будет вечеринка. Вы придёте?**	oo nahss **boo**deet veech^{y}ee**reen**kah. vi preed^{y}**ot**^{y}eh
That's very kind of you.	**Это очень любезно.**	**eh**tah **o**ch^{y}een^{y} l^{y}oo**b**^{y}**ehz**nah
Great. I'd love to come.	**Отлично. Приду с удовольствием.**	aht**leech**^{y}nah. pree**doo** s oodah**vol**^{y}**st**vee^{y}ehm
What time shall we come?	**В котором часу нам прийти?**	f kah**tor**rahm ch^{y}ee**ssoo** nahm preey**tee**
May I bring a friend?	**Можно привести приятеля?**	**mozh**nah preevees**tee** pree^{y}**ah**teel^{y}ah
I'm afraid we've got to go now.	**К сожалению, нам пора.**	k sahzhahl^{y}**eh**nee^{y}oo nahm pah**rah**
Next time you must come to visit us.	**В следующий раз вы должны нас навестить.**	f **sl**^{y}**eh**doo^{y}ooshch^{y}eey rahs vi dahlzh**ni** nahss nahvees**teet**^{y}

Dating *Свидания*

Do you mind if I smoke?	**Вы не возражаете, если я закурю?**	vi nee vahzrah**zha**eet^{y}eh ^{y}**eh**slee ^{y}ah zahkoor^{y}**oo**
Would you like a cigarette?	**Не хотите ли сигарету?**	nee khah**teet**^{y}eh lee seegahr^{y}**eh**too
Do you have a light, please?	**Нет ли у вас спичек/зажигалки?**	n^{y}eht lee oo vahss **spee**ch^{y}eek/zahzhi**gahl**kee
Why are you laughing?	**Почему вы смеётесь?**	pahch^{y}ee**moo** vi smee^{y}**o**t^{y}ehs^{y}
Is my Russian that bad?	**Я так плохо говорю по-русски?**	^{y}ah tahk **plo**khah gahvahr^{y}**oo** pah **roos**kee
Do you mind if I sit (down) here?	**Разрешите присесть сюда?**	rahzree**shit**^{y}eh prees^{y}**ehst**^{y} s^{y}oo**dah**
Can I get you a drink?	**Вы хотите что-нибудь выпить?**	vi khah**teet**^{y}eh **shto**-neebood^{y} **vi**ppeet^{y}
Are you free this evening?	**Вы свободны сегодня вечером?**	vi svah**bod**ni see**vod**n^{y}ah **v**^{y}**eh**ch^{y}eerahm

Would you like to go out with me tonight?	**Хотите, пойдём куда-нибудь сегодня вечером?**	khah**teet**^{y}eh pigh**d^{y}om** koo**dah**-nee**bood**^{y} see**vodn**^{y}ah **v^{y}eh**-ch^{y}eerahm
Would you like to go dancing?	**Хотите танцевать?**	khah**teet**^{y}eh tahntseh**vaht**^{y}
I know a good restaurant.	**Я знаю хороший ресторан.**	^{y}ah **znah**^{y}oo khah**ro**shiy reestah**rahn**
Shall we go to the cinema (movies)?	**Давайте пойдём в кино.**	dah**vight**^{y}eh pigh**d^{y}om** f kee**no**
Would you like to go for a walk?	**Пойдём немного погуляем?**	pigh**d^{y}om** neem**nog**gah pahgoo**l^{y}ah**^{y}ehm
Where shall we meet?	**Где мы встретимся?**	gd^{y}eh mi **fstr^{y}eh**teemsah
I'll pick you* up at your hotel.	**Я зайду за вами/тобой в гостиницу.**	^{y}ah zigh**doo** zah **vah**mee/tah**boy** v gah**stee**neetsoo
I'll call for you* at 8.	**Я зайду за вами/тобой в восемь часов.**	^{y}ah zigh**doo** zah **vah**mee/tah**boy** v **vo**sseem^{y} ch^{y}ee**ssof**
May I take you* home?	**Можно вас/тебя проводить домой?**	**mozh**nah vahss/tee**b^{y}ah** prahvah**deet**^{y} dah**moy**
Can I see you again tomorrow?	**Мы увидимся завтра?**	mi oo**vee**deemsah **zahf**trah
I hope we'll meet again.	**Я надеюсь, что мы встретимся ещё.**	^{y}ah nah**d^{y}eh**^{y}oos^{y} shto mi **fstr^{y}eh**teemsah ee**shch^{y}o**

. . . and you might answer:

With great pleasure!	**С большим удовольствием!**	z bahl^{y}**shim** oodah**vol^{y}st**vee^{y}ehm
Thank you, but I'm busy.	**Спасибо, но я занят/занята.**	spah**ssee**bah no ^{y}ah **zah**neet/**zah**neetah
No, I'm not interested.	**Нет, это меня не интересует.**	n^{y}eht **eh**tah meen**^{y}ah** nee eenteeree**ssoo**eet
Leave me alone, please.	**Оставьте меня в покое!**	ah**stahv**^{y}t^{y}eh meen**^{y}ah** f pah**koy**eh
Thank you. It's been a wonderful evening.	**Спасибо за чудесный вечер.**	spah**ssee**bah zah ch^{y}oo**d^{y}eh**sniy **v^{y}eh**ch^{y}eer
I've enjoyed myself.	**Я хорошо провёл (провела) время.**	^{y}ah khahrah**sho** prah**v^{y}ol** (prahvee**lah**) **vr^{y}eh**m^{y}ah

* The polite form for "you" is **вы**, the familiar form is **ты**.
See also GRAMMAR, page 159.

Shopping guide

This shopping guide is designed to help you find what you want with ease, accuracy and speed. It features:

1. A list of all major shops, stores and services (p. 98).
2. Some general expressions required when shopping to allow you to be specific and selective (p. 100).
3. Full details of the shops and services most likely to concern you. Here you'll find advice, alphabetical lists of items and conversion charts listed under the headings below.

		page
Bookshop/ Stationer's	books, magazines, newspapers, stationery	104
Camping equipment	all items required for camping	106
Chemist's (drugstore)	medicine, first-aid, cosmetics, toilet articles	108
Clothes shop	clothes and accessories, shoes	112
Electrical/ leisure	hi-fi equipment, electrical appliances	119
Grocery/ Supermarket	some general expressions, weights, measures and packaging	120
Jeweller's/ Watchmaker's	jewellery, watches, watch repairs	121
Optician	glasses, lenses, binoculars	123
Photography	cameras, films, developing, accessories	124
Tobacconist's	smoker's supplies	126
Miscellaneous	souvenirs, records, cassettes, toys	127

LAUNDRY, see page 29/HAIRDRESSER'S, see page 30

Shops and useful addresses* *Магазины и полезные адреса*

Most shops are open from 8 a.m. to 8 p.m. or from 9 a.m. to 9 p.m., some close for lunch, usually between 1 and 2 p.m. The most famous department stores are *GOOM* and *TSOOM* in Moscow and *Gostinny Dvor* in St. Petersburg.

Is there a(n) ... near here ...?	**Есть ли здесь поблизости ...?**	^{y}ehst^y lee zd^{y}ehs^y pah**blee**zahstee
antique shop	**антикварный магазин**	ahntee**kvahr**niy mahgah**zeen**
art gallery	**картинная галерея**	kahr**teen**nah^{y}ah gahleer^y**eh**^{y}ah
baker's	**булочная**	**boo**lahch^{y}nah^{y}ah
beauty salon	**косметический кабинет**	kahsm^{y}eh**tee**ch^{y}eeskeey kahbeen^y**eht**
Beryozka (hard-currency shop)	**Берёзка**	beer^y**os**kah
bookshop	**книжный магазин**	**kneezh**niy mahgah**zeen**
butcher's	**мясной магазин**	mees**noy** mahgah**zeen**
cake shop	**кондитерская**	kahn**dee**t^{y}ehrskah^{y}ah
camera shop	**магазин фото-товаров**	mahgah**zeen** **fotto**-tah**vah**rahf
chemist's	**аптека**	ahpt^y**eh**kah
confectioner's	**кондитерская**	kahn**dee**t^{y}ehrskah^{y}ah
dairy	**молочная**	mah**loch**^{y}nah^{y}ah
delicatessen	**гастроном**	gahstrah**nom**
dentist	**зубной врач**	zoob**noy** vrahch^y
department store	**универмаг**	ooneev^{y}ehr**mahk**
drugstore	**аптека**	ahpt^y**eh**kah
dry cleaner's	**химчистка**	kheem**ch^{y}eest**kah
electrical goods shop	**магазин электро-товаров**	mahgah**zeen** ehl^{y}ehktrah-tah**vah**rahf
fishmonger's	**рыбный магазин**	**rib**niy mahgah**zeen**
florist's	**цветочный магазин**	tsvee**toch**^{y}niy mahgah**zeen**
furrier's	**магазин меховых изделий**	mahgah**zeen** meekhah**vikh** eezd^y**eh**leey
greengrocer's	**овощной магазин**	ahvahshch^y**noy** mahgah**zeen**
grocery	**бакалея/продукты**	bahkahl^y**eh**^{y}ah/prah**dook**ti
hairdresser's ladies/men	**парикмахерская женская/мужская**	pahreek**mah**kheerskah^{y}ah **zhehns**kah^{y}ah/moosh s**kah**^{y}ah
hat shop	**магазин головных уборов**	mahgah**zeen** gahlahv**nikh** oo**bor**rahf

*Most shops just carry the name of the article sold, e.g. **ХЛЕБ** (bread), **РЫБА** (fish), **ОБУВЬ** (shoes), **ЦВЕТЫ** (flowers), etc.

hospital	больница	bahl^y**nee**tsah
information bureau	справочное бюро/ справки	**sprah**vahch^{y}nah^{y}eh b^y**ooro**/ **sprahf**kee
jeweller's	ювелирный магазин	^{y}oovee**leer**niy mahgah**zeen**
launderette	прачечная самообслуживания	**prah**ch^{y}eech^{y}nah^{y}ah sahmahahp**sloo**zhivvahnee^{y}ah
laundry	прачечная	**prah**ch^{y}eech^{y}nah^{y}ah
library	библиотека	beebleeah**t^{y}eh**kah
market	рынок	**ri**nnahk
music shop	нотный магазин	**not**niy mahgah**zeen**
newsstand	газетный киоск/ союзпечать	gah**z^{y}eht**niy kee**osk**/ sah^{y}oospee**ch^{y}aht^y**
optician	оптика	**op**teekah
pastry shop	кондитерская	kahn**deet^y**ehrskah^{y}ah
perfumery	парфюмерия	pahrf^{y}oomee**ree^y**ah
photographer	фотография	fahtah**grah**fee^{y}ah
police station	отделение милиции	ahtdee**l^{y}eh**nee^{y}eh mee**lee**tsi^{y}ee
post office	почта	**poch^y**tah
savings bank	сберкасса	zb^{y}ehr**kah**ssah
second-hand books	букинистический магазин	bookeenees**tee**ch^{y}eeskeey mahgah**zeen**
second-hand shop	комиссионный магазин	kahmees**s^{y}on**niy mahgah**zeen**
shoemaker's (repairs)	ремонт обуви	ree**mont** **o**boovee
shoe shop	магазин обуви	mahgah**zeen** **o**boovee
shopping centre	торговый центр	tahr**go**vviy tsehntr
souvenir shop	магазин сувениров	mahgah**zeen** soovee**neer**ahf
sporting goods shop	спорттовары	sporttah**vah**ri
stationer's	культтовары	kool^{y}ttah**vah**ri
supermarket	универсам	ooneev^{y}ehr**sahm**
telegraph office	телеграф	teelee**grahf**
tobacconist's	табак	tah**bahk**
toy shop	магазин игрушек	mahgah**zeen** ee**groo**shehk
travel agency	бюро путешествий	b^y**ooro** pootee**shehst**veey
vegetable store	овощной магазин	ahvahshch^y**noy** mahgah**zeen**
veterinarian	ветеринар	veeteeree**nahr**
watchmaker's	часовая мастерская	ch^{y}eessah**vah**^{y}ah mahsteer**skah**^{y}ah
wine merchant	винный магазин	**veen**niy mahgah**zeen**

ВХОД	ENTRANCE
ВЫХОД	EXIT
ЗАПАСНОЙ ВЫХОД	EMERGENCY EXIT

General expressions *Общие выражения*

Where? *Где?*

Where's there a good shop for ...?	**Где хороший магазин для ...?**	gd^yeh khah**ro**shiy mahgah**zeen** dl^yah
Where can I find a ...?	**Где мне найти ...?**	gd^yeh mn^yeh nigh**tee**
Where's the main shopping area?	**Где большие магазины?**	gd^yeh bahl^y**shi**^yeh mahgah**zee**ni
Is it far from here?	**Это далеко отсюда?**	**eh**tah dahlee**ko** ahts^y**oo**dah
How do I get there?	**Как мне туда попасть?**	kahk mn^yeh too**dah** pah**pahst**^y
Where can I buy ...?	**Где можно купить ...?**	gd^yeh **mozh**nah koo**peet**^y

УЦЕНЕННЫЕ ТОВАРЫ SALE

Service *Обслуживание*

Can you help me?	**Будьте добры!**	**boot**^ytee dah**bri**
I'm just looking.	**Я только смотрю.**	^yah **tol**^ykah smahtr^y**oo**
Do you sell/ have ...?	**Продают ли у вас/ Есть ли у вас ...?**	prahdah^y**oot** lee oo vahss/ ^yehst^y lee oo vahss
I'd like ...	**Я бы хотел(а) ...**	^yah bi khaht^y**ehl**(ah)
Can you show me some ...?	**Покажите мне, пожалуйста ...**	pahkah**zhit**^yeh mn^yeh pah**zhahl**stah
Do you have any ...?	**Есть ли у вас ...?**	^yehst^y lee oo vahss
Where's the ... department?	**Где отдел ...?**	gd^yeh ahtd^y**ehl**
Where is the lift (elevator)/escalator?	**Где лифт/эскалатор?**	gd^yeh leeft/ehskah**lah**tahr

That one *Тот*

Can you show me ...?	**Покажите мне, пожалуйста ...**	pahkah**zhit**^yeh mn^yeh pah**zhahl**stah
this/that	**это/то**	**eh**tah/to
the one in the window	**тот в витрине**	tot v vee**treen**^yeh

Defining the article *Описание предмета*

I'd like a ... one.	**Я хотел(а) бы...**	^{y}ah khaht^{y}**ehl**(ah) bi
big	**большой**	bahl^{y}**shoy**
cheap	**дешёвый**	dee**shov**viy
dark	**тёмный**	**t^{y}om**niy
good	**хороший**	khah**ro**shiy
heavy	**тяжёлый**	tee**zhol**liy
large	**крупный**	**kroop**niy
light (weight)	**лёгкий**	**l^{y}okh**keey
light (colour)	**светлый**	**sv^{y}eht**liy
oval	**овальный**	ah**vahl^{y}**niy
rectangular	**прямоугольный**	pr^{y}ahmahoo**gol^{y}**niy
round	**круглый**	**kroog**liy
small	**маленький**	**mah**leen^{y}keey
square	**квадратный**	kvah**draht**niy
sturdy	**крепкий**	**kr^{y}ehp**keey
I don't want anything too expensive.	**Я не хочу ничего слишком дорогого.**	^{y}ah nee khah**ch^{y}oo** neech^{y}ee**vo sleesh**kahm dahrah**gov**vah

I prefer ... *Я предпочитаю...*

Can you show me some others?	**Покажите мне, пожалуйста, ещё другие.**	pahkah**zhit^{y}**eh mn^{y}eh pah**zhahl**stah eesh**ch^{y}o** droo**gee^{y}**eh
Haven't you anything ...?	**Нет ли у вас чего-нибудь...?**	n^{y}eht lee oo vahss ch^{y}ee**vo**neebood^{y}
cheaper/better	**подешевле/получше**	pahdee**shehv**l^{y}eh/pah**looch^{y}**sheh
larger/smaller	**побольше/поменьше**	pah**bol^{y}**sheh/pah**m^{y}ehn^{y}**sheh

How much? *Сколько?*

How much is this?	**Сколько это стоит?**	**skol^{y}**kah **eh**tah **sto**eet
I don't understand.	**Я не понимаю.**	^{y}ah nee pahnee**mah^{y}**oo
Please write it down.	**Напишите, пожалуйста.**	nahpee**shit^{y}**eh pah**zhahl**stah
I don't want to spend more than 20 rubles.	**Я не хочу истратить больше 20 рублей.**	^{y}ah nee khah**ch^{y}oo** eestrah**teet^{y} bol^{y}**sheh 20 roo**bl^{y}ay**

NUMBERS, see page 147 / COLOURS, see page 113

Decision *Решение*

It's not quite what I want.	**Это не совсем то, что я хочу.**	**eh**tah nee sahfs^{y}**ehm** to shto ^{y}ah khah**ch^{y}oo**
No, I don't like it.	**Нет, мне это не нравится.**	n^{y}eht mn^{y}eh **eh**tah nee **nrah**veetsah
I'll take it.	**Я возьму это.**	^{y}ah vahz^{y}**moo eh**tah

Ordering *Заказы*

Can you order it for me?	**Будьте добры, закажите.**	**boot**^{y}tee dah**bri** zahkah**zhit**^{y}eh
How long will it take?	**Сколько это займёт времени?**	**skol**^{y}kah **eh**tah zigh**m^{y}ot** **vr^{y}eh**meenee

Delivery *Доставка*

I'll take it with me.	**Я возьму это с собой.**	^{y}ah vahz^{y}**moo eh**tah s sah**boy**
Deliver it to the ... Hotel.	**Отправьте, пожалуйста, в гостиницу ...**	aht**prahv**^{y}t^{y}eh pah**zhahl**stah v gah**stee**neetsoo
Please send it to this address.	**Отправьте, пожалуйста, по этому адресу.**	aht**prahv**^{y}t^{y}eh pah**zhahl**stah pah **eh**tahmoo **ah**dreessoo
Will I have any difficulty with the customs?	**Будут ли у меня трудности на таможне?**	**boo**doot lee oo meen**^{y}ah** **trood**nahstee nah tah**mozh**nee

Paying *Оплата*

When shopping in foreign-currency shops, you pay in the normal way. In other shops, however, you have to memorize the price of the item you want to buy, pay the exact amount at the cash desk, and pick up the item you want using your receipt.

How much is it?	**Сколько это стоит?**	**skol**^{y}kah **eh**tah **sto**eet
Can I pay by traveller's cheque/credit card?	**Могу ли я платить дорожными чеками/кредитной карточкой?**	mah**goo** lee ^{y}ah plah**teet**^{y} dah**rozh**nimmee **ch^{y}eh**kahmee/kree**deet**nigh **kahr**tahch^{y}kigh
Do you accept dollars/pounds?	**Вы принимаете доллары/фунты?**	vi preenee**might**^{y}eh **dol**lahri/**foon**ti
Haven't you made a mistake in the bill?	**Вы не ошиблись в счёте?**	vi nee ah**shib**lees^{y} f **shch^{y}o**ttee

Anything else? *Ещё что-нибудь?*

No, thanks, that's all.	**Нет, спасибо, это всё.**	n^{y}eht spahs**see**bah **eh**tah fs^{y}o
Yes, I want ...	**Да, я хочу ...**	dah ^{y}ah khah**ch^{y}oo**
Show me ...	**Покажите мне ...**	pahkah**zhit**^{y}eh mn^{y}eh
May I have a bag, please?	**Дайте мне, пожалуйста, сумку.**	**digh**tee mn^{y}eh pah**zhahl**stah **soom**koo
Could you wrap it up for me, please?	**Заверните, пожалуйста.**	zahveer**neet**^{y}eh pah**zhahl**stah
May I have a receipt?	**Будьте добры, чек.**	**boot**^{y}tee dah**bri** ch^{y}ehk

Complaints *Жалобы*

Can you please exchange this?	**Нельзя ли это обменять?**	neel^{y}**z^{y}ah** lee **eh**tah ahbmeen**^{y}aht^{y}**
I want to return this.	**Я хочу это возвратить.**	^{y}ah khah**ch^{y}oo eh**tah vahzvrah**teet^{y}**
I'd like a refund. Here's the receipt.	**Я хотел(а) бы, чтобы мне вернули деньги. Вот чек.**	^{y}ah khaht^{y}**ehl**(ah) bi **shto**bbi mn^{y}eh veer**noo**lee **d^{y}ehn^{y}**gee. vot ch^{y}ehk

Слушаю вас.	Can I help you?
Что бы вы хотели?	What would you like?
Какой/Какое ... вы хотите?	What ... would you like?
цвет/размер качество/количество	colour/shape quality/quantity
Извините, этого у нас нет.	I'm sorry, we don't have any.
Всё распродано.	We're out of stock.
Заказать для вас?	Shall we order it for you?
Ещё что-нибудь?	Anything else?
... рублей, пожалуйста.	That's ... rubles, please.
Платите в кассу.	Pay at the cash desk, please.

Bookshop – Stationer's *Книги – Культтовары*

You'll find Russian newspapers, magazines, envelopes and postcards at newsstands with the inscription *"СОЮЗПЕЧАТЬ"*. For foreign newspapers and magazines, have a look on the newsstand in your hotel.

Where's the nearest ...?	**Где ближайший ...?**	gd^y^eh blee**zhigh**shiy
bookshop	**книжный магазин**	**kneezh**niy mahgah**zeen**
newsstand	**газетный киоск**	gahz**^y^ehtniy** kee**osk**
second-hand bookshop	**букинистический магазин**	bookeenees**teech**^y^ehskee^y^ mahgah**zeen**
stationer's	**писчебумажный магазин**	peeshch^y^ehboo**mahzh**niy mahgah**zeen**
Where can I buy an English-language newspaper?	**Где мне купить английскую газету?**	gd^y^eh mn^y^eh koo**peet^y^** ahn**gleeys**koo^y^oo gahz**^y^eh**too
Where's the guidebook section?	**Где отдел путеводителей?**	gd^y^eh aht**d^y^ehl** pooteevah**deet**^y^ehl^y^ay
Where do you keep the English books?	**Где у вас английские книги?**	gd^y^eh oo vahss ahn**gleeys**kee^y^eh **knee**gee
Do you have any of Tolstoy's books in English?	**Есть ли у вас книги Толстого на английском языке?**	^y^ehst^y^ lee oo vahss **knee**gee tahls**to**vvah nah ahn**gleeys**kahm eezik**^y^eh**
I'd like ...	**Я хотел(а) бы ...**	^y^ah khaht**^y^ehl**(ah) bi
address book	**записную книжку для адресов**	zahpees**noo**^y^oo **kneesh**koo dl^y^ah ahdree**ssof**
ball-point pen	**шариковую ручку**	**shah**reekahvoo^y^oo **rooch^y^**koo
book	**книгу***	**knee**goo
calendar	**календарь**	kahleen**dahr^y^**
children's book	**детскую книгу**	**d^y^ehts**koo^y^oo **knee**goo
crayons	**карандаши**	kahrahndah**shi**
diary	**записную книжку**	zahpees**noo**^y^oo **kneesh**koo
dictionary	**словарь**	slah**vahr^y^**
Russian-English	**русско-английский**	**roo**skah-ahn**gleeys**keey
English-Russian	**англо-русский**	**ahn**glah-**roo**skeey
pocket dictionary	**карманный словарь**	kahr**mahn**niy slah**vahr^y^**

* "I'd like" is followed by the accusative case in Russian. The nominative case of **книгу** is **книга** (**knee**gah). See also GRAMMAR section, page 158.

drawing paper	бумагу для рисования	boo**mah**goo dl^{y}ah reessah**vah**nee^{y}ah
drawing pins	чертёжные кнопки	ch^{y}eert^y**ozhni**^{y}eh **knop**kee
envelopes	конверты	kahn**v^{y}ehr**ti
eraser	резинка	ree**zeen**kah
exercise book	тетрадь	tee**trahd^y**
felt-tip pen	фломастер	flah**mah**steer
fountain pen	авторучку	ahftah**rooch^y**koo
glue	клей	kl^{y}ay
grammar book	учебник	oo**ch^{y}ehb**neek
guidebook	путеводитель	pooteevah**dee**teel^y
ink	чернила	ch^{y}eer**nee**lah
black/red/blue	чёрные/красные/синие	**ch^{y}or**ni^{y}eh/**krahs**ni^{y}eh/**see**nee^{y}eh
magazine	журнал	zhoor**nahl**
map	план/схему	plahn/**skh^{y}eh**moo
map of the town	план города	plahn **gor**rahdah
road map	карту дорог	**kahr**too dah**rok**
notebook	записную книжку	zahpees**noo**^{y}oo **kneesh**koo
note paper	почтовую бумагу	pahch^y**tov**voo^{y}oo boo**mah**goo
paintbox	краски	**krahs**kee
paper	бумагу	boo**mah**goo
paperback	книжку карманного формата	**kneesh**koo kahr**mahn**nahvah fahr**mah**tah
paperclips	скрепки	**skr^{y}ehp**kee
paste	клей	kl^{y}ay
pen	ручку	**rooch^y**koo
pencil	карандаш	kahrahn**dahsh**
pencil sharpener	точилку	tahch^y**eel**koo
phrasebook	разговорник	rahzgah**vor**neek
pocket calculator	карманную счётную машинку	kahr**mahn**noo^{y}oo **shch^{y}ot**noo^{y}oo mah**shin**koo
postcards	открытки	aht**krit**kee
refill (for a pen)	чернила для авторучки	ch^{y}eer**nee**lah dl^{y}ah ahftah**rooch^y**kee
rubber	резинка	ree**zeen**kah
ruler	линейку	leen^y**ay**koo
Scotch tape	скотч	skotch
staples	скрепки	**skr^{y}ehp**kee
string	бечёвку, верёвку	beech^y**of**koo, veer^y**of**koo
thumbtacks	чертёжные кнопки	ch^{y}eert^y**ozhni**^{y}eh **knop**kee
travel guide	путеводитель	pooteevah**deet^y**ehl^y
typewriter ribbon	ленту для пишущей машинки	**l^{y}ehn**too dl^{y}ah **pee**shooshch^{y}ay mah**shin**kee
wrapping paper	обёрточную бумагу	ah**b^{y}or**tahch^{y}noo^{y}oo boo**mah**goo
writing pad	блокнот	blah**knot**

Camping equipment *Оборудование для кемпинга*

Where can I buy/hire camping equipment?	**Где можно купить/ взять напрокат оборудование для кемпинга?**	gd^{y}eh **mozh**nah koo**peet^y**/ vz^{y}aht^y nahprah**kaht** ahbah**roo**dahvahnee^{y}eh dl^{y}ah **kehm**peengah
I need …	**Мне надо …**	mn^{y}eh **nah**dah
bottle-opener	**штопор/открывалка**	**shto**ppahr/ahtkri**vahl**kah
bucket	**ведро**	vee**dro**
butane gas	**газ в баллонах**	gahs v bah**lo**nnahkh
campbed	**складная кровать**	sklahd**nah^y**ah krah**vaht^y**
can opener	**консервный нож**	kahns^y**ehrv**niy nosh
candles	**свечки**	**sv^{y}ehch^y**kee
(folding) chair	**(складной) стул**	(sklahd**noy**) stool
charcoal	**древесный уголь**	dreev^y**ehs**niy **oo**gahl^y
clothes pegs	**защипки**	zah**shch^{y}eep**kee
compass	**компас**	**kom**pahss
cool box	**сумка-термос**	**soom**kah-**tehr**mahss
corkscrew	**штопор**	**shto**ppahr
crockery	**посуда**	pah**ssoo**dah
cutlery	**прибор**	pree**bor**
deck chair	**шезлонг**	shehz**long**
first-aid kit	**аптечка**	ahpt^y**ehch^y**kah
fishing tackle	**рыболовные снасти**	ribah**lov**ni^{y}eh **snahs**tee
flashlight	**карманный фонарик**	kahr**mahn**niy fah**nah**reek
(food) box	**пластмассовая коробка (для еды)**	plahst**mahss**ahvah^{y}ah kah**rop**kah (dl^{y}ah ee**di**)
frying pan	**сковородка**	skahvah**rot**kah
groundsheet	**подстилка под палатку**	paht**steel**kah paht pah**laht**koo
hammer	**молоток**	mahlah**tok**
hammock	**гамак**	gah**mahk**
ice-bag	**пузырь для льда**	poo**zir^y** dl^{y}ah l^{y}dah
kerosene	**керосин**	keerah**seen**
knapsack	**рюкзак**	r^{y}ook**zahk**
lamp	**лампа**	**lahm**pah
lantern	**фонарь**	fah**nahr^y**
matches	**спички**	**speech^y**kee
mattress	**матрас**	mah**trahss**
methylated spirits	**денатурированный спирт**	deenahtooree**ro**vvanniy speert
mosquito net	**сетка от комаров**	**s^{y}eht**kah aht kahmah**rof**
pail	**ведро**	vee**dro**
paper napkins	**бумажные салфетки**	boo**mahzh**ni^{y}eh sahl**f^{y}eht**kee
paraffin	**керосин**	keerah**seen**
penknife	**перочинный ножик**	peerah**ch^{y}een**niy **no**zhik

CAMPING, see page 32

picnic basket	**корзина для пикника**	kahr**zee**nah dl^{y}ah peek**nee**kah
plastic bag	**полиэтиленовый мешочек**	pahleeehteel**^{y}eh**nahviy mee**shoch**^{y}ehk
rope	**верёвка**	veer**^{y}of**kah
rucksack	**рюкзак**	r^{y}ook**zahk**
saucepan	**кастрюля**	kah**str^{y}ool**^{y}ah
scissors	**ножницы**	**nozh**neetsi
screwdriver	**отвёртка**	aht**v^{y}ort**kah
sleeping bag	**спальный мешок**	**spahl**^{y}niy mee**shok**
stew pot	**кастрюля**	kah**str^{y}ool**^{y}ah
stove	**печка**	**p^{y}ehch**^{y}kah
(folding) table	**(складной) стол**	(sklahd**noy**) stoll
tent	**палатка**	pah**laht**kah
tent pegs	**палаточные колышки**	pah**lah**tahch^{y}ni^{y}eh **ko**llishkee
tent pole	**палаточный столб**	pah**lah**tahch^{y}niy stolp
tinfoil	**алюминиевая фольга**	ahl^{y}oo**meen**^{y}ehvah^{y}ah **fol**^{y}gah
tin opener	**консервный нож**	kahns**^{y}ehr**vniy nosh
tongs	**клещи**	**kl^{y}eh**shch^{y}ee
tool kit	**набор инструментов**	nah**bor** eenstroom**^{y}ehn**tahf
torch	**карманный фонарик**	kahr**mahn**niy fah**nah**reek
vacuum flask	**термос**	**tehr**mahss
washing powder	**стиральный порошок**	steer**ahl**^{y}niy pahrah**shok**
water flask	**бак для воды**	bahk dl^{y}ah vah**di**
wood alcohol	**денатурированный спирт**	deenahtooree**ro**vvanniy speert

Crockery *Посуда*

cups	**чашки**	**ch^{y}ahsh**kee
glasses	**стаканы**	stah**kah**ni
mugs	**кружки**	**kroosh**kee
plates	**тарелки**	tahr**^{y}ehl**kee
saucers	**блюдца**	**bl^{y}ood**tsah

Cutlery *Прибор*

forks	**вилки**	**veel**kee
knives	**ножи**	nah**zhi**
spoons	**ложки**	**losh**kee
teaspoons	**чайные ложки**	**ch^{y}igh**ni^{y}eh **losh**kee
plastic	**пластмасса**	plahst**mahs**sah
stainless steel	**нержавеющая сталь**	neerzhah**v^{y}eh**^{y}oo-shch^{y}ah^{y}ah stahl^y

Chemist's (Drugstore) *Аптека*

For medicine of any kind, you must go to an *аптека* (ahp-**t^{y}eh**kah). Russian chemist's don't stock the wide range of goods that you find in Britain or the United States. Medical treatment is free in Russia, but you do have to pay for medicine.

For toilet articles, you have to go to a *парфюмерия* – pahr-f^{y}oomee**ree**^{y}ah.

For reading ease, this section has been divided into two parts:

1. Pharmaceutical—medicine, first-aid, etc.
2. Toiletry—toilet articles, cosmetic.

General questions *Общие вопросы*

Where's the nearest (all-night) chemist's?	**Где ближайшая (дежурная) аптека?**	gd^{y}eh blee**zhigh**shah^{y}ah (dee**zhoor**nah^{y}ah) ahpt^{y}**eh**kah
What time does the chemist's open/close?	**Во сколько открывается/закрывается аптека?**	vah **skol^{y}**kah ahtkri**vvah**eetsah/zahkri**vvah**eetsah ahpt^{y}**eh**kah

1—Pharmaceutical *Лекарства*

I'd like something for ...	**Дайте мне, пожалуйста, что-нибудь от ...**	**digh**t^{y}eh mn^{y}eh pah**zhahl**stah **shto**-neebood^{y} aht
cold	**простуды**	prah**stoo**di
cough	**кашля**	**kahshl**^{y}ah
hay fever	**сенной лихорадки**	seen**noy** leekhah**raht**kee
headache	**головной боли**	gahlahv**noy bo**lee
insect bites	**укусов насекомых**	oo**koo**ssahf nahssee**ko**mmikh
nausea	**тошноты**	tahshnah**ti**
sunburn	**солнечного ожога**	**sol**neech^{y}nahvah ahz**ho**ggah
travel sickness	**морской болезни**	mahrs**koy** bah**l^{y}eh**znee
upset stomach	**расстройства желудка**	rahss**troy**stvah zhi**loot**kah
Can you prepare this prescription for me?	**Вы можете приготовить это лекарство?**	vi **mo**zhit^{y}eh preegah**to**vveet^{y} **eh**tah lee**kahrs**tvah
Can I get it without a prescription?	**Можно получить это без рецепта?**	**mozh**nah pahloo**ch^{y}eet^{y} eh**tah b^{y}ehz reet**seh**ptah
Shall I wait?	**Мне подождать?**	mn^{y}eh pahdah**zhdaht^{y}**

DOCTOR, see page 137

analgesic	**болеутоляющие таблетки**	boleeootahl^y**ah**^{y}oosh-ch^{y}ee^{y}eh tah**bl^{y}eht**kee
antiseptic cream	**антисептическая мазь**	ahnteeseep**tee**ch^{y}eeskah^{y}ah mahz^y
aspirin	**аспирин**	ahspee**reen**
bandage	**гигиенический бинт**	geegee^{y}eh**nee**ch^{y}eeskeey beent
elastic bandage	**эластичный бинт**	ehlahs**tee**ch^{y}niy beent
Band-Aids	**пластырь**	**plah**stir^y
condoms	**презервативы**	preezeervah**tee**vi
contraceptives	**противозачаточные средства**	prahteevahzah**ch^{y}ah**tahch^y-ni^{y}eh **sr^{y}ehts**tvah
corn plasters	**мозольный пластырь**	mah**zol^y**niy **plah**stir^y
cotton wool (absorbent cotton)	**вата**	**vah**tah
cough drops	**таблетки от кашля**	tah**bl^{y}eht**kee aht **kahsh**l^{y}ah
disinfectant	**дезинфицирующее средство**	deezeenfeet**sir**oo^{y}oosh-ch^{y}eh^{y}eh **sr^{y}ehts**tvah
ear drops	**ушные капли**	oosh**ni**^{y}eh **kah**plee
Elastoplast	**пластырь**	**plah**stir^y
eye drops	**глазные капли**	glahz**ni**^{y}eh **kah**plee
gauze	**марля**	**mahr**l^{y}ah
insect repellent	**средство от комаров**	**sr^{y}ehts**tvah aht kahmah**rof**
iodine	**йод**	^{y}ot
laxative	**слабительное**	slah**bee**teel^{y}nah^{y}eh
mouthwash	**полоскание для рта**	pahlahs**kah**nee^{y}eh dl^{y}ah rtah
nose drops	**капли от насморка**	**kah**plee aht **nahs**mahrkah
sanitary towels (napkins)	**гигиенические салфетки**	geegee^{y}eh**nee**ch^{y}eeskee^{y}eh sahl**f^{y}eht**kee
sleeping pills	**снотворное**	snah**tvor**nah^{y}eh
suppositories	**свечи**	**sv^{y}eh**ch^{y}ee
... tablets	**таблетки от ...**	tah**bl^{y}eht**kee aht
thermometer	**термометр, градусник**	teer**mom**^{y}ehtr, **grah**doossneek
throat lozenges	**таблетки для горла**	tah**bl^{y}eht**kee dl^{y}ah **gor**lah
tranquillizers	**успокоительное**	oospahkah**ee**teel^{y}nah^{y}eh
vitamin pills	**витамины**	veetah**mee**ni

ОТРАВА/ЯД	POISON
НАРУЖНОЕ	FOR EXTERNAL USE ONLY

PARTS OF THE BODY, see page 138

2 – Toiletry *Туалетные принадлежности*

Many toiletries and cosmetics cannot be bought in Russia, so stock up before going.

Do you have any ...?	**Есть ли у вас...?**	^{y}ehst^y lee oo vahss
after-shave lotion	**одеколон после бритья**	ahdeekah**lon pos**lee breet^y**ah**
astringent lotion	**вяжущее средство**	**v^{y}ah**zhooshch^{y}eh^{y}eh **sr^{y}ehts**tvah
bath salts	**экстракт для ванны**	ehk**strahkt** dl^{y}ah **vahn**ni
blusher (rouge)	**румяна**	room^y**ah**nah
bubble bath	**пена для ванны**	**p^{y}eh**nah dl^{y}ah **vahn**ni
cologne	**тройной одеколон**	trigh**noy** ahdeekah**lon**
cream	**крем**	kr^{y}ehm
cleansing cream	**крем для снятия косметики**	kr^{y}ehm dl^{y}ah **sn^{y}ah**tee^{y}ah kahs**m^{y}eh**teekee
foundation cream	**крем-тон**	kr^{y}ehm-**ton**
moisturizing cream	**питательный крем**	pee**tah**teel^{y}niy kr^{y}ehm
night cream	**ночной крем**	nahch^y**noy** kr^{y}ehm
deodorant	**дезодорант**	deezahdah**rahnt**
eyebrow pencil	**карандаш для бровей**	**kahrahndahsh** dl^{y}ah brah**v^{y}ay**
eye liner	**тушь для век**	toosh^y dl^{y}ah v^{y}ehk
eye shadow	**тени для век**	**t^{y}eh**nee dl^{y}ah v^{y}ehk
face powder	**пудра**	**poo**drah
hand cream	**крем для рук**	kr^{y}ehm dl^{y}ah rook
lipsalve	**гигиеническая губная помада**	geegee^{y}eh**nee**ch^{y}eeskah^{y}ah goob**nah**^{y}ah pah**mah**dah
lipstick	**губная помада**	goob**nah**^{y}ah pah**mah**dah
make-up	**косметика**	kahs**m^{y}eh**teekah
make-up remover	**лосьон**	lahs**^{y}on**
mascara	**тушь для ресниц**	toosh^y dl^{y}ah rees**neets**
nail brush	**щёточка для ногтей**	**shch^{y}o**ttahch^{y}kah dl^{y}ah nahg**t^{y}ay**
nail file	**пилочка**	**pee**lahch^{y}kah
nail polish	**лак для ногтей**	lahk dl^{y}ah nahg**t^{y}ay**
nail polish remover	**ацетон**	ahtseh**ton**
nail scissors	**ножницы для ногтей**	**nozh**neetsi dl^{y}ah nahg**t^{y}ay**
perfume	**духи**	doo**khee**
powder	**пудра**	**poo**drah
razor	**бритва**	**breet**vah
razor blades	**лезвия**	**l^{y}ehz**vee^{y}ah
rouge	**румяна**	room^y**ah**nah
safety pins	**английские булавки**	ahn**gleey**skee^{y}eh boo**lahf**kee

shaving brush	кисточка для бритья	keestahch^{y}kah dl^{y}ah breet^{y}ah
shaving cream	крем для бритья	kr^{y}ehm dl^{y}ah breet^{y}ah
soap	мыло	millah
sponge	губка	goopkah
sun-tan cream	крем для загара	kr^{y}ehm dl^{y}ah zahgahrah
sun-tan oil	масло для загара	mahslah dl^{y}ah zahgahrah
talcum powder	тальк	tahl^{y}k
toilet paper	туалетная бумага	tooahl^{y}ehtnah^{y}ah boomahgah
toilet water	одеколон	ahdeekahlon
toothbrush	зубная щётка	zoobnah^{y}ah shch^{y}otkah
toothpaste	зубная паста	zoobnah^{y}ah pahstah
towel	полотенце	pahlaht^{y}ehntseh
tweezers	пинцет	peentseht

For your hair *Для волос*

bobby pins	заколки	zahkolkee
colour shampoo	красящий шампунь	krahseeshch^{y}eey shahmpoon^{y}
comb	расчёска	rahsch^{y}oskah
curlers	бигуди	beegoodee
dye	краска	krahskah
hairbrush	щётка (для волос)	shch^{y}otkah (dl^{y}ah vahloss)
hairgrips	заколки	zahkolkee
hair lotion	жидкость для волос	zhitkahst^{y} dl^{y}ah vahloss
hair pins	шпильки	shpeel^{y}kee
hair slide	заколка для волос	zahkolkah dl^{y}ah vahloss
hair spray	лак	lahk
setting lotion	фиксатор	feeksahtahr
shampoo	шампунь	shahmpoon^{y}
for dry/greasy (oily) hair	для сухих/жирных волос	dl^{y}ah sookheekh/zhirnikh vahloss
tint	оттенок	ahtt^{y}ehnahk
wig	парик	pahreek

For the baby *Для ребёнка*

baby food	продукты детского питания	prahdookti d^{y}ehtskahvah peetahnee^{y}ah
dummy (pacifier)	соска/пустышка	soskah/poostishkah
feeding bottle	детский рожок	d^{y}ehtskeey rahzhok
nappies (diapers)	пелёнки	peel^{y}onkee

Clothing *Одежда*

If you want to buy something specific, prepare yourself in advance. Look at the list of clothing on page 116. Get some idea of the size, colour and material you want. They're all listed on the next few pages.

I'd like a pullover for ...	**Я хотел(а) бы свитер для ...**	^{y}ah khaht^y**ehl**(ah) bi **svee**tehr dl^{y}ah
a woman/a man	**женщины/мужчины**	**zhehn**shch^{y}eeni/ moo**shch^{y}ee**ni
a 10-year-old boy	**десятилетнего мальчика**	deeseeteel^y**eht**neevah **mahl**^{y}ch^{y}eekah
a 10-year-old girl	**десятилетней девочки**	deeseeteel^y**eht**n^{y}ay d^y**eh**vahch^{y}kee
I like the one in the window.	**Мне нравится тот, который на витрине.**	mn^{y}eh **nrah**veetsah tot kahtorriy nah veetreen^{y}eh

Size *Размер*

Women *Женские размеры*

Dresses/Suits						
American	8	10	12	14	16	18
British	10	12	14	16	18	20
Russian	36	38	40	42	44	46

Stockings						
American / British	8	8½	9	9½	10	10½
Russian	0	1	2	3	4	5

Shoes				
American	6	7	8	9
British	4½	5½	6½	7½
Russian	36	37	38	40

Men *Мужские размеры*

Suits/Overcoats						
American / British	36	38	40	42	44	46
Russian	46	48	50	52	54	56

Shirts				
American / British	15	16	17	18
Russian	38	41	43	45

Shoes									
American / British	5	6	7	8	8½	9	9½	10	11
Russian	38	39	41	42	43	43	44	44	45

I take size 38.	**У меня размер 38.**	oo meen^{y}**ah** rahzm^{y}**ehr** 38
Could you measure me?	**Можете ли снять с меня мерку?**	**mo**zhit^{y}eh lee sn^{y}**aht**^{y} s meen^{y}**ah** **m^{y}ehr**koo
I don't know the Russian sizes.	**Я не знаю русских размеров.**	^{y}ah nee **znah**^{y}oo **roos**keekh rahzm^{y}**eh**rahf

Colour *Цвет*

I'd like something in red.	**Я хотел(а) бы что-нибудь красное.**	^{y}ah khaht^{y}**ehl**(ah) bi **shto**neebood^{y} **krahs**nah^{y}eh
I'd like ...	**Я хотел(а) бы ...**	^{y}ah khaht^{y}**ehl**(ah) bi
a lighter shade	**более светлый оттенок**	**bo**lee **sv^{y}eht**liy ahtt^{y}**eh**nahk
a darker shade	**более тёмный оттенок**	**bo**lee **t^{y}om**niy ahtt^{y}**eh**nahk
something to match this	**что-нибудь в тон к этому**	**shto**neebood^{y} f ton k **eh**tahmoo
something colourful	**что-нибудь яркое**	**shto**neebood^{y} ^{y}**ahr**ka^{y}eh
I don't like the colour.	**Мне этот цвет не нравится.**	mn^{y}eh **eh**taht tsv^{y}eht nee **nrah**veetsah

beige	**бежевый**	**b^{y}eh**zhehviy
black	**чёрный**	**ch^{y}or**niy
blue	**синий**	**see**neey
brown	**коричневый**	kah**reech^{y}**neeviy
golden	**золотистый**	zahlah**tees**tiy
green	**зелёный**	zeel^{y}**o**nniy
grey	**серый**	**s^{y}eh**riy
orange	**оранжевый**	ah**rahn**zhiviy
pink	**розовый**	**ro**zahviy
purple	**яркокрасный**	^{y}ahrkah**krahs**niy
red	**красный**	**krahs**niy
silver	**серебряный**	seer^{y}**eh**breeniy
turquoise	**бирюзовый**	beer^{y}oo**zo**viy
white	**белый**	**b^{y}eh**liy
yellow	**жёлтый**	**zhol**tiy
light ...	**светло-...**	**sv^{y}eht**lah-
dark ...	**тёмно-...**	**t^{y}om**nah-

одноцветный (ahdnah**tsv^{y}eht**niy)

в полоску (f pah**los**koo)

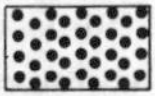

в горошек (v gah**ro**shehk)

в клетку (f **kl^{y}eht**koo)

с узором (s oo**zo**rahm)

Fabric/Material *Ткань/Материал*

Do you have anything in ...?	**Есть ли у вас что-нибудь из...?**	^{y}ehst^{y} lee oo vahss **shto**neebood^{y} eez
What fabric is it?	**Какая это ткань?/ Какой это материал?**	kah**kah**^{y}ah **eh**tah tkahn^{y}/ kah**koy eh**tah mahteeree**ahl**

cambric	**батист**	bah**teest**
camel-hair	**верблюжья шерсть**	veer**bl^{y}**oozh^{y}ah shehrst^{y}
chiffon	**шифон**	shif**fon**
corduroy	**вельвет**	veel^{y}**v^{y}eht**
cotton	**бумажная ткань**	boo**mahzh**nah^{y}ah tkahn^{y}
crepe	**креп**	kr^{y}ehp
denim	**бумажное полотно**	boo**mahzh**nah^{y}eh pahlaht**no**
felt	**фетр**	f^{y}ehtr
flannel	**фланель, байка**	flahn^{y}**ehl^{y}**, **bigh**kah
gabardine	**габардин**	gahbahr**deen**
lace	**кружево**	**kroo**zhehvah
leather	**кожа**	**ko**zhah
linen	**полотно**	pahlaht**no**
poplin	**поплин**	pah**pleen**
satin	**атлас**	aht**lahss**
silk	**шёлк**	sholk
suede	**замша**	**zahm**shah
towelling (terrycloth)	**махровая ткань**	mah**khro**vah^{y}ah tkahn^{y}
velvet	**бархат**	**bahr**khaht
velveteen	**вельвет**	veel^{y}**v^{y}eht**
wool	**шерсть**	shehrst^{y}

Is that ...?	**Это...?**	**eh**tah
handmade	**ручная работа**	rooch^{y}**nah**^{y}ah rah**bo**ttah
imported	**импортное**	eem**port**nah^{y}eh
made here	**отечественное производство**	aht^{y}**eh**ch^{y}eestv^{y}ehnnah^{y}eh praheez**votst**vah
I'd like something thinner.	**Я хотел(а) бы что-нибудь потоньше.**	^{y}ah khaht^{y}**ehl**(ah) bi **shto**neebood^{y} pah**ton**^{y}sheh
Do you have anything of better quality?	**Есть ли у вас что-нибудь лучшего качества?**	^{y}ehst^{y} lee oo vahss **shto**neebood^{y} **looch^{y}**shivah **kah**ch^{y}eestvah

Is it ...?	**Это ...?**	ehtah
pure cotton pure wool synthetic colourfast crease (wrinkle) resistant	**чистый хлопок** **чистая шерсть** **синтетика** **не линяет** **не мнётся**	ch^{y}eestiy khlopahk ch^{y}eestah^{y}ah shehrst^{y} seentehteekah nee leen^{y}ah^{y}eht nee mn^{y}otsah
Is it hand washable/ machine washable?	**Можно это стирать/ стирать в машине?**	mozhnah ehtah steeraht^{y}/ steeraht^{y} v mahshin^{y}eh
Will it shrink?	**Это садится?**	ehtah sahdeetsah

... talking about fabrics:

I'd like 2 metres of this fabric.	**Я хотел(а) бы 2 метра этой ткани.**	^{y}ah khaht^{y}ehl(ah) bi 2 m^{y}ehtrah ehtigh tkahnee
How much is that per metre?	**Сколько стоит метр?**	skol^{y}kah sto^{y}eet m^{y}ehtr

1 centimetre	= 0.39 in.	1 inch	= 2.54 cm.
1 metre	= 39.37 in.	1 foot	= 30.5 cm.
10 metres	= 32.81 ft.	1 yard	= 0.91 m.

A good fit? *Хорошо сидит?*

Can I try it on?	**Можно померить?**	mozhnah pahm^{y}ehreet^{y}
Where's the fitting room?	**Где примерочная?**	gd^{y}eh preem^{y}ehrahch^{y}-nah^{y}ah
Is there a mirror?	**Есть ли у вас зеркало?**	^{y}ehst^{y} lee oo vahss z^{y}ehrkahlah
It fits very well.	**Очень хорошо сидит.**	och^{y}een^{y} khahrahsho see-deet
It doesn't fit.	**Не годится.**	nee gahdeetsah
It's too ...	**Слишком ...**	sleeshkahm
short/long tight/loose	**коротко/длинно** **узко/широко**	korrahtkah/dleennah ooskah/shirrahko
How long will it take to alter?	**Сколько времени займёт переделка?**	skol^{y}kah vr^{y}ehmeenee zighm^{y}ot peereed^{y}ehlkah

NUMBERS, see page 147

Clothes *Одежда*

I'd like ...	**Я хотел(а) бы...**	^{y}ah khaht^y**ehl**(ah) bi
anorak	**спортивную куртку**	spahr**teev**noo^{y}oo **koort**koo
bathing cap	**купальную шапочку**	koo**pahl^y**noo^{y}oo **shah**pahch^{y}koo
bathing suit	**купальник**	koo**pahl^y**neek
bathrobe	**купальный халат**	koo**pahl^y**niy khah**laht**
bikini	**бикини**	bee**kee**nee
blouse	**блузку**	**bloos**koo
bra	**бюстгальтер**	b^{y}ooz**khahl^y**tehr
braces	**подтяжки**	pahtt^y**ahsh**kee
briefs	**трусы, трусики**	troo**ssi**, **troo**seekee
cap	**кепку**	**k^{y}eh**pkoo
cardigan	**вязаный жакет**	**v^{y}ah**zahniy zhah**k^{y}eht**
children's clothes	**детскую одежду**	**d^{y}ehts**koo^{y}oo ahd^y**ehzh**doo
coat	**пальто**	pahl^y**to**
dress	**платье**	**plaht^y**eh
dressing gown	**халат**	khah**laht**
evening dress (woman's)	**вечернее платье**	veech^y**ehr**nee^{y}eh **plaht^y**eh
fur coat	**шубу**	**shoo**boo
fur hat	**меховую шапку**	meekhah**voo^y**oo **shahp**koo
girdle	**пояс**	**po^y**ahss
gloves	**перчатки**	peer**ch^{y}aht**kee
handkerchief	**носовой платок**	nahssah**voy** plah**tok**
hat	**шляпу**	**shl^{y}ah**poo
jacket	**куртку**	**koort**koo
jacket (man's)	**пиджак**	peed**zhahk**
jeans	**джинсы**	**dzheen**si
jersey	**вязаную кофту**	**v^{y}ah**zahnoo^{y}oo **kof**too
jumper (Br.)	**свитер**	**svee**tehr
kneesocks	**гольфы**	**gol^y**fi
leather jacket	**кожаную куртку**	**ko**zhahnoo^{y}oo **koort**koo
nightdress	**ночную рубашку**	nahch^y**noo^y**oo roo**bahsh**koo
overalls	**комбинезон**	kahmbeenee**zon**
pair of ...	**пару...**	**pah**roo
panties	**трусики**	**troo**seekee
pants (Am.)	**брюки**	**br^{y}oo**kee
panty girdle	**ремень**	ree**m^{y}ehn^y**
panty hose	**колготы**	kahl**go**tti
pullover	**свитер, пуловер**	**svee**tehr, poolo**veer**
round-neck	**с круглым воротом**	s **kroog**lim **vo**rahtahm
V-neck	**с вырезом**	s **vir^y**ehzahm
with long/short sleeves	**с длинными/короткими рукавами**	s **dleen**nimmee/kah**rot**keemee rookah**vah**mee

pyjamas	**пижаму**	pee**zhah**moo
raincoat	**плащ**	plahshch^{y}
scarf	**шарф**	shahrf
shirt	**рубашку**	roo**bahsh**koo
shorts	**шорты**	**shor**ti
skirt	**юбку**	^{y}**oop**koo
sleeveless pullover	**безрукавку**	beezroo**kahf**koo
slip	**комбинацию**	kahmbee**nah**tsi^{y}oo
socks	**носки**	nahs**kee**
sports jacket	**спортивную куртку**	spahr**teev**noo^{y}oo **koort**koo
stockings	**чулки**	ch^{y}ool**kee**
suit (man's/woman's)	**костюм**	kahs**t^{y}oom**
suspenders (Am.)	**подтяжки**	paht**t^{y}ahsh**kee
sweater	**свитер**	**svee**tehr
sweatshirt	**спортивный пуловер**	spahr**teev**niy poo**lo**veer
swimming trunks	**плавки**	**plahf**kee
swimsuit	**купальник**	koo**pahl^{y}**neek
tie	**галстук**	**gahl**stook
tights	**колготы**	kahl**go**tti
tracksuit	**тренировочный костюм**	treeneero**vahch^{y}**niy kahs**t^{y}oom**
trousers	**брюки**	**br^{y}oo**kee
T-shirt	**майку**	**migh**koo
umbrella	**зонтик**	**zon**teek
underpants	**трусы**	troo**ssi**
undershirt	**майку**	**migh**koo
underwear	**нижнее бельё**	**neezh**nee^{y}eh beel^{y}**o**
vest (Am.)	**жилет**	zhil^{y}**eht**
vest (Br.)	**майку**	**migh**koo
waistcoat	**жилет**	zhil^{y}**eht**

belt	**пояс, ремень**	**po**^{y}ahss, reem^{y}**ehn**^{y}
buckle	**пряжка**	**pr^{y}ahsh**kah
button	**пуговица**	**poo**gahveetsah
collar	**ворот**	**vo**raht
elastic	**резинка**	ree**zeen**kah
lining	**подкладка**	paht**klaht**kah
pocket	**карман**	kahr**mahn**
press stud (snap fastener)	**кнопка**	**knop**kah
zip (zipper)	**молния**	**mol**nee^{y}ah

Shoes *Обувь*

I'd like ...	**Я хотел(а) бы...**	^{y}ah khaht^{y}**ehl**(ah) bi
boots	**сапоги**	sahpah**gee**
felt boots	**валенки**	**vah**leenkee
children's shoes	**детскую обувь**	**d^{y}ehts**koo^{y}oo **o**boov^{y}
moccasins	**мокасины**	mahkah**ssee**ni
plimsolls	**тапочки**	**tah**pahch^{y}kee
sandals	**сандалии**	sahn**dah**lee^{y}ee
shoes	**туфли/ботинки**	**too**flee/bah**teen**kee
flat	**на низком каблуке**	nah **nees**kahm kahblook^{y}**eh**
with a heel	**на высоком каблуке**	nah vi**sso**kahm kahblook^{y}**eh**
with leather soles	**на коже**	nah **ko**zheh
with rubber soles	**на резине**	nah reez**een**^{y}eh
slippers	**тапки, тапочки**	**tah**pkee, **tah**pahch^{y}kee
These are too ...	**Эти слишком...**	**eh**tee **sleesh**kahm
narrow/wide	**узкие/широкие**	**oo**skee^{y}eh/shi**rro**kee^{y}eh
large/small	**большие/маленькие**	bahl^{y}**shi**^{y}eh/**mah**leen^{y}kee^{y}eh
Do you have a larger/ smaller size?	**Есть ли на номер больше/меньше?**	^{y}ehst^{y} lee nah **no**mmeer **bol**^{y}sheh/**m^{y}ehn**^{y}sheh
Do you have the same in black?	**Есть ли у вас такие же чёрного цвета?**	^{y}ehst^{y} lee oo vahss tah**kee**^{y}eh zheh **ch^{y}or**nahvah **tsv^{y}eh**tah
cloth	**ткань**	tkahn^{y}
leather	**кожа**	**ko**zhah
rubber	**резина**	ree**zee**nah
suede	**замша**	**zahm**shah
Is it genuine leather?	**Это настоящая кожа?**	**eh**tah nahstah^{y}**ah**shch^{y}ah^{y}ah **ko**zhah
I need some shoe polish/shoelaces.	**Мне нужен гуталин/ мне нужны шнурки.**	mn^{y}eh **noo**zhehn gootah**leen**/ mn^{y}eh noozh**ni** shnoor**kee**

Shoe repairs *Ремонт обуви*

Can you repair these shoes?	**Можно починить эти туфли?**	**mozh**nah pahch^{y}ee**neet**^{y} **eh**tee **too**flee
I'd like new soles and heels.	**Мне нужны новые подмётки и набойки.**	mn^{y}eh noozh**ni** **no**vi^{y}eh pahd**m^{y}o**tkee ee nah**boy**kee
Can you stitch this?	**Можно это зашить?**	**mozh**nah **eh**tah zah**shit**^{y}
When will they be ready?	**Когда будут готовы?**	kahg**dah** **boo**doot gah**to**vvi

COLOURS, see page 113

Electrical appliances *Электротовары*

While 220 volts AC, 50 cycles, tends to be standard, you'll still find 110–120 volts AC, 50 cycles, in some places. Western plugs are not always the same as Russian ones, but large hotels often have sockets suited to Western plugs. If you're planning on travelling around, it's wise to buy an adapter before leaving for those appliances you're taking with you. Adapters are hard to find in Russia.

This is broken. Can you repair it?	**Это не работает. Можно починить?**	**eh**tah nee rah**bo**ttah^{y}eht. **mozh**nah pahch^{y}**eeneet**^{y}
Do you have a battery for this?	**Есть ли у вас батарейка для этого?**	^{y}ehst^{y} lee oo vahss bahtahr^{y}**ay**kah dl^{y}ah **eh**tahvah
Can you show me how it works?	**Покажите мне, пожалуйста, как это действует.**	pahkah**zhit**^{y}eh mn^{y}eh pah**zhahl**stah kahk **eh**tah d^{y}**ayst**voo^{y}eht
I'd like ...	**Я хотел(а) бы ...**	^{y}ah khaht^{y}**ehl**(ah) bi
adapter	**адаптер**	ah**dahp**tehr
amplifier	**усилитель**	oossee**lee**teel^{y}
battery	**батарейку**	bahtahr^{y}**ay**koo
bulb	**лампочку**	**lahm**pahch^{y}koo
clock	**часы**	ch^{y}**eessi**
hair dryer	**фен**	f^{y}ehn
(travelling) iron	**(дорожный) утюг**	(dah**rozh**niy) oot^{y}**ook**
kettle	**чайник**	**ch^{y}igh**neek
lamp	**лампу**	**lahm**poo
lead	**шнур**	shnoor
plug	**штепсель**	**sht^{y}ehps**^{y}ehl^{y}
portable ...	**портативный ...**	pahrtah**teev**niy
radio	**приёмник**	pree^{y}**om**neek
record player	**проигриватель**	prah**ee**greevahteel^{y}
shaver	**электробритву**	ehl^{y}ehktrah**breet**voo
speakers	**громкоговорители**	**grom**kahgahvahreeteelee
(cassette) tape recorder	**(кассетный) магнитофон**	(kah**ss^{y}eht**niy) mahgneetah**fon**
television	**телевизор**	teelee**vee**zahr
transformer	**трансформатор**	trahnsfahr**mah**tahr
video cassette	**видео-кассету**	**vee**deho-kah**ss^{y}eh**too
video recorder	**видеомагнитофон**	veedehomahgneetah**fon**

Grocery *Продукты*

I'd like a loaf of bread, please.	**Дайте мне, пожалуйста, буханку хлеба.**	**dight**^{y}eh mn^{y}eh pah**zhahl**stah boo**khahn**koo **khl^{y}eh**bah
What sort of cheese do you have?	**Какие у вас сорта сыра?**	kah**kee**^{y}eh oo vahss sahr**tah si**rrah
A piece of ...	**Кусок ...**	koo**ssok**
that one	**этого**	**eh**tahvah
the one on the shelf	**того на полке**	tah**vo** nah **polk**^{y}eh
May I help myself?	**Я могу взять сам(а)?**	^{y}ah mahgoo vz^{y}aht^{y} sahm(**ah**)
I'd like ...	**Я хотел(а) бы ...**	^{y}ah khaht**^{y}ehl**(ah) bi
a kilo of apples	**килограмм яблок**	keelah**grahm ^{y}ah**blahk
half a kilo of tomatoes	**полкило помидоров**	pahlkee**lo** pahmee**do**rahf
1½ kilos of potatoes	**полтора кило картошки**	pahltah**rah** kee**lo** kahr**tosh**kee
100 grams of butter	**сто грамм масла**	sto grahm **mahs**lah
a litre/bottle of milk	**литр/бутылку молока**	leetr/boo**til**koo mahlah**kah**
10 eggs	**десяток яиц**	dee**ss^{y}ah**tahk ^{y}**aheets**
a packet of tea	**пачку чая**	**pahch^{y}**koo **ch^{y}ah**^{y}ah
a jar of jam	**банку варенья**	**bahn**koo vahr**^{y}ehn**^{y}ah
a tin (can) of peaches	**банку персиков**	**bahn**koo **p^{y}ehr**seekahf
a jar of mustard	**баночку горчицы**	**bah**nahch^{y}koo gahr**ch^{y}ee**tsi
a box of chocolates	**коробку шоколадных конфет**	kah**rop**koo shahkah**lahd**nikh kahn**f^{y}eht**
a packet of biscuits	**пачку печенья**	**pahch^{y}**koo pee**ch^{y}ehn**^{y}ah

Weights and measures
1 kilogram or kilo (kg) = 1000 grams (g) 100 g = 3.5 oz. ½ kg = 1.1 lb. 200 g = 7.0 oz. 1 kg = 2.2 lb. 1 oz. = 28.35 g 1 lb. = 453.60 g
1 litre (l) = 0.88 imp. quarts = 1.06 U.S. quarts 1 imp. quart = 1.14 l 1 U.S. quart = 0.95 l 1 imp. gallon = 4.55 l 1 U.S. gallon = 3.8 l

FOOD, see also page 63

Jeweller's—Watchmaker's *Ювелирные изделия – Часы*

Could I see that, please?	**Покажите это, пожалуйста.**	pahkah**zhit**^{y}eh **eh**tah pah**zhahl**stah
I'd like something in silver/gold.	**Я хотел(а) бы что-нибудь из серебра/золота.**	^{y}ah khaht^{y}**ehl**(ah) bi **shto**nee**bood**^{y} ees seeree**brah**/**zol**lahtah
I'd like to buy a small present.	**Мне нужно купить маленький подарок.**	mn^{y}eh **noozh**nah koo**peet**^{y} **mah**leen^{y}keey pah**dah**rahk
I don't want anything too expensive.	**Что-нибудь не очень дорогое, пожалуйста.**	**shto**neebood^{y} nee **och**^{y}een^{y} dahrah**go**^{y}eh pah**zhahl**stah
Is this real silver?	**Это настоящее серебро?**	**eh**tah nahstah^{y}**ahshch**^{y}eh^{y}eh seeree**bro**
How many carats is this?	**Сколько здесь каратов?**	**skol**^{y}kah zd^{y}**ehs**^{y} kah**rah**tahf
Can you repair this watch?	**Можно починить эти часы?**	**mozh**nah pahch^{y}ee**neet**^{y} **eh**tee ch^{y}**ees**si
It is fast/slow.	**Они спешат/отстают.**	ah**nee** spee**shaht**/ahtstah^{y}**oot**
I'd like ...	**Я хотел(а) бы ...**	^{y}ah khaht^{y}**ehl**(ah) bi
alarm clock	**будильник**	boo**deel**^{y}neek
bangle	**браслет**	brahs**l**^{y}**eht**
bracelet	**браслет**	brahs**l**^{y}**eht**
brooch	**брошь, брошку**	brosh^{y}, **brosh**koo
chain	**цепочку**	tseh**poch**^{y}koo
charm	**брелок**	bree**lok**
cigarette case	**портсигар**	portsee**gahr**
cigarette lighter	**зажигалку**	zahzhi**gahl**koo
clips	**клипсы**	**kleep**si
clock	**настольные часы**	nah**stol**^{y}ni^{y}eh ch^{y}**ees**si
cross	**крестик**	**kr**^{y}**ehs**teek
earrings	**серьги**	**s**^{y}**ehr**^{y}gee
gem	**самоцвет**	sahmah**tsv**^{y}**eht**
jewellery	**ювелирные изделия**	^{y}ooveel**eer**ni^{y}eh eez**d**^{y}**eh**lee^{y}ah
necklace	**ожерелье**	ahzhir^{y}**ehl**^{y}eh
pearl necklace	**жемчужное ожерелье**	zhim**ch**^{y}**oozh**nah^{y}eh ahzhir^{y}**ehl**^{y}eh
pendant	**кулон**	koo**lon**
pin	**булавку**	boo**lahf**koo
powder compact	**пудреницу**	**poo**dreeneetsoo
ring	**кольцо**	kahl^{y}**tso**
wedding ring	**обручальное кольцо**	ahbroo**ch**^{y}**ahl**^{y}nah^{y}eh kahl^{y}**tso**

silverware	столовое серебро	stahlovvah^{y}eh seereebro
tie pin	булавку для галстука	boolahfkoo dl^{y}ah gahl-stookah
watch	часы	ch^{y}eessi
automatic	электронные	ehleektronni^{y}eh
digital	с цифрами	s tsifrahmee
pocket	карманные	kahrmahnni^{y}eh
quartz	кварцевые	kvahrtsivi^{y}eh
with a second hand	с секундной стрелкой	s seekoondnigh str^{y}ehl-kigh
waterproof	водонепроницаемые	vahdahneeprahneetsah-^{y}ehmi^{y}eh
watchstrap	браслет для часов	brahsl^{y}eht dl^{y}ah ch^{y}eessof
wristwatch	ручные часы	rooch^{y}ni^{y}eh ch^{y}eessi
What kind of stone is it?	Что это за камень?	shto ehtah zah kahmeen^{y}

amber	янтарь	eentahr^{y}
amethyst	аметист	ahmeeteest
chromium	хром	khrom
copper	медь	m^{y}ehd^{y}
coral	коралл	kahrahl
crystal	хрусталь	khroostahl^{y}
diamond	бриллиант	breeleeahnt
ebony	чёрное дерево	ch^{y}ornah^{y}eh d^{y}ehreevah
emerald	изумруд	eezoomroot
enamel	эмаль	ehmahl^{y}
glass	стекло	steeklo
gold	золото	zollahtah
gold plate	позолоченный	pahzahloch^{y}eenniy
ivory	слоновая кость	slahnovvah^{y}ah kost^{y}
jade	нефрит	neefreet
onyx	оникс	ahneeks
pearl	жемчуг	zhehmch^{y}ook
pewter	олово	olahvah
platinum	платина	plahteenah
ruby	рубин	roobeen
sapphire	сапфир	sahpfeer
silver	серебро	seereebro
silver plate	серебряный	seer^{y}ehbreeniy
stainless steel	нержавеющая сталь	neerzhahv^{y}eh^{y}oosh-ch^{y}ah^{y}ah stahl^{y}
topaz	топаз	tahpahs
turquoise	бирюза	beer^{y}oozah

Optician *Оптика*

I've broken my glasses.	**У меня разбились очки.**	oo meen^y**ah** rahz**bee**lees^y ahch^y**kee**
Can you repair them?	**Можно их починить?**	**mozh**nah eekh pahch^{y}ee**neet^y**
When will they be ready?	**Когда они будут готовы?**	kahg**dah** ah**nee** **boo**doot gah**to**vvi
Can you change the lenses?	**Можно поменять стёкла?**	**mozh**nah pahmeen**^{y}aht^y** st^y**ok**lah
I'd like tinted lenses.	**Мне нужны тёмные стёкла.**	mn^{y}eh noozh**ni** **t^{y}om**ni^{y}eh st^y**ok**lah
The frame is broken.	**Оправа сломана.**	ah**prah**vah **slom**mahnah
I'd like a spectacle case.	**Мне нужен футляр для очков.**	mn^{y}eh **noo**zhehn foot**l^{y}ahr** dl^{y}ah ahch^y**kof**
I'd like a magnifying glass.	**Мне нужна лупа.**	mn^{y}eh noozh**nah** **loo**pah
I'd like to have my eyesight checked.	**Я хотел(а) бы проверить зрение.**	^{y}ah khaht**^{y}ehl**(ah) bi prahv**^{y}eh**reet^y **zr^{y}eh**nee^{y}eh
I'm short-sighted/ long-sighted.	**У меня близорукость/ дальнозоркость.**	oo meen**^{y}ah** bleezah**roo**kahst^y/ dahl^{y}nah**zor**kahst^y
I'd like some contact lenses.	**Мне нужны контактные линзы.**	mn^{y}eh noozh**ni** kahn**tahkt**ni^{y}eh **leen**zi
I've lost one of my contact lenses.	**Я потерял(а) одну линзу.**	^{y}ah pahteer**^{y}ahl**(ah) ahd**noo** **leen**zoo
Could you give me another one?	**Можете ли вы мне дать другую?**	**mo**zhit^{y}eh lee vi mn^{y}eh daht^y droo**goo**^{y}oo
I have hard/soft lenses.	**У меня твёрдые/ мягкие линзы.**	oo meen**^{y}ah** **tv^{y}or**di^{y}eh/ **m^{y}ahkh**kee^{y}eh **leen**zi
Do you have any contact lens fluid?	**Есть ли у вас жидкость для контактных линз?**	^{y}ehst^y lee oo vahss **zhit**kahst^y dl^{y}ah kahn**tahkt**nikh leens
I'd like to buy a pair of sunglasses.	**Я хотел(а) бы купить тёмные очки.**	^{y}ah khaht**^{y}ehl**(ah) bi koo**peet^y** **t^{y}om**ni^{y}eh ahch^y**kee**
May I look in a mirror?	**У вас есть зеркало?**	oo vahss ^{y}ehst^y **z^{y}ehr**kahlah
I'd like to buy a pair of binoculars.	**Я хотел(а) бы купить бинокль.**	^{y}ah khaht**^{y}ehl**(ah) bi koo**peet^y** beeno**kl^y**
How much is it?	**Сколько стоит?**	**skol^y**kah **sto**eet

Photography *Фотография*

Make sure you take enough film from home. If you have to buy film, then get it processed before leaving, as it is difficult to process Russian film in the West. Don't photograph objects of a military nature, airports or harbours. When in doubt, better ask:

May I take a picture of this/of you?	**Это можно снимать?/ Можно вас снять?**	**eh**tah **mozh**nah snee**maht^{y}**/ **mozh**nah vahss sn^{y}aht^{y}

Cameras *Фотоаппараты*

I'd like a(n) ... camera.	**Я хотел(а) бы ... фотоаппарат.**	^{y}ah khaht**^{y}ehl**(ah) bi ... fotahahpah**raht**
automatic	**автоматический**	ahftahmah**tee**ch^{y}eeskeey
inexpensive	**недорогой**	needahrah**goy**
simple	**простой**	prah**stoy**
Show me some cine (movie) cameras, please.	**Покажите мне, пожалуйста, кинокамеру.**	pahkah**zhit**^{y}eh mn^{y}eh pah**zhahl**stah keenah**kah**meeroo
I'd like to have some passport photos taken.	**Мне нужно сфотографироваться на паспорт.**	mn^{y}eh **noozh**nah sfahtahgrah**fee**rahvaht^{y}sah nah **pahss**pahrt

Film* *Плёнка*

I'd like a ... film for this camera.	**Дайте мне, пожалуйста, ... плёнку для этого аппарата.**	**dight**^{y}eh mn^{y}eh pah**zhahl**stah ... **pl^{y}on**koo dl^{y}ah **eh**tahvah ahpah**rah**tah
black and white	**чёрно-белую**	**ch^{y}or**nah-b**^{y}eh**loo^{y}oo
colour	**цветную**	tsveet**noo**^{y}oo
colour slide	**цветную для слайдов**	tsveet**noo**^{y}oo dl^{y}ah **sligh**dahf
cartridge	**катушка**	kah**toosh**kah
roll film	**роликовая плёнка**	**ro**leekahvah^{y}ah **pl^{y}on**kah
20/36 exposures	**двадцать/тридцать шесть кадров**	**dvah**tsaht^{y}/**tree**tsaht^{y} shehst^{y} **kah**drahf
this size	**этого размера**	**eh**tahvah rahz**m^{y}eh**rah
artificial light type	**для искусственного света**	dl^{y}ah ees**koost**v^{y}ehnnahvah **sv^{y}eh**tah
daylight type	**для дневного света**	dl^{y}ah dneev**no**vvah **sv^{y}eh**tah

---

* The sensitivity of Russian films is measured in GOST units: 90 GOST = 21 DIN/100 ASA, 180 GOST = 24 DIN/200 ASA.

Processing *Проявление*

How much do you charge for processing?	**Сколько стоит проявить плёнку?**	**skol^{y}kah stoeet praheeveet^{y} pl^{y}onkoo**
I'd like 5 prints of each negative.	**Я хотел(а) бы по 5 фотографий с каждого негатива.**	^{y}ah khaht^{y}ehl(ah) bi pah 5 fahtahgrahfeey s kahzhdahvah neegahteevah
Will you enlarge this, please?	**Я хотел(а) бы увеличить это.**	^{y}ah khaht^{y}ehl(ah) bi ooveeleech^{y}eet^{y} ehtah
When will the photos be ready?	**Когда будут готовы фотографии?**	kahgdah boodoot gahtovvi fahtahgrahfee^{y}ee

Accessories *Фотопринадлежности*

I need a(n) ...	**Мне нужен/нужна...**	mn^{y}eh noozhehn/noozhnah
battery	**батарейка**	bahtahr^{y}aykah
cable release	**тросик**	trosseek
camera case	**футляр для фотоаппарата**	footl^{y}ahr dl^{y}ah fotahahpahrahtah
(electronic) flash	**(электронная) вспышка**	(ehleektronnah^{y}ah) fspishkah
filter	**фильтр**	feel^{y}tr
for black and white	**для чёрно-белой плёнки**	dl^{y}ah ch^{y}ornah-b^{y}ehligh pl^{y}onkee
for colour	**для цветной плёнки**	dl^{y}ah tsveetnoy pl^{y}onkee
lens	**объектив**	ahb^{y}eekteef
telephoto lens	**телеобъектив**	t^{y}ehl^{y}ehahb^{y}eekteef
lens cap	**крышка объектива**	krishkah ahb^{y}eekteevah
lens shade	**бленда**	bl^{y}ehndah
tripod	**штатив**	shtahteef

Repairs *Ремонт*

Can you repair this camera?	**Можно починить этот аппарат?**	mozhnah pahch^{y}eeneet^{y} ehtaht ahpahraht
The film is jammed.	**Плёнку заело.**	pl^{y}onkoo zah^{y}ehlah
The ... doesn't work.	**...не работает.**	... nee rahbottah^{y}eht
exposure counter	**выдержка**	viddeershkah
film winder	**перемотка**	peereemotkah
light meter	**экспонометр**	ehkspahnomeetr
rangefinder	**дальномер**	dahl^{y}nahm^{y}ehr
shutter	**затвор**	zahtvor

NUMBERS, see page 147

Tobacconist's *Табак*

Cigarettes and tobacco are sold at tobacco kiosks (табак – tah**bahk**) or in tobacconist's. (Tobacconist's do not sell sweets, postcards or stamps.) Western cigarettes can only be found in Beryozka shops or in hotels, but for a taste of the exotic, why not try the Russian *папиросы* (pahpee**ro**ssi) or other popular brands like "Ява" or "Столичные".

Remember that smoking is not permitted in many public places, like the foyers of theatres and cinemas and some restaurants.

A packet of cigarettes, please.	**Пачку сигарет, пожалуйста.**	**pahch^y**koo seegahr^y**eht** pah**zhahl**stah
Do you have any American/English cigarettes?	**У вас есть американские/английские сигареты?**	oo vahss ^{y}ehst^y ahmeeree**kahns**kee^{y}eh/ahn**gleeys**kee^{y}eh seegahr^y**eh**tee
Do you have a/any ...?	**У вас есть ...?**	oo vahss ^{y}ehst^y
chewing gum	**жвачка**	**zhvahch^y**kah
cigarette holder	**мундштук**	moon(d)**shtook**
cigarettes	**сигареты**	seegahr^y**eh**tee
filter-tipped	**с фильтром**	s **feel^y**trahm
without filter	**без фильтра**	bees **feel^y**trah
mild/strong	**лёгкие/крепкие**	**l^{y}okh**kee^{y}eh/**kr^{y}ehp**kee^{y}eh
menthol	**с ментолом**	s meen**to**lahm
cigars	**сигары**	see**gah**ri
lighter	**зажигалка**	zahzhi**gahl**kah
lighter fluid/gas	**жидкий газ/газ для зажигалки**	**zhit**keey gahs/gahs dl^{y}ah zahzhi**gahl**kee
matches	**спички**	**speech^y**kee
pipe	**трубка**	**troop**kah
pipe cleaners	**прибор для чистки трубки**	pree**bor** dl^{y}ah **ch^{y}eest**kee **troop**kee
pipe tobacco	**табак (для трубки)**	tah**bahk** (dl^{y}ah **troop**kee)
wick	**фитиль**	fee**teel^y**
May I smoke here?	**Можно здесь курить?**	**mozh**nah zd^{y}ehs^y koo**reet^y**

НЕ КУРИТЬ
NO SMOKING

Miscellaneous

Souvenirs *Сувениры*

When buying antiques, travellers should bear in mind that anything from before 1917 is generally considered to be a national treasure and may not be taken out of the country. Thus, you can only export antique paintings, sculpture, antique samovars and icons after securing permission from the Ministry of Culture and upon payment of customs duties.

You'll find a whole range of items at the Beryozka stores where all purchases must be made in foreign currency. Wooden dolls and flower-printed shawls make nice souvenirs, as well as books, posters and records.

Here are some more ideas for souvenir shopping:

abacus	**счёты**	**shch^{y}o**tti
amber	**янтарь**	een**tahr^{y}**
balalaika	**балалайка**	bahlah**ligh**kah
caviar	**икра**	ee**krah**
ceramics	**керамика**	kee**rah**meekah
chess set	**шахматы**	**shahkh**mahti
fur hat	**меховая шапка**	meekhah**vah^{y}**ah **shahp**kah
icon	**икона**	ee**ko**nnah
lace	**кружево**	**kroo**zhivah
Palekh boxes	**Палехские шкатулки**	**pah**leekhskee^{y}eh shkah**tool**-kee
perfume	**духи**	doo**khee**
poster	**плакат**	plah**kaht**
rugs from Tekin	**текинские ковры**	tee**keen**skee^{y}eh kah**vri**
Russian cigarettes	**папиросы**	pahpee**ro**ssi
samovar	**самовар**	sahmah**vahr**
shawl	**платок**	plah**tok**
stamps	**марки**	**mahr**kee
vodka	**водка**	**vot**kah
wood carving	**резьба по дереву**	reez^{y}**bah** pah **d^{y}eh**reevoo
wooden doll	**матрёшка**	mah**tr^{y}osh**kah
wooden spoons	**деревянные ложки**	deeree**v^{y}ah**nni^{y}eh **losh**kee

Records – Cassettes *Пластинки – Кассеты*

Do you have any records by ...?	**Есть ли у вас пластинки ...?**	**^{y}ehst^{y}** lee oo **vahss** plah**steen**kee

I'd like a ...	**Я хотел(а) бы...**	^{y}ah khaht^{y}ehl(ah) bi
cassette	**кассету**	kahss^{y}ehtoo
video cassette	**видео-кассету**	veedeeo-kahss^{y}ehtoo
Do you have any songs by ...?	**Есть ли у вас песни...?**	^{y}ehst^{y} lee oo vahss p^{y}ehsnee
Can I listen to this record?	**Можно прослушать эту пластинку?**	mozhnah prahslooshaht^{y} ehtoo plahsteenkoo
chamber music	**камерная музыка**	kahmeernah^{y}ah moozikah
classical music	**классическая музыка**	klahsseech^{y}eeskah^{y}ah moozikah
folk music	**народная музыка**	nahrodnah^{y}ah moozikah
instrumental music	**инструментальная музыка**	eenstroomeentahl^{y}nah^{y}ah moozikah
jazz	**джаз**	dzhahz
light music	**лёгкая музыка**	l^{y}okhkah^{y}ah moozikah
orchestral music	**оркестровая музыка**	ahrkeestrovah^{y}ah moozikah
pop music	**поп-музыка**	pop-moozikah

Toys *Игрушки*

I'd like a toy/ game ...	**Я хотел(а) бы игрушку/игру...**	^{y}ah khaht^{y}ehl(ah) bi eegrooshkoo/eegroo
for a boy	**для мальчика**	dl^{y}ah mahl^{y}ch^{y}eekah
for a 5-year-old girl	**для пятилетней девочки**	dl^{y}ah peeteel^{y}ehtn^{y}ay d^{y}ehvahch^{y}kee
ball	**мяч**	m^{y}ahch^{y}
bucket and spade (pail and shovel)	**ведёрко и совок**	veed^{y}orkah ee sahvok
building blocks (bricks)	**кубики**	koobeekee
card game	**игральные карты**	eegrahl^{y}ni^{y}eh kahrti
chess set	**шахматы**	shahkhmahti
doll	**куклу**	kookloo
electronic game	**электронную игру**	ehleektronnoo^{y}oo eegroo
flippers	**ласты**	lahsti
roller skates	**ролики**	roleekee
snorkel	**(дыхательную) трубку**	(dikhahteel^{y}noo^{y}oo) troopkoo
teddy bear	**мишку**	meeshkoo
wooden toys	**деревянные игрушки**	deereev^{y}ahnni^{y}eh eegrooshkee

Your money: banks—currency

General

All foreign currency must be declared at customs. Keep the declaration form, for you must present it each time you change dollars or pounds into roubles (keep the respective receipts as well) and on departure. It's forbidden to import or export roubles. Currency transactions are permitted only at banks and official currency-exchange desks at hotels, airports, etc.

Opening hours

Moscow Bank for Foreign Trade: open Monday to Friday, 9.30 a.m. to 1 p.m. Currency-exchange desks are open considerably longer. Remember to carry your passport and currency declaration form when changing money.

Currency

The monetary unit is the rouble (рубль —roobl^y), divided into 100 kopecks (копейка—kah**p^{y}ay**kah). The abbreviations are р. and к. Banknotes: 1, 3, 5, 10, 15, 25, 50, 100, 500, 1000 and 5000 roubles. Coins: 1, 2, 3, 5, 10, 15, 20 and 50 kopecks; 1 rouble.

All well-known traveller's cheques are recognized at official currency-exchange desks and at most foreign-currency shops. International credit cards are accepted in some Russian shops as well as in hotels and foreign-currency shops. Foreign currency, particularly US Dollars, is required in many restaurants and hotel bars, and most shops selling Western goods.

Where can I change some money?	**Где можно обменять валюту?**	gd^{y}eh **mozh**nah ahbmee**n^{y}aht^y** vahl^y**oo**too
May I have a form for an international money order?	**Можно бланк для международного почтового перевода?**	**mozh**nah blahnk dl^{y}ah meezhdoonah**rod**nahvah pahch^{y}tah**vo**vvah peeree**vo**ddah

At the bank *В банке*

I'd like to change some dollars/ pounds.	**Я хотел(а) бы обменять доллары/фунты.**	^{y}ah khaht^{y}**ehl**(ah) bi ahb-meen^{y}**aht^{y} do**llahri/ **foon**ti
I'd like to cash a traveller's cheque.	**Я хотел(а) бы разменять дорожный чек.**	^{y}ah khaht^{y}**ehl**(ah) bi rahz-meen^{y}**aht^{y}** dah**rozh**niy ch^{y}ehk
Here's my passport.	**Вот мой паспорт.**	vot moy **pahs**pahrt
What's the exchange rate?	**Какой валютный курс?**	kah**koy** vahl^{y}**oot**niy koors
How much commission do you charge?	**Сколько вы берёте за обмен?**	**skol**^{y}kah vi beer^{y}**ot**^{y}eh zah ahb**m^{y}ehn**
Can you telex my bank in London?	**Можете ли вы послать телекс моему банку в Лондоне?**	**mo**zhit^{y}eh lee vi pah**slaht^{y} t^{y}eh**leeks mahee**moo bahn**koo v **lon**don^{y}eh
I have a/an/some ...	**У меня ...**	oo meen^{y}**ah**
bank account	**счёт в банке**	shch^{y}ot v **bahn**k^{y}eh
check card	**чековая карточка**	**ch^{y}eh**kahvah^{y}ah **kahr**-tahch^{y}kah
credit card	**кредитная карточка**	kree**deet**nah^{y}ah **kahr**-tahch^{y}kah
introduction from ...	**рекомендательное письмо ...**	reekahmeen**dah**teel^{y}nah^{y}eh pees^{y}**mo**
letter of credit	**аккредитив**	ahkkreedee**teef**
I'm expecting some money from ... Has it arrived yet?	**Для меня должны быть деньги из ... Они уже пришли?**	dl^{y}ah meen^{y}**ah** dahlzh**ni** bit^{y} **d^{y}ehn**^{y}gee eez ... ah**nee** oo**zheh** pree**shlee**
Give me ... 50-rouble notes (bills) and some small change, please.	**Дайте мне, пожалуйста, ... пятидесятирублёвок, остальное мелочью.**	**digh**tee mn^{y}eh pah**zhahl**-stah ... peeteedeessee**tee**-roo**bl^{y}o**vvahk ahstahl^{y}**no**^{y}eh **m^{y}eh**lahch^{y}oo
Give me ... large notes and the rest in small notes.	**Дайте мне пожалуйста ... крупных купюр, а остальное мелкими купюрами.**	**digh**tee mn^{y}eh pah**zhahl**-stah ... **kroop**nikh koop^{y}**oor** ah ahstahl^{y}**no**^{y}eh **m^{y}ehl**-keemee koop^{y}**oo**rahmee
I'd like to ...	**Я хотел(а) бы ...**	^{y}ah khaht^{y}**ehl**(ah) bi
open an account	**открыть счёт**	aht**krit^{y}** shch^{y}ot
withdraw ... roubles	**снять со счёта ... рублей**	sn^{y}aht^{y} sah **shch^{y}o**ttah ... roo**bl^{y}ay**
Where should I sign?	**Где мне подписать?**	gd^{y}eh mn^{y}eh pahtpee**ssaht^{y}**

NUMBERS, see page 147

I want to deposit this in my account.	**Я хочу внести это на счёт.**	^{y}ah khah**ch^{y}oo** vnees**tee** **eh**tah nah shch^{y}ot

Business terms *Деловые выражения*

My name is ...	**Моя фамилия ...**	mah^{y}**ah** fah**mee**lee^{y}ah
Here's my card.	**Вот моя визитная карточка.**	vot mah^{y}**ah** vee**zeet**nah^{y}ah **kahr**tahch^{y}kah
I have an appointment with ...	**Я договорился/договорилась с ...**	^{y}ah dahgahvah**reel**sah/ dahgahvah**reel**ahs^{y} s
Can you give me an estimate of the cost?	**Можете ли вы дать мне предварительную смету расходов?**	**mo**zhit^{y}eh lee vi daht^{y} mn^{y}eh preedvah**ree**teel^{y}noo^{y}oo **sm^{y}eh**too rahs**khod**dahf
What's the rate of inflation?	**Какая у вас инфляция?**	kah**kah**^{y}ah oo vahss een**fl^{y}ah**tsi^{y}ah
Can you provide me with an interpreter/ a secretary?	**Можете ли вы найти мне переводчика/ секретаршу?**	**mo**zhit^{y}eh lee vi nigh**tee** mn^{y}eh peeree**vod**ch^{y}eekah/ seekree**tahr**shoo
Where can I make photocopies?	**Где мне сделать фотокопии?**	gd^{y}eh mn^{y}eh **zd^{y}eh**laht^{y} fahtah**ko**ppee^{y}ee

amount	**сумма**	**soo**mmah
balance	**баланс**	bah**lahnss**
capital	**капитал**	kahpee**tahl**
cheque	**чек**	ch^{y}ehk
cheque book	**чековая книжка**	**ch^{y}eh**kahvah^{y}ah **kneesh**kah
contract	**договор, контракт**	dahgah**vor**, kahn**trahkt**
expenses	**расходы**	rahs**kho**ddi
interest	**процент**	prah**tsehnt**
investment	**капиталовложение**	kahpeetahlahvlah**zheh**nee^{y}eh
invoice	**счёт, фактура**	shch^{y}ot, fahk**too**rah
loss	**убыток**	oo**bi**ttahk
mortgage	**ипотека**	eepah**t^{y}eh**kah
payment	**платёж**	plah**t^{y}osh**
percentage (rate of interest)	**процентная ставка**	prah**tsehnt**nah^{y}ah **stahf**kah
profit	**доход, прибыль**	dah**khot**, **pree**bil^{y}
purchase	**покупка, купля**	pah**koop**kah, **koo**pl^{y}ah
sale	**продажа**	prah**dah**zhah
share	**акция**	**ahk**tsi^{y}ah
transfer	**перевод**	peeree**vot**
value	**стоимость, цена**	**sto**eemahst^{y}, tsin**nah**

At the post office *На почте*

The main post offices in Moscow and St. Petersburg offer round-the-clock service. Other post offices are generally open from 9 a.m. to 6 or 7 p.m. Major hotels have their own branches of the post office for postal, telegraph, telex and telephone services. International money orders can only be cashed at banks.

You'll find postcards and envelopes at hotels, post offices and newsstands. Letter boxes are painted blue.

Where's the nearest post office?	**Где ближайшая почта?**	gd^{y}eh blee**zhigh**shah^{y}ah **poch^{y}**tah
Where's the main post office?	**Где почтамт?**	gd^{y}eh pahch^{y}**tahmt**
What time does the post office open/close?	**Во сколько открывается/закрывается почта?**	vah **skol^{y}**kah ahtkri**vvah**eetsah/zahkri**vvah**eetsah **poch^{y}**tah
Where's the letter box (mailbox)?	**Где почтовый ящик?**	gd^{y}eh pahch^{y}**tov**viy **^{y}ah**shch^{y}eek
Where can I buy postcards/envelopes/stamps?	**Где можно купить открытки/конверты/марки?**	gd^{y}eh **mozh**nah koo**peet^{y}** aht**krit**kee/kahn**v^{y}ehr**ti/ **mahr**kee
Could you give me a stamp for this letter/postcard, please?	**Дайте мне, пожалуйста, марку на это письмо/эту открытку.**	**dight**^{y}eh mn^{y}eh pah**zhahl**stah **mahr**koo nah **eh**tah pees^{y}**mo**/**eh**too aht**krit**koo
A 3-kopeck/5-kopeck stamp, please.	**Пожалуйста, марку за 3 копейки/5 копеек.**	pah**zhahl**stah **mahr**koo zah 3 kah**p^{y}ay**kee/ 5 kah**p^{y}eh**^{y}ehk
What's the postage for a letter to the United States?	**Сколько стоит письмо в Соединённые Штаты?**	**skol^{y}**kah **sto**eet pees^{y}**mo** f sah^{y}eedeen**^{y}on**ni^{y}eh **shtah**ti
What's the postage for a postcard to Great Britain?	**Сколько стоит открытка в Англию?**	**skol^{y}**kah **sto**eet aht**krit**kah v **ahn**glee^{y}oo
I'd like to send this parcel.	**Я хотел(а) бы послать эту посылку.**	^{y}ah khaht**^{y}ehl**(ah) bi pah**slaht^{y}** **eh**too pah**ssil**koo

ПОЧТОВЫЕ МАРКИ	STAMPS
ПОСЫЛКИ	PARCELS

NUMBERS, see page 147

airmail	**авиапочта/авиа**	ahveeahpoch^{y}tah/ahveeah
express (special delivery)	**экспресс/с нарочным**	ehkspr^{y}ehss/s nahrahch^{y}nim
recorded delivery	**с уведомлением о вручении**	s ooveedahml^{y}ehnee^{y}ehm ah vrooch^{y}ehnee^{y}ee
registered letter	**заказное письмо**	zahkahzno^{y}eh pees^{y}mo

Where is the poste restante (general delivery) counter?	**Где окошко до востребования?**	gd^{y}eh ahkoshkah dah vahstr^{y}ehbahvahnee^{y}ah
Is there any mail for me? My name is …	**Нет ли для меня писем? Моя фамилия …**	n^{y}eht lee dl^{y}ah meen^{y}ah peess^{y}ehm. mah^{y}ah fahmeelee^{y}ah
Here's my passport.	**Вот мой паспорт.**	vot moy pahspahrt

The address *Адрес*

Russian addresses are written back to front, i.e. you start with the country, then the city, the street, and end with the name. But when sending letters or postcards abroad, you can write the address as usual.

Telegrams *Телеграммы*

From where can I send a telegram/telex?	**Откуда можно послать телеграмму/телекс?**	ahtkoodah mozhnah pahslaht^{y} teeleegrahmmoo/t^{y}ehleeks
I'd like to send a telegram.	**Я хочу послать телеграмму.**	^{y}ah khahch^{y}oo pahslaht^{y} teeleegrahmmoo
May I have an international message form, please?	**Международный бланк, пожалуйста.**	meezhdoonahrodniy blahnk pahzhahlstah
How much is it per word?	**Сколько стоит слово?**	skol^{y}kah stoeet slovvah
How long will a telegram to London take?	**Сколько времени идёт телеграмма в Лондон?**	skol^{y}kah vr^{y}ehmeenee eed^{y}ot teeleegrahmmah v london
How much will this telex cost?	**Сколько будет стоить этот телекс?**	skol^{y}kah boodeet stoeet^{y} ehtaht t^{y}ehleeks

Telephone *Телефон*

When phoning from a public telephone, insert the required money (coins to the value of 15 kopecks) **before** picking up the receiver. Long-distance calls can only be made from your hotel or by going to the telephone and telegraph office. International calls are best booked through the hotel service desk, and if possible, well in advance. There are no phone books available! You can get somebody's number at an enquiry booth in the street, called справочное бюро (**sprah**vahch^{y}nah^{y}eh b^{y}oo**ro**) or simply справки (**sprahf**kee) but only if you know the person's name, address and date of birth.

General questions *Общие вопросы*

Where's the telephone?	**Где телефон?**	gd^{y}eh teelee**fon**
Where's the nearest public telephone (telephone booth)?	**Где ближайший телефон-автомат/ таксофон?**	gd^{y}eh blee**zhigh**shiy teelee**fon**-ahftah**maht**/ tahksah**fon**
I'd like to book a phone call to England.	**Я хотел(а) бы заказать разговор с Англией.**	^{y}ah khaht^y**ehl**(ah) bi zahkah**zaht^y** rahzgah**vor** s **ahn**glee^{y}ay
Will I have to wait long?	**Мне долго ждать?**	mn^{y}eh **dol**gah zhdaht^y

If you are calling from a post office, you might hear the following phrases:

Какой номер?	What number (are you calling)?
Сколько минут хотите говорить?	How many minutes do you want to speak?
Подождите!	Wait, please!
Ваш разговор в кабине номер 4.	Your call is in cabin number 4.
Время кончилось.	The time is over.

May I use your phone?	**Можно от вас позвонить?**	**mozh**nah aht vahss pahzvah**neet**^{y}
I'd like to make a ... call.	**Я хотел(а) бы ...разговор.**	^{y}ah khaht^y**ehl**(ah) bi ... rahzgah**vor**
long-distance	**междугородный**	m^{y}ehzhdoogah**rod**niy
international	**международный**	m^{y}ehzhdoonah**rod**niy
Can I dial direct?	**Я могу сам(а) набрать?**	^{y}ah mah**goo** sah**m(ah)** nah**braht**^{y}
The dialling code is ...	**Код (города) ...**	koht (**go**rrahdah)

Speaking *У телефона*

Hello!	**Алло!/Слушаю!**	**ahl^{y}o/sloo**shah^{y}oo
This is ... speaking.	**Это говорит ...**	**eh**tah gahvah**reet**
I'd like to speak to ...	**Позовите, пожалуйста ...**	pahzah**veet**^{y}eh pah**zhahl**stah
I'd like extension 24.	**Добавочный 24, пожалуйста.**	dah**bah**vahch^{y}niy 24, pah**zhahl**stah
Who is speaking?	**Кто говорит?**	kto gahvah**reet**
I don't understand.	**Я не понимаю.**	^{y}ah nee pahnee**mah**^{y}oo
Do you speak English?	**Вы говорите по-английски?**	vi gahvah**reet**^{y}eh pah ahn**gleey**skee
Could you speak louder/more slowly, please?	**Говорите громче/медленнее, пожалуйста.**	gahvah**reet**^{y}eh **gromch**^{y}eh/**m^{y}eh**dleennee pah**zhahl**stah
Could you spell it?	**Скажите по буквам, пожалуйста.**	skah**zhit**^{y}eh pah **book**vahm pah**zhahl**stah

Bad luck *Вам не повезло*

You gave me the wrong number.	**Вы мне дали неправильный номер.**	vi mn^{y}eh **dah**lee nee**prah**veel^{y}niy **no**mmeer
We have been interrupted.	**Нас прервали.**	nahss preer**vah**lee
I can't get through.	**Я не могу дозвониться.**	^{y}ah nee mah**goo** dahzvah**neet**^{y}sah
Will I have to wait long?	**Мне долго ждать?**	mn^{y}eh **dol**gah zhdaht^y

ALPHABET, see page 6

He's/She's not there *Его/Её нет*

When will he/she be back?	**Когда он/она вернётся?**	kahg**dah** onn/ah**nah** veern^{y}**o**tsah
Will you tell him/her I called?	**Передайте ему/ей, пожалуйста, что я звонил(а).**	peeree**dight**^{y}eh ee**moo**/^{y}ay pah**zhahl**stah shto ^{y}ah zvah**neel**(ah)
My name is ...	**Меня зовут ...**	meen^{y}**ah** zah**voot**
Would you ask him/her to call me?	**Попросите его/её, пожалуйста, позвонить мне.**	pahprah**sseet**^{y}eh ee**vo**/ee^{y}**o** pah**zhahl**stah pahzvah**neet**^{y} mn^{y}eh
Would you take a message, please?	**Передайте, пожалуйста, что ...**	peeree**dight**^{y}eh pah**zhahl**stah shto
I'll call again/later.	**Я позвоню ещё раз/попозже.**	^{y}ah pahzvah**n**^{y}**oo** ee**shch**^{y}**o** rahs/pah**pozz**heh

Charges* *Плата*

What was the cost of that call?	**Сколько стоит разговор?**	**skol**^{y}kah **sto**eet rahzgah**vor**
I'd like to pay for the call.	**Я хочу заплатить за разговор.**	^{y}ah khah**ch**^{y}**oo** zahplah**teet**^{y} zah rahzgah**vor**

Вас вызывают по телефону.	There's a call for you.
Не вешайте трубку.	Please hold the line.
Какой номер вам нужен?	What number are you calling?
Минуточку!	Just a moment, please.
Линия занята.	The line's engaged.
Никто не отвечает.	There's no answer.
Его/Её сейчас нет.	He's/She's out at the moment.
У вас неправильный номер.	You've got the wrong number.
Телефон поменялся.	This number is no longer valid.
Телефон не работает.	The phone is out of order.

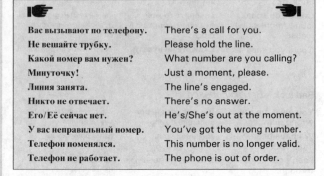

* You usually have to pay in advance for your calls.

Doctor

Medical treatment is free of charge in Russia, but you'll have to pay for medicine.

General *Общие понятия*

Can you get me a doctor?	Вы можете вызвать мне врача?	vi **mo**zhit^{y}eh **viz**vaht^{y} mn^{y}eh vrah**ch^{y}ah**
Is there a doctor here?	Есть ли здесь врач?	^{y}ehst^{y} lee zd^{y}ehs^{y} vrahch^{y}
I need a doctor quickly.	Мне срочно нужен врач.	mn^{y}eh **sroch^{y}**nah **noo**zhehn vrahch^{y}
Where can I find a doctor who speaks English?	Где мне найти врача, который говорит по-английски?	gd^{y}eh mn^{y}eh nigh**tee** vrah**ch^{y}ah** kah**to**rriy gahvah**reet** pah ahng**leeys**kee
Where's the surgery (doctor's office)/ clinic?	Где кабинет врача/ поликлиника?	gd^{y}eh kahbeen**^{y}eht** vrah**ch^{y}ah**/pahleek**lee**neekah
What are the surgery (office) hours?	В какие часы приём больных?	f kah**kee**^{y}eh ch^{y}ee**ssi** pree**^{y}om** bahl^{y}**nikh**
Could the doctor come to see me here?	Может ли врач прийти ко мне?	**mo**zhit lee vrahch^{y} preey**tee** kah mn^{y}eh
What time can the doctor come?	Когда врач может прийти?	kahg**dah** vrahch^{y} **mo**zhit preey**tee**
Can you recommend a/an ...?	Можете ли вы посоветовать мне ...?	**mo**zhit^{y}eh lee vi pahsah**v^{y}eh**tahvaht^{y} mn^{y}eh
I need a ...	Мне нужен ...	mn^{y}eh **noo**zhehn
general practitioner	терапевт	teerap**^{y}ehft**
children's doctor	педиатр	peedee**ahtr**
eye specialist	глазной врач	glahz**noy** vrahch^{y}
gynaecologist	гинеколог	geenee**ko**llahk
Can I have an appointment ...?	Я хотел(а) бы записаться на приём ...	^{y}ah khaht**^{y}ehl**(ah) bi zahpee**saht^{y}**sah nah pree**^{y}om**
immediately	незамедлительно	neezahmee**dlee**t^{y}ehl^{y}nah
tomorrow	на завтра	nah **zahf**trah
as soon as possible	как можно скорее	kahk **mozh**nah skahr**^{y}eh**^{y}eh

CHEMIST'S, see page 108

Parts of the body *Части тела*

arm	**рука**	roo**kah**
artery	**артерия**	ahrt^y**eh**ree^{y}ah
back	**спина**	spee**nah**
bladder	**мочевой пузырь**	mahch^y**eevoy** poo**zir**^{y}
bone	**кость**	kost^y
bowel/bowels	**кишка/кишки**	keesh**kah**/keesh**kee**
breast	**грудь**	grood^y
cheek	**щека**	shch^{y}ee**kah**
chest	**грудная клетка**	grood**nah**^{y}ah **kl^{y}eht**kah
ear/ears	**ухо/уши**	**oo**khah/**oo**shi
elbow	**локоть**	**lo**kkaht^y
eye	**глаз**	glahs
face	**лицо**	lee**tso**
finger	**палец**	**pah**leets
foot	**нога**	nah**gah**
genitals	**половые органы**	pahlah**vi**^{y}eh **or**gahni
hand	**рука**	roo**kah**
head	**голова**	gahlah**vah**
heart	**сердце**	s^y**ehr**tseh
jaw	**челюсть**	**ch^{y}eh**l^{y}oost^y
joint	**сустав**	soos**tahf**
kidney	**почка**	**poch^y**kah
knee	**колено**	kahl^y**eh**nah
leg	**нога**	nah**gah**
lip	**губа**	goo**bah**
liver	**печень**	**p^{y}eh**ch^{y}ehn^y
lungs	**лёгкие**	**l^{y}o**khkee^{y}eh
mouth	**рот**	rot
muscle	**мышца**	**mish**tsah
neck	**шея**	**sheh**^{y}ah
nerve	**нерв**	n^{y}ehrf
nervous system	**нервная система**	**n^{y}ehr**vnah^{y}ah seest^y**eh**mah
nose	**нос**	noss
rib	**ребро**	ree**bro**
shoulder	**плечо**	plee**ch^{y}o**
skin	**кожа**	**ko**zhah
spine	**позвоночник**	pahzvah**noch^y**neek
stomach	**живот/желудок**	zhi**vot**/zhi**loo**dahk
tendon	**сухожилие**	sookhah**zhilee**^{y}eh
thigh	**бедро**	bee**dro**
throat	**горло**	**gor**lah
toe	**палец ноги**	**pah**leets nah**gee**
tongue	**язык**	ee**zik**
tonsils	**миндалины**	meen**dah**leeni
vein	**вена**	**v^{y}eh**nah

Accident – Injury *Несчастный случай – Травма*

There's been an accident.	Несчастный случай.	nee**shch^{y}ahst**niy **slooch^{y}**igh
My child has had a fall.	Мой ребёнок упал.	moy reeb^{y}onnahk oo**pahl**
He/She has hurt his/her head.	Он/Она повредил(а) себе голову.	on/ah**nah** pahvree**deel**(ah) seeb^{y}**eh** **gol**lahvoo
He's/She's unconscious.	Он/Она потерял(а) сознание.	on/ah**nah** pahteer^{y}**ahl**(ah) sah**znah**n^{y}eh
He's/She's bleeding heavily.	У него/неё сильное кровотечение.	oo nee**vo**/nee^{y}**o** **seel**^{y}na^{y}eh krahvahtee**ch^{y}eh**nee^{y}eh
He's/She's seriously injured.	У него/неё серьёзное повреждение.	oo nee**vo**/nee^{y}**o** see^{y}**oz**-nah^{y}eh pahvreezh**d^{y}eh**-nee^{y}eh
His/Her arm is broken.	Он/Она сломал(а) руку.	on/ah**nah** slah**mahl**(ah) **roo**koo
His/Her ankle is swollen.	У него/неё опухла лодыжка.	oo nee**vo**/nee^{y}**o** ah**pookh**lah lah**dish**kah
I've been stung by a wasp/bee.	Меня ужалила оса/пчела.	meen^{y}**ah** oo**zhah**leelah ah**ssah**/pch^{y}ee**lah**
I've got something in my eye.	Мне что-то попало в глаз.	mn^{y}eh **shto**tah pah**pah**lah v glahs
Could you have a look at this ...?	Посмотрите, пожалуйста, ...	pahsmah**tree**t^{y}eh pah**zhahl**stah
bite	укус	oo**koos**
blister	волдырь	vahl**dir^{y}**
boil	нарыв/фурункул	nah**rif**/foo**roon**kool
bruise	ушиб	oo**ship**
burn	ожог	ah**zhok**
cut	порез	pah**r^{y}ehs**
graze	ссадину	**ssah**deenoo
lump	шишку	**shish**koo
rash	сыпь	sip^{y}
sting	укус	oo**koos**
swelling	опухоль	**o**pookhahl^{y}
wound	рану	**rah**noo
I can't move my ...	Я не могу двинуть ...	^{y}ah nee mah**goo** **dvee**noot^{y}
It hurts.	Мне больно.	mn^{y}eh **bol^{y}**nah
What should I do?	Что мне делать?	shto mn^{y}eh **d^{y}eh**laht^{y}

Что у вас болит?	Where does it hurt?
Какая (это) боль?	What kind of pain is it?
тупая/острая **постоянная**	dull/sharp constant
Нужно сделать рентген.	You'll have to have an X-ray.
Это ...	It's ...
сломано/растянуто **вывихнуто/разорвано**	broken/sprained dislocated/torn
Вы растянули мышцу.	You've pulled a muscle.
Нужно наложить гипс.	You'll have to have a plaster.
У вас заражение (Заражения нет).	It's (not) infected.
Вам слелали прививку против столбняка?	Have you been vaccinated against tetanus?
Я вам дам антисептическое/ болеутоляющее средство.	I'll give you an antiseptic/ a painkiller.

Illness *Болезнь*

I'm not feeling well.	**Я плохо себя чувствую.**	^{y}ah **plo**khah see**b^{y}ah** **ch^{y}oost**voo^{y}oo
I'm ill.	**Я болен/больна.**	^{y}ah **bo**leen/bahl^{y}**nah**
I feel dizzy/ faint.	**У меня кружится голова.**	oo meen^{y}**ah** **kroo**zhitsah gahlah**vah**
I feel nauseous/ shivery.	**Меня тошнит/ Меня знобит.**	meen^{y}**ah** tahsh**neet**/ meen^{y}**ah** znah**beet**
I've got a fever.	**У меня жар.**	oo meen^{y}**ah** zhahr
My temperature is 38 degrees.	**У меня температура – 38.**	oo meen^{y}**ah** teempeerah**too**rah 38
I've been vomiting.	**Меня рвало.**	meen^{y}**ah** rvah**lo**
I'm constipated/ I've got diarrhoea.	**У меня запор/ У меня понос.**	oo meen^{y}**ah** zah**por**/ oo meen^{y}**ah** pah**noss**
My ... hurts/hurt.	**У меня болит/болят...**	oo meen^{y}**ah** bah**leet**/bahl^{y}**aht**
It hurts here.	**Здесь болит.**	zd^{y}ehs^{y} bah**leet**

PARTS OF THE BODY, see page 138

I've got ...	**У меня...**	oo meen^y**ah**
asthma	**астма**	**ahst**mah
cramps	**судороги/спазмы**	**soo**dahrahgee/**spahz**mi
indigestion	**расстройство желудка**	rahs**stroyst**vah zhi**loot**kah
nosebleed	**кровотечение из носа**	krahvahtee**ch^{y}eh**nee^{y}eh eez **nos**sah
palpitations	**сердцебиение**	s^{y}ehrtsehbee^y**eh**nee^{y}eh
rheumatism	**ревматизм**	r^{y}ehvmah**teezm**
sunstroke	**солнечный удар**	**sol**neech^{y}niy oo**dahr**
I've got ...	**У меня болит...**	oo meen^y**ah** bah**leet**
backache	**спина**	spee**nah**
headache	**голова**	gahlah**vah**
stomach ache	**живот/желудок**	**zhivot**/zhi**loo**dahk
I have difficulties breathing.	**Мне трудно дышать.**	mn^{y}eh **trood**nah di**shaht^y**
I have a pain in my chest.	**У меня боль в груди.**	oo meen^y**ah** bol^y v groo**dee**
I had a heart attack 5 years ago.	**У меня был сердечный приступ 5 лет назад.**	oo meen^y**ah** bill seer**d^{y}ehch^y**niy **pree**stoop 5 l^{y}eht nah**zaht**
My blood pressure is too high/low.	**У меня слишком высокое/низкое давление.**	oo meen^y**ah** **sleesh**kahm vis**so**kah^{y}eh/**nees**kah^{y}eh dah**vl^{y}eh**nee^{y}eh
I'm allergic to ...	**У меня аллергия на...**	oo meen^y**ah** ahl^y**ehr**gee^{y}ah nah
I'm a diabetic.	**У меня диабет.**	oo meen^y**ah** deeah**b^{y}eht**

Women's section *У гинеколога*

I have period pains.	**У меня болезненная менструация.**	oo meen^y**ah** bahl^y**ehz**neennah^{y}ah meenstroo**ah**tsi^{y}ah
I have a vaginal infection.	**У меня воспаление влагалища.**	oo meen^y**ah** vahspahl^y**eh**nee^{y}eh vlah**gah**leeshch^{y}ah
I'm on the pill.	**Я принимаю противозачаточные пилюли.**	^{y}ah preenee**mah**^{y}oo prahteevahzah**ch^{y}ah**tahch^{y}ni^{y}eh peel^y**oo**lee
I haven't had my period for 2 months.	**У меня нет менструации уже 2 месяца.**	oo meen^y**ah** n^{y}eht meenstroo**ah**tsi^{y}ee oo**zheh** 2 **m^{y}eh**sseetsah
I'm (3 months) pregnant.	**Я беременна (на третьем месяце).**	^{y}ah beer^y**eh**meennah (nah **tr^{y}eh**t^{y}eem **m^{y}eh**sseetseh)

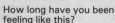

Давно вы так себя чувствуете?	How long have you been feeling like this?
Это у вас впервые?	Is it the first time you've had this?
Я вам измерю температуру/ давление.	I'll take your temperature/ blood pressure.
Засучите рукав, пожалуйста.	Roll up your sleeve, please.
Разденьтесь, пожалуйста (до пояса).	Please undress (down to the waist).
Ложитесь сюда, пожалуйста.	Please lie down over here.
Откройте рот.	Open your mouth.
Сделайте глубокий вдох.	Breathe deeply.
Покашляйте, пожалуйста.	Cough, please.
Где у вас болит?	Where does it hurt?
У вас…	You've got (a/an) …
аппендицит	appendicitis
венерическая болезнь	venereal disease
воспаление…	inflammation of …
воспаление лёгких	pneumonia
цистит	cystitis
гастрит	gastritis
грипп	flu
желтуха	jaundice
корь	measles
отравление	(food) poisoning
Это (не) заразно.	It's (not) contagious.
Я вам сделаю укол/инъекцию.	I'll give you an injection.
Надо сделать анализ крови/ кала/мочи.	I want a specimen of your blood/stools/urine.
Вы должны 5 дней полежать в постели.	You must stay in bed for 5 days.
Я вас пошлю к специалисту.	I want you to see a specialist.
Я вас направлю в стационар на исследование.	I want you to go to the hospital for a general check-up.

At the doctor's—Treatment *У врача – Лечение*

This is my usual medicine.	**Я обычно принимаю это лекарство.**	^{y}ah ah**bich**^{y}nah preenee**mah**^{y}oo **eh**tah lee**kahrst**vah
Can you give me a prescription for this?	**Выпишите мне, пожалуйста, рецепт.**	**vi**peeshit^{y}eh mn^{y}eh pah**zhahl**stah ree**tsehpt**
Can you prescribe a/an/some ...?	**Пропишите мне, пожалуйста...**	prahpee**shit**^{y}eh mn^{y}eh pah**zhahl**stah
antidepressant	**антидепрессивное средство**	ahnteedeeprees**seev**nah^{y}eh **sr**^{y}**ehts**tvah
sleeping pills	**снотворное**	snah**tvor**nah^{y}eh
tranquillizer	**успокоительное**	oospahkah**ee**teel^{y}nah^{y}eh
I'm allergic to antibiotics/penicilline.	**Я не переношу антибиотики/пенициллин.**	^{y}ah nee peereenah**shoo** ahnteebee**ot**teekee/peeneetsil**leen**
I don't want anything too strong.	**Что-нибудь не очень сильное.**	**shto**-neebood^y nee **och**^{y}een^y **seel**^{y}nah^{y}eh
How many times a day should I take it?	**Сколько раз в день надо принимать?**	**skol**^{y}kah rahs v d^{y}ehn^y **nah**dah preenee**maht**^{y}
Must I swallow them whole?	**Надо глотать по целой таблетке?**	**nah**dah glah**taht**^{y} pah **tseh**ligh tah**bl**^{y}**eht**k^{y}eh

Как вы лечитесь?	What treatment are you having?
Какое вы принимаете лекарство?	What medicine are you taking?
Инъекции или таблетки?	By injection or orally?
Принимайте это лекарство по 2 чайных ложки...	Take 2 teaspoons of this medicine ...
Принимайте по 3 таблетки, запивая водой...	Take 3 tablets with a glass of water ...
раз в день/3 раза в день	once a day/3 times a day
перед каждой едой	before each meal
после каждой еды	after each meal
утром/вечером	in the morning/at night
каждые 3 часа/5 часов	every 3/5 hours
в случае боли	if there is any pain
4 дня/10 дней	for 4/10 days

CHEMIST'S, see page 108 / NUMBERS, see page 147

Fee *Плата*

Medical care is free of charge, but you have to pay for the medicine.

How much do I owe you?	**Сколько я вам должен/должна?**	skol^{y}kah ^{y}ah vahm dolzhin/dahlzhnah
Can I have a medical certificate?	**Мне нужно медицинское свидетельство.**	mn^{y}eh noozhnah meedeetsinskah^{y}eh sveed^{y}ehteel^{y}stvah

Hospital *Больница*

Please notify my family.	**Сообщите, пожалуйста, моей семье.**	sahahpshch^{y}eet^{y}eh pahzhahlstah mah^{y}ay seem^{y}eh
What are the visiting hours?	**Когда часы посещений?**	kahgdah ch^{y}eessi pahsseeshch^{y}ehneey
When can I get up?	**Когда я смогу вставать?**	kahgdah ^{y}ah smahgoo fstahvaht^{y}
When will the doctor come?	**Когда придёт врач?**	kahgdah preed^{y}ot vrahch^{y}
I don't feel well.	**Я плохо себя чувствую.**	^{y}ah plokhah seeb^{y}ah ch^{y}oostvoo^{y}oo
I'm in pain.	**У меня боли.**	oo meen^{y}ah bolee
I can't eat/sleep.	**Я не ем/не сплю.**	^{y}ah nee ^{y}ehm/nee spl^{y}oo
Where is the bell?	**Где звонок?**	gd^{y}eh zvahnok

doctor/surgeon	**врач/хирург**	vrahch^{y}/kheeroork
nurse	**медсестра**	meetseestrah
patient	**пациент/пациентка**	pahtsi^{y}ehnt/pahtsi^{y}ehntkah
anaesthesia	**наркоз**	nahrkos
blood transfusion	**переливание крови**	peereeleevahnee^{y}eh krovee
injection	**укол/инъекция**	ookol/een^{y}ehktsi^{y}ah
operation	**операция**	ahpeerahtsi^{y}ah
bed	**кровать/постель**	krahvaht^{y}/pahst^{y}ehl^{y}
bedpan	**утка**	ootkah
thermometer	**термометр/градусник**	teermom^{y}ehtr/grahdoosneek

Dentist *Зубной врач*

Can you recommend a good dental clinic?	**Не знаете ли вы хорошую стоматологическую поликлинику?**	nee **znah**eet^{y}eh lee vi khah**ro**shoo^{y}oo stahmahtahlah**gee**ch^{y}eeskoo^{y}oo pahlee**klee**neekoo
What are the surgery (office) hours?	**Когда приёмные часы?**	kahg**dah** pree^y**om**ni^{y}eh ch^{y}ee**ssi**
Can I have an appointment?	**Я хотел(а) бы записаться на приём.**	^{y}ah khaht^y**ehl**(ah) bi zahpee**saht**^{y}sah nah pree^y**om**
How long will I have to wait?	**Сколько мне придётся ждать?**	**skol**^{y}kah mn^{y}eh pree**d**^{y}**o**tsah zhdaht^y
I think it's my turn.	**Теперь моя очередь.**	teep^y**ehr**^{y} mah^y**ah** **och**^{y}eereed^y
I have a toothache.	**У меня болит зуб.**	oo meen^y**ah** bah**leet** zoop
I have an abscess.	**У меня нарывает.**	oo meen^y**ah** nahri**vah**^{y}eht
This tooth hurts.	**Этот зуб болит.**	**eh**taht zoop bah**leet**
at the top	**сверху**	**sv**^{y}**ehr**khoo
at the bottom	**снизу**	**snee**zoo
in the front	**спереди**	**sp**^{y}**eh**reedee
at the back	**сзади**	**zzah**dee
I have a broken tooth.	**У меня сломался зуб.**	oo meen^y**ah** slah**mahl**sah zoop
Can you fix it temporarily?	**Нельзя ли его временно залечить?**	neel^y**z**^{y}**ah** lee eevo **vr**^{y}**eh**meennah zahlee**ch**^{y}**ee**t^y
I don't want it pulled out.	**Если возможно, не вырывайте его.**	^{y}**ehs**lee vahz**mozh**nah nee virri**vvight**^{y}eh eevo
Could you give me an anaesthetic?	**Можно сделать обезболивание?**	**mozh**nah **zd**^{y}**eh**laht^y ahbeez**bo**leevahnee^{y}eh
I've lost a filling.	**Выпала пломба.**	**vi**ppahlah **plom**bah
My gums ...	**Десна ...**	dees**nah**
are very sore	**очень воспалена**	**och**^{y}een^y vahspahlee**nah**
are bleeding	**кровоточит**	krahvahtah**ch**^{y}**eet**
I've broken my denture.	**У меня сломался протез.**	oo meen^y**ah** slah**mahl**sah prah**tehs**
Can you repair my denture?	**Можно починить протез?**	**mozh**nah pahch^{y}ee**neet**^{y} prah**tehs**
When will it be ready?	**Когда он будет готов?**	kahg**dah** on **boo**deet gah**tof**

Reference section

Where do you come from? *Откуда вы?*

I'm from ...	**Я из ...**	^{y}ah eez
the USA	**Соединённых Штатов**	sighdeen^{y}onnikh **shtah**tahf
Great Britain	**Великобритании**	veleekahbree**tah**nee

Countries *Страны*

Austria	**Австрия**	**ahf**stree^{y}ah
Belarus	**Беларус**	b^{y}el**aroos**
Bulgaria	**Болгария**	bahl**gah**ree^{y}ah
Canada	**Канада**	kah**nah**dah
China	**Китай**	kee**tigh**
Commonwealth of Independent States (CIS)	**Содружество независимых государств (СНГ)**	sah**droo**zhestvah n^{y}ezah**visi**mikh gahsoo**dahrs**tv (ehs en gay)
England	**Англия**	**ahn**glee^{y}ah
Finland	**Финляндия**	feen**l^{y}ahn**dee^{y}ah
France	**Франция**	**frahn**tsi^{y}ah
Germany	**Германия**	geer**mah**nee^{y}ah
Great Britain	**Великобритания**	veleekahbree**tah**nee^{y}ah
Hungary	**Венгрия**	**v^{y}ehn**gree^{y}ah
India	**Индия**	**een**dee^{y}ah
Ireland	**Ирландия**	eer**lahn**dee^{y}ah
Italy	**Италия**	ee**tah**lee^{y}ah
Japan	**Япония**	ee**po**nnee^{y}ah
Mongolia	**Монголия**	mahn**go**lee^{y}ah
Poland	**Польша**	**pol**^{y}shah
Russia	**Россия**	rahs**si**^{y}ah
Scotland	**Шотландия**	shaht**lahn**dee^{y}ah
South Africa	**Южная Африка**	**^{y}oozh**nah^{y}ah **ahf**reekah
Spain	**Испания**	ees**pah**nee^{y}ah
Sweden	**Швеция**	**shv^{y}eh**tsi^{y}ah
Switzerland	**Швейцария**	shveey**tsah**ree^{y}ah
Turkey	**Турция**	**toor**tsi^{y}ah
Ukraine	**Украина**	ookrah**ee**nah
USA	**Соединённые Штаты Америки (США)**	sighdeen^{y}onni^{y}eh **shtah**ti ahm^{y}**eh**reekee (s-shah)
USSR (former)	**(бывший) СССР**	(**biv**shiy) ehs ehs ehs ehr
Africa/Asia	**Африка/Азия**	**ahf**reekah/**ah**zee^{y}ah
Australia	**Австралия**	ahf**strah**lee^{y}ah
Europe	**Европа**	eev**ro**ppah
North America	**Северная Америка**	**s^{y}eh**veernah^{y}ah ahm^{y}**eh**reekah
South America	**Латинская Америка**	lah**teens**kah^{y}ah ahm^{y}**eh**reekah

Numbers *Числа*

0	**ноль**	nol^Y
1	**один/одна/одно**	ah**deen**/ahd**nah**/ahd**no**
2	**два/две**	dvah/dv^{Y}eh
3	**три**	tree
4	**четыре**	ch^{Y}ee**tir**ree
5	**пять**	p^{Y}aht^Y
6	**шесть**	shehst^Y
7	**семь**	s^{Y}ehm^Y
8	**восемь**	**vo**sseem^Y
9	**девять**	**d^{Y}eh**veet^Y
10	**десять**	**d^{Y}eh**sseet^Y
11	**одиннадцать**	ah**dee**nahtsaht^Y
12	**двенадцать**	dvee**nah**tsaht^Y
13	**тринадцать**	tree**nah**tsaht^Y
14	**четырнадцать**	ch^{Y}ee**tir**nahtsaht^Y
15	**пятнадцать**	peet**nah**tsaht^Y
16	**шестнадцать**	shis**nah**tsaht^Y
17	**семнадцать**	seem**nah**tsaht^Y
18	**восемнадцать**	vahsseem**nah**tsaht^Y
19	**девятнадцать**	deeveet**nah**tsaht^Y
20	**двадцать**	**dvah**tsaht^Y
21	**двадцать один**	**dvah**tsaht^Y ah**deen**
22	**двадцать два**	**dvah**tsaht^Y dvah
23	**двадцать три**	**dvah**tsaht^Y tree
24	**двадцать четыре**	**dvah**tsaht^Y ch^{Y}ee**tir**ree
25	**двадцать пять**	**dvah**tsaht^Y p^{Y}aht^Y
26	**двадцать шесть**	**dvah**tsaht^Y shehst^Y
27	**двадцать семь**	**dvah**tsaht^Y s^{Y}ehm^Y
28	**двадцать восемь**	**dvah**tsaht^Y **vo**sseem^Y
29	**двадцать девять**	**dvah**tsaht^Y **d^{Y}eh**veet^Y
30	**тридцать**	**tree**tsaht^Y
31	**тридцать один**	**tree**tsaht^Y ah**deen**
32	**тридцать два**	**tree**tsaht^Y dvah
33	**тридцать три**	**tree**tsaht^Y tree
40	**сорок**	**so**rrahk
41	**сорок один**	**so**rrahk ah**deen**
42	**сорок два**	**so**rrahk dvah
43	**сорок три**	**so**rrahk tree
50	**пятьдесят**	peedee**ss^{Y}aht**
51	**пятьдесят один**	peedee**ss^{Y}aht** ah**deen**
52	**пятьдесят два**	peedee**ss^{Y}aht** dvah
53	**пятьдесят три**	peedee**ss^{Y}aht** tree
60	**шестьдесят**	shizdee**ss^{Y}aht**
61	**шестьдесят один**	shizdee**ss^{Y}aht** ah**deen**
62	**шестьдесят два**	shizdee**ss^{Y}aht** dvah

70	**семьдесят**	**s^{y}ehm**deess^{y}aht
71	**семьдесят один**	**s^{y}ehm**deess^{y}aht ah**deen**
72	**семьдесят два**	**s^{y}ehm**deess^{y}aht dvah
80	**восемьдесят**	**vo**sseemdeess^{y}aht
81	**восемьдесят один**	**vo**sseemdeess^{y}aht ah**deen**
82	**восемьдесят два**	**vo**sseemdeess^{y}aht dvah
90	**девяносто**	deevee**no**stah
91	**девяносто один**	deevee**no**stah ah**deen**
92	**девяносто два**	deevee**no**stah dvah
100	**сто**	sto
101	**сто один**	sto ah**deen**
102	**сто два**	sto dvah
110	**сто десять**	sto **d^{y}eh**sseet^{y}
120	**сто двадцать**	sto **dvah**tsaht^{y}
130	**сто тридцать**	sto **tree**tsaht^{y}
140	**сто сорок**	sto **so**rrahk
150	**сто пятьдесят**	sto peedee**ss^{y}aht**
160	**сто шестьдесят**	sto shizdee**ss^{y}aht**
170	**сто семьдесят**	sto **s^{y}ehm**deess^{y}aht
180	**сто восемьдесят**	sto **vo**sseemdeess^{y}aht
190	**сто девяносто**	sto deevee**no**stah
200	**двести**	**dv^{y}eh**stee
300	**триста**	**tree**stah
400	**четыреста**	ch^{y}ee**ti**rreestah
500	**пятьсот**	peet**sot**
600	**шестьсот**	shi**ssot**
700	**семьсот**	seem**sot**
800	**восемьсот**	vosseem**sot**
900	**девятьсот**	deeveet**sot**
1000	**тысяча**	**ti**sseech^{y}ah
1100	**тысяча сто**	**ti**sseech^{y}ah sto
1200	**тысяча двести**	**ti**sseech^{y}ah **dv^{y}eh**stee
2000	**две тысячи**	dv^{y}eh **ti**sseech^{y}ee
5000	**пять тысяч**	p^{y}aht^{y} **ti**sseech^{y}
10 000	**десять тысяч**	**d^{y}eh**sseet^{y} **ti**sseech^{y}
100 000	**сто тысяч**	sto **ti**sseech^{y}
1 000 000	**миллион**	meelee**on**
1 000 000 000	**миллиард**	meelee**ahrt**

N.B.: After numbers ending in 2, 3 or 4 (including 2, 3, 4), the following noun goes into the Genitive singular case (e.g. 2 *of rouble* – два рубл**я** – dvah roo**bl^{y}ah**). All other numbers (except 1 and those ending in 1) are followed by the Genitive plural (e.g. 5 *of roubles* – пять рубл**ей** – p^{y}aht^{y} roo**bl^{y}ay**).

first	**первый**	p^{y}ehrviy
second	**второй**	ftahroy
third	**третий**	tr^{y}ehteey
fourth	**четвёртый**	ch^{y}eetv^{y}ortiy
fifth	**пятый**	p^{y}ahtiy
sixth	**шестой**	shistoy
seventh	**седьмой**	seed^{y}moy
eighth	**восьмой**	vahs^{y}moy
ninth	**девятый**	deev^{y}ahtiy
tenth	**десятый**	deess^{y}ahtiy
once	**один раз**	ahdeen rahs
twice	**два раза/дважды**	dvah rahzah/dvahzhdi
three times	**три раза/трижды**	tree rahzah/treezhdi
a half	**половина**	pahlahveenah
half (adj.)	**пол**	pol
a quarter	**четверть**	ch^{y}ehtv^{y}ehrt^{y}
one third	**треть**	tr^{y}eht^{y}
one per cent	**один процент**	ahdeen prahtsehnt
3,4%	**три и четыре десятых процента**	tree ee ch^{y}eetirree dee-ss^{y}ahtikh prahtsehntah

Year and age *Год и возраст*

year	**год**	got
leap year	**високосный год**	veessahkosniy got
decade	**десятилетие**	deesseeteel^{y}ehtee^{y}eh
century	**век/столетие**	v^{y}ehk/stahl^{y}ehtee^{y}eh
this year	**в этом году**	v ehtahm gahdoo
last year	**в прошлом году**	f proshlahm gahdoo
next year	**в будущем году**	v boodooshch^{y}eem gahdoo
2 years ago	**два года назад**	dvah goddah nahzaht
in one year	**через год**	ch^{y}eerees got
for one year	**на год**	nah got
in the 16th century	**в шестнадцатом веке**	f shisnahtsahtahm v^{y}ehk^{y}eh
in the 20th century	**в двадцатом веке**	v dvahtsahtahm v^{y}ehk^{y}eh
in 1981	**в тысяча девятьсот восемьдесят первом году**	f tisseech^{y}ah deeveetsot vosseemdeess^{y}aht p^{y}ehrvahm gahdoo
in 1992	**в тысяча девятьсот девяносто втором году**	f tisseech^{y}ah deeveetsot deeveenostah ftahrom gahdoo
in 2003	**в две тысячи третьем году**	v dv^{y}eh tisseech^{y}ee tr^{y}eh-t^{y}eem gahdoo

How old are you?	**Сколько вам/тебе лет?**	**skol**^{y}kah vahm/tee**b^{y}eh** l^{y}eht
I'm 30 years old.	**Мне тридцать лет.**	mn^{y}eh **tree**tsaht^y l^{y}eht
He/She was born in 1960.	**Он родился/Она родилась в 1960-ом году.**	on rah**deel**sah/ah**nah** rahdee**lahs^y** f tissee**ch^{y}ah** deeveet**sot** shizdee**ss^{y}ah**tahm gah**doo**
Children under 16 are not admitted.	**Дети до шестнадцати лет не допускаются.**	**d^{y}eh**tee do shis**naht**sahtee l^{y}eht nee dahpoos**kah**^{y}ootsah

Seasons *Времена года*

spring/summer	**весна/лето**	vees**nah/l^{y}eh**tah
autumn/winter	**осень/зима**	**o**sseen^y/zee**mah**
in spring	**весной**	vees**noy**
during the summer	**летом**	**l^{y}eh**tahm
in autumn	**осенью**	**o**sseen^{y}oo
during the winter	**зимой**	zee**moy**
high season	**разгар сезона**	rahz**gahr** see**zo**nnah
low season	**не сезон**	nee see**zon**

Months *Месяцы*

January	**январь**	een**vahr^y**
February	**февраль**	feev**rahl^y**
March	**март**	mahrt
April	**апрель**	ah**pr^{y}ehl^y**
May	**май**	migh
June	**июнь**	ee**^{y}oon^y**
July	**июль**	ee**^{y}ool^y**
August	**август**	**ahv**goost
September	**сентябрь**	seent**^{y}ahbr^y**
October	**октябрь**	ahkt**^{y}ahbr^y**
November	**ноябрь**	nah**^{y}ahbr^y**
December	**декабрь**	dee**kahbr^y**
in September	**в сентябре**	f seentee**br^{y}eh**
since October	**с октября**	s ahktee**br^{y}ah**
the beginning of January	**в начале января**	v nah**ch^{y}ahl**^{y}eh eenvah**r^{y}ah**
the middle of February	**в середине февраля**	f seeree**deen**^{y}eh feevrah**l^{y}ah**
the end of March	**в конце марта**	f kahn**tseh mahr**tah

Days and date *День и число*

What day is it today?	**Какой сегодня день?**	kah**koy** see**vo**dn^{y}ah d^{y}ehn^y
Sunday	**воскресенье**	vahskree**ss^{y}eh**n^{y}eh
Monday	**понедельник**	pahnee**d^{y}ehl^y**neek
Tuesday	**вторник**	**ftor**neek
Wednesday	**среда**	sree**dah**
Thursday	**четверг**	ch^{y}eet**v^{y}ehrk**
Friday	**пятница**	**p^{y}aht**neetsah
Saturday	**суббота**	soo**bo**ttah
What date is it today?	**Какое сегодня число?**	kah**ko**^{y}eh see**vo**dn^{y}ah ch^{y}ee**slo**
It's ...	**Сегодня ...**	see**vo**dn^{y}ah
July 1	**первое июля**	**p^{y}ehr**vah^{y}eh ee^y**oo**l^{y}ah
March 17	**семнадцатое марта**	seem**nah**tsahtah^{y}eh **mahr**tah
in the morning	**утром**	**oo**trahm
during the day	**днём**	dn^{y}om
in the afternoon	**после обеда/днём**	**pos**lee ah**b^{y}eh**dah/dn^{y}om
in the evening	**вечером**	**v^{y}eh**ch^{y}ehrahm
at night	**ночью**	**noch^y**yoo
yesterday	**вчера**	fch^{y}ee**rah**
today	**сегодня**	see**vo**dn^{y}ah
tomorrow	**завтра**	**zahf**trah
the day after tomorrow	**послезавтра**	poslee**zahf**trah
the next day	**на другой день**	nah droo**goy** d^{y}ehn^y
two days ago	**два дня назад**	dvah dn^{y}ah nah**zaht**
in three days' time	**через три дня**	**ch^{y}ee**rees tree dn^{y}ah
last week	**на прошлой неделе**	nah **prosh**ligh need**^{y}eh**lee
next week	**на следующей/будущей неделе**	nah **sl^{y}eh**doo^{y}ooshch^{y}ay/**boo**dooshch^{y}ay need**^{y}eh**lee
for two weeks	**на две недели**	nah dv^{y}eh need**^{y}eh**lee
birthday	**день рождения**	d^{y}ehn^y rahzh**d^{y}eh**nee^{y}ah
day off	**выходной день**	vikhahd**noy** d^{y}ehn^y
holiday	**праздник**	**prahz**neek
holidays (vacation)	**отпуск**	**ot**poosk
school holidays	**каникулы**	kah**nee**koolli
weekday	**будний день**	**bood**neey d^{y}ehn^y
weekend	**конец недели/викенд**	kahn**^{y}ehts** need**^{y}eh**lee/vee**kehnt**
working day	**рабочий день**	rah**bo**ch^{y}eey d^{y}ehn^y

Public holidays *Праздники*

January 1	**Новый Год**	New Year's Day
March 8	**Международный Женский День**	International Women's Day
May 1, 2	**1-е мая**	May Day(s)
May 9	**День Победы**	Victory in Europe Day
October 7	**День Конституции**	Constitution Day
November 7, 8	**Праздник Октябрьской Революции**	Revolution Days

Christmas *(Рождество)* is not officially observed, nor are Easter *(Пасха)* and Whitsuntide *(Троица)*.

Greetings and wishes *Приветствия и пожелания*

Happy holiday! (general)	**С праздником!**	s **prahz**neekahm
Congratulations (with all my heart)!	**Поздравляю (от всей души)!**	pahzdrah**vl^{y}ah^{y}**oo (aht fs^{y}ay doo**shi**)
All the best!/ Best wishes!	**Всего хорошего!/ Всего доброго!**	fsee**vo** khah**ro**shehvah/ fsee**vo do**brahvah
Good luck!	**Желаю удачи/успехов!**	zhil**lah^{y}**oo oo**dah**ch^{y}ee/ oos**p^{y}eh**khahf
Happy New Year!	**С Новым Годом!**	s **no**vvim **go**ddahm
Happy birthday!	**С днём рождения!**	s dn^{y}om rahzh**d^{y}eh**nee^{y}ah
Have a good trip!	**Счастливого пути!**	shch^{y}ahst**lee**vahvah poo**tee**
Have a good holiday!	**Желаю хорошо отдохнуть!**	zhil**lah^{y}**oo khahrah**sho** ahddahkh**noot^{y}**
I wish you ...	**Желаю вам/тебе...**	zhil**lah^{y}**oo vahm/tee**b^{y}eh**
Best regards from my wife!	**Привет от жены!**	pree**v^{y}eht** aht zhin**ni**
My regards to your husband!	**Передайте привет мужу!**	peeree**dight^{y}**eh pree**v^{y}eht** **moo**zhoo
Get well soon!	**Поправляйтесь!/ Поправляйся!**	pahprah**vl^{y}igh**tees^{y}/ pahprah**vl^{y}ighs^{y}**ah
Take care!	**Будьте здоровы!/ Будь здоров!**	**boot^{y}**tee zdah**ro**vvi/ boot^{y} zdah**rof**

What time is it? *Который час?/Сколько времени?*

Excuse me. Can you tell me the time?	Будьте добры! Который час?	**boot^{y}**tee dah**bri**. kah**to**rriy ch^{y}ahss
It's ...	Сейчас...	seech^{y}**ahss**
five past one	пять минут второго	p^{y}aht^{y} mee**noot** ftah**ro**vvah
ten past two	десять минут третьего	**d^{y}eh**sseet^{y} mee**noot** **tr^{y}eh**t^{y}eevah
a quarter past three	четверть четвёртого	**ch^{y}eh**tv^{y}ehrt^{y} ch^{y}eet**v^{y}or**tahvah
twenty past four	двадцать минут пятого	**dvah**tsaht^{y} mee**noot** **p^{y}ah**tahvah
twenty-five past five	двадцать пять минут шестого	**dvah**tsaht^{y} p^{y}aht^{y} mee**noot** shis**to**vvah
half past six	пол седьмого	pol seed^{y}**mo**vvah
twenty-five to seven	без двадцати пяти семь	b^{y}ehz dvahtsah**tee** pee**tee** s^{y}ehm^{y}
twenty to eight	без двадцати восемь	b^{y}ehz dvahtsah**tee** **vo**sseem^{y}
a quarter to nine	без четверти девять	b^{y}ehz **ch^{y}eh**tv^{y}ehrtee **d^{y}eh**veet^{y}
ten to ten	без десяти десять	b^{y}ehz deessee**tee** **d^{y}eh**sseet^{y}
five to eleven	без пяти одиннадцать	b^{y}ehz pee**tee** ah**dee**nahtsaht^{y}
twelve o'clock (noon/midnight)	двенадцать часов (полдень/полночь)	dvee**nah**tsaht^{y} ch^{y}ee**ssof** (**pol**deen^{y}/**pol**nahch^{y})
The train leaves at ...	Поезд уходит в...	**po**eezd oo**kho**ddeet v
13.04 (1.04 p.m.)	тринадцать (часов) четыре (минуты)	tree**nah**tsaht^{y} (ch^{y}ee**ssof**) ch^{y}ee**ti**ree (mee**noo**ti)
12.40 (0.40 a.m.)	двенадцать (часов) сорок (минут)	dvee**nah**tsaht^{y} (ch^{y}ee**ssof**) **so**rrahk (mee**noot**)
after/afterwards	после/потом	**po**slee/pah**tom**
before/beforehand	до/раньше	do/**rahn^{y}**sheh
early	рано	**rah**nah
in time	вовремя	**vo**vr^{y}ehm^{y}ah
late	поздно	**poz**nah
hour	час	ch^{y}ahss
minute	минута	mee**noo**tah
second	секунда	see**koon**dah
quarter of an hour	четверть часа	**ch^{y}eh**tv^{y}ehrt^{y} ch^{y}ee**ssah**
half an hour	полчаса	polch^{y}ee**ssah**
I'm sorry I'm late.	Простите за опоздание.	prah**steet^{y}**eh zah ahpahz**dah**nee^{y}eh

Common abbreviations *Употребительные сокращения*

АЗС	**автозаправочная станция**	petrol station
бульв.	**бульвар**	boulevard
г.	**год/город/грамм**	year/city/gram
д.	**дом**	house
ж.	**женский**	ladies
и т.д.	**и так далее**	etc.
им.	**имени**	of the name of ...
к., корп.	**корпус**	building
кв.	**квартира**	apartment
коп.	**копейка**	kopeck
м.	**метр/мужской**	metre/gentlemen
наб.	**набережная**	quay, pier
пл.	**площадь**	square
пр., просп.	**проспект**	avenue
р.	**рубль**	rouble
ул.	**улица**	street
ч.	**час**	hour

N.B.: You will notice that many words in modern Russian are made up of abbreviations of other words, e.g. госиздат (государственное издалельство – state edition); Ин'яз (Институт иностранных языков – institute of foreign languages), and so on.

Signs and notices *Надписи и объявления*

Берегись	Caution
Внимание	Attention
...воспрещается	... forbidden
Вход/Выход	Entrance/Exit
Женский туалет (Ж)	Ladies (toilet)
Заказано	Reserved
Закрыто (на ремонт)	Closed (for repairs)
Запасной выход	Emergency exit
Медпункт	First-aid post
Мужской туалет (М)	Gentlemen (toilet)
Не курить	No smoking
Опасно для жизни	Danger of death
Осторожно собака	Beware of the dog
От себя/К себе	Push/Pull
Переход	Crossing
(Руками) не трогать	Do not touch
Скорая помощь	Ambulance
Справки/Справочное бюро	Information
Туалет (М) (Ж)	Toilet (G) (L)

Emergency *Крайний случай/Крайняя необходимость*

Call the police	Позовите милицию/ Позвоните в милицию	pahzah**vee**tee mee**lee**tsi^{y}oo/ pahzvah**nee**tee v mee**lee**tsi^{y}oo
Consulate	консульство	**kon**sool^{y}stvah
DANGER	ОПАСНО	ah**pahs**nah
Embassy	посольство	pah**sol^{y}**stvah
FIRE	ПОЖАР	pah**zhahr**
Gas	газ	gahs
Get a doctor	Позовите врача	pahzah**vee**tee vrah**ch^{y}ah**
Go away	Уходите	ookhah**dee**tee
HELP!	НА ПОМОЩЬ!	nah **pom**mahshch^{y}
Get help quickly	Позовите быстро кого-нибудь на помощь	pahzah**vee**tee **bis**trah kah**vo**-neebood^{y} nah **pom**mahshch^{y}
I'm ill	Я болен/больна	^{y}ah **bo**leen^{y}/bahl^{y}**nah**
I'm lost	Я заблудился/ Я заблудилась	^{y}ah zahbloo**deel**sah/ ^{y}ah zahbloo**dee**lahs^{y}
Leave me alone	Оставьте меня в покое	ah**stahv^{y}**tee meen**^{y}ah** f pah**koy**
LOOK OUT	ОСТОРОЖНО	ahstah**rozh**nah
Poison	отрава/яд	ah**trah**vah/^{y}aht
POLICE	МИЛИЦИЯ	mee**lee**tsi^{y}ah
Stop him/her!	Держи его/её!	deer**zhi** ee**vo**/ee**^{y}o**
STOP THIEF!	ДЕРЖИ ВОРА!	deer**zhi vor**rah

Lost property – Theft *Пропажи и находки – Кражи*

Where's the ...?	Где ...?	gd^{y}eh
lost-property (lost and found) office	бюро находок	b^{y}ooro nah**kho**dahk
police station	отделение милиции	ahddeel**^{y}eh**n^{y}eh mee**lee**tsi^{y}ee
I want to report a theft.	Я хочу заявить о краже.	^{y}ah khah**ch^{y}oo** zahee**veet^{y}** ah **krah**zheh
My ... has been stolen.	У меня украли ...	oo meen**^{y}ah** ook**rah**lee
I've lost my ...	Я потерял/потеряла ...	^{y}ah pahteer**^{y}ahl**/pahteer**^{y}ah**lah
handbag	сумочку	**soo**mahch^{y}koo
keys	ключи	**kl^{y}oo**ch^{y}ee
money	деньги	**d^{y}ehn^{y}**gee
passport	паспорт	**pahs**pahrt
wallet	бумажник	boo**mahzh**neek

CAR ACCIDENTS, see page 79

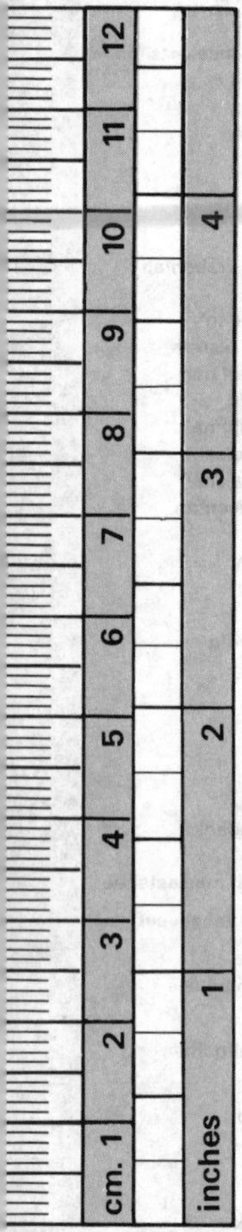

Conversion tables

Centimetres and inches

To change centimetres into inches, multiply by .39.

To change inches into centimetres, multiply by 2.54.

	in.	feet	yards
1 mm.	0.039	0.003	0.001
1 cm.	0.39	0.03	0.01
1 dm.	3.94	0.32	0.10
1 m.	39.40	3.28	1.09

	mm.	cm.	m.
1 in.	25.4	2.54	0.025
1 ft.	304.8	30.48	0.305
1 yd.	914.4	91.44	0.914

(32 metres = 35 yards)

Temperature

To convert centigrade into degrees Fahrenheit, multiply centigrade by 1.8 and add 32.

To convert degrees Fahrenheit into centigrade, subtract 32 from Fahrenheit and divide by 1.8.

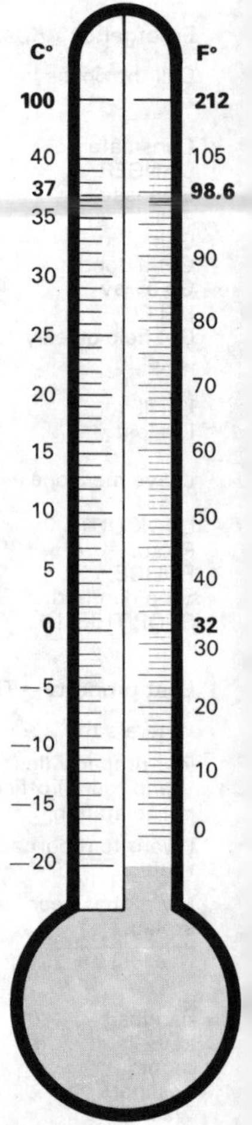

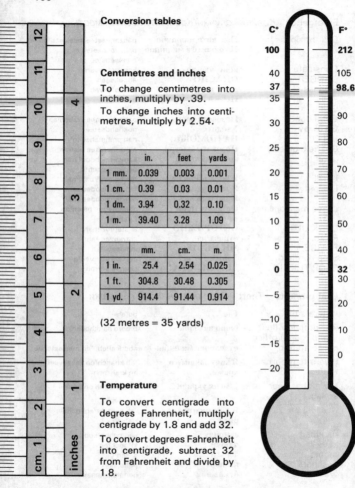

SIZES, see page 112 / YARDS AND INCHES, see page 115 /
WEIGHTS AND MEASURES, see page 120

A very basic grammar*

Nouns

There are three genders in Russian: masculine, feminine and neuter. There are no articles. You can usually determine the gender of a noun by its ending. Here are some basic rules to follow:

Masculine: all nouns ending in a consonant and **-й**:

стол	table	**нож**	knife	**музе́й**	museum

Feminine: most nouns ending in **-а** and **-я**:

кни́га	book	**неде́ля**	week

Neuter: nouns ending in **-о** and **-е**:

окно́	window	**по́ле**	field

Nouns ending in **-ь** can be either masculine or feminine.

учи́тель (m.)	teacher	**пло́щадь** (f.)	square

Plural: Although there are many exceptions, most masculine and feminine nouns end in **-и** or **-ы**, while neuter nouns generally end in **-а** and **-я**. Here are some examples:

столы́	tables
кни́ги	books
поля́	fields

Many words are stressed differently in the plural form:

нож – ножи́	knife – knives
рука́ – ру́ки	hand – hands
окно́ – о́кна	window – windows

Declension

The endings of nouns vary according to their use in a sentence. There are six different cases in Russian. The examples below show you how to use them:

*To help you pronounce the words correctly, we indicate the stress by an accent (') in this section of the book.

The **nominative** (N)* refers to the subject of the sentence – the person or thing performing the action:

Де́вушка чита́ет.	*The girl* is reading.
Окно́ откры́то.	*The window* is open.

The **genitive** (G) is used to designate a person to whom, or an object to which, somebody or something belongs or refers (it can often be translated by "of" in English):

улы́бка *де́вушки*	the smile *of the girl*
ча́шка *ча́я*	a cup *of tea*

The **dative** (D) designates the person/object to whom/which something is given or done:

Я даю́ э́то *де́вушке.*	I give it *to the girl.*

The **accusative** (A) usually denotes the direct object of an action:

Я люблю́ *э́ту де́вушку.*	I love *that girl.*
Я пишу́ *телегра́мму.*	I write *a telegramme.*

The **instrumental** (I) answers the questions "by whom?", "by what means?", "how?", etc.:

Э́тот расска́з напи́сан *де́вушкой.*	This story has been written *by the girl.*
Он пи́шет *карандашо́м.*	He writes *with a pencil.*

The **prepositional** (P) is always used with a preposition. The most common are **в, на** (on, in) and **о** (about):

Кни́га *на столе́.*	The book is *on the table.*
Мы говори́м *о де́вушке.*	We're speaking *about the girl.*

All prepositions (i.e. on, of, with, at, etc.) are governed by one or more cases. See also the examples on page 15.

Adjectives

Adjectives agree in number and gender with the noun they modify. There is only one plural ending for all three genders. The table below shows the declension of nouns and adjectives:

*The capital letters designate the cases. See also page 15.

	Masculine (quiet evening)	Feminine (nice girl)	Neuter (important matter)
sing. N	**ти́хий ве́чер**	**ми́лая де́вушка**	**ва́жное де́ло**
G	**ти́хого ве́чера**	**ми́лой де́вушки**	**ва́жного де́ла**
D	**ти́хому ве́черу**	**ми́лой де́вушке**	**ва́жному де́лу**
A	**ти́хий ве́чер**	**ми́лую де́вушку**	**ва́жное де́ло**
I	**ти́хим ве́чером**	**ми́лой де́вушкой**	**ва́жным де́лом**
P	**ти́хом ве́чере**	**ми́лой де́вушке**	**ва́жном де́ле**
plur. N	**ти́хие вечера́**	**ми́лые де́вушки**	**ва́жные дела́**
G	**ти́хих вечеро́в**	**ми́лых де́вушек**	**ва́жных дел**
D	**ти́хим вечера́м**	**ми́лым де́вушкам**	**ва́жным дела́м**
A	**ти́хие вечера́**	**ми́лых де́вушек**	**ва́жные дела́**
I	**ти́хими вечера́ми**	**ми́лыми де́вушками**	**ва́жными дела́ми**
P	**ти́хих вечера́х**	**ми́лых де́вушках**	**ва́жных дела́х**

Personal pronouns

	I	you	he	she	it	we	you	they
N	**я**	**ты**	**он**	**она́**	**оно́**	**мы**	**вы**	**они́**
G	**меня́**	**тебя́**	**его́**	**её**	**его́**	**нас**	**вас**	**их**
D	**мне**	**тебе́**	**ему́**	**ей**	**ему́**	**нам**	**вам**	**им**
A	**меня́**	**тебя́**	**его́**	**её**	**его́**	**нас**	**вас**	**их**
I	**мной**	**тобо́й**	**им**	**ей**	**им**	**на́ми**	**ва́ми**	**и́ми**
P	**мне**	**тебе́**	**нём**	**ней**	**нём**	**нас**	**вас**	**них**

Note: There are two forms for "you" in Russian: **ты** (plural: **вы**) is used when talking to relatives, close friends and children, and between young people; **Вы** (written with a capital **В**) is used in all other cases.

Possessive pronouns

They agree with the noun in number and gender and are declined like adjectives.

	Masculine	Feminine	Neuter	Plural
my	**мой**	**моя́**	**моё**	**мои**
your	**твой**	**твоя́**	**твоё**	**твои́**
his/its	**его́**	**его́**	**его́**	**его́**
her	**её**	**её**	**её**	**её**
our	**наш**	**на́ша**	**на́ше**	**на́ши**
your	**ваш**	**ва́ша**	**ва́ше**	**ва́ши**
their	**их**	**их**	**их**	**их**

Verbs

The infinitive of many verbs ends in **-ть**. Here are three verbs in the present tense:

	чита́ть (to read)	**люби́ть** (to love)	**сказа́ть** (to say)
я	**чита́ю**	**люблю́**	**скажу́**
ты	**чита́ешь**	**лю́бишь**	**ска́жешь**
он/она/оно	**чита́ет**	**лю́бит**	**ска́жет**
мы	**чита́ем**	**лю́бим**	**ска́жем**
вы	**чита́ете**	**лю́бите**	**ска́жете**
они	**чита́ют**	**лю́бят**	**ска́жут**

…and three useful irregular verbs:

	хоте́ть (to want)	**мочь** (can/may)	**идти** (to go)
я	**хочу́**	**могу́**	**иду́**
ты	**хо́чешь**	**мо́жешь**	**идёшь**
он/она/оно	**хо́чет**	**мо́жет**	**идёт**
мы	**хоти́м**	**мо́жем**	**идём**
вы	**хоти́те**	**мо́жете**	**идёте**
они	**хотя́т**	**мо́гут**	**иду́т**

To be/To have

These two verbs cannot be translated directly into English. The verb "to be" (**быть**) is not used in the present tense:

I'm a student.	**Я студе́нт.**	(literally: "I – student".)
It is cold.	**Хо́лодно.**	(literally: "cold")

"To be" is used, however, in the future and past tense:

I *will be* in Moscow.	**Я *бу́ду* в Москве́.**
I *was* in Moscow.	**Я *был(а́)* в Москве́.**

"To have" is expressed by using the preposition **у**, followed by the genitive case, plus "**есть**" (3rd person singular of the verb "to be"), plus the possessed object at the nominative case:

		(literally:)
I have a car.	**У меня́ есть маши́на.**	"At me there is a car."
You have a dog.	**У тебя́ есть соба́ка.**	"At you there is a dog."
The brother has a house.	**У бра́та есть дом.**	"At the brother's there is a house."

Some more remarks about verbs...

The following explanations and examples are intended to give you some general ideas and indications on one of the most difficult chapters of Russian grammar: the verb.

There are three tenses: past, present and future.
In the **past tense,** the verb agrees in gender and number with the subject of the sentence, i.e. there is a masculine, a feminine, a neuter and a plural form. For regular verbs, you just take off the infinitive ending **-ть** and add **-л** for masculine, **-ла** for feminine, **-ло** for neuter and **-ли** for plural:

ex: **сказáть** (to say)	**он сказáл**	he said
	она сказáла	she said
	мы сказáли	we said
любúть (to love)	**я любúл**	I loved (when a man is speaking)
	я любúла	I loved (when a woman is speaking)

Almost every verb in Russian occurs in two different forms, called **aspects**:
– the **imperfective aspect** is used for continuous, repeated or uncompleted action. For the present tense, one always uses the imperfective form of the verb.
– the **perfective aspect** is used for a temporarily limited, single or finished action.

Thus, every verb has two infinitives, one for each aspect. The perfective infinitive is usually formed by adding a prefix to the imperfective infinitive or by changing its ending, e.g.:
to read: imperfective form – **читáть**
perfective form – **прочитáть**
to open: imperfective form – **открывáть**
perfective form – **откры́ть**

N.B. For space reasons, we only give one of the two aspects in our dictionary. You will find out how it's used by looking up the phrase on the cross-referenced page.

Dictionary
and alphabetical index

English–Russian

f feminine *m* masculine *nt* neuter *pl* plural

For adjectives where only the masculine ending (-ый, -ий or -ой) is given, the feminine and neuter endings are -ая, -ое (see GRAMMAR section).

abbreviation сокращение *nt* sahkrah**shch^{y}eh**nee^{y}eh 154
able, to be *(can)* мочь moch^{y} 13, 160
about *(approximately)* примерно preem^{y}**ehr**nah 79
above наверху nahveer**khoo** 62
abscess нарыв *m* nah**rif** 145
absorbent cotton вата *f* **vah**tah 109
accept, to принимать preenee**maht^{y}** 102; *(take)* брать braht^{y} 62
accident несчастный случай *m* nee**shch^{y}ahst**niy **sloo**ch^{y}igh 79, 139
account счёт *m* shch^{y}ot 130, 131
actor актёр *m* ahk**t^{y}or** 86
adapter адаптер *m* ah**dahp**tehr 119
address адрес *m* **ah**dreess 21, 31, 76, 79, 98, 102, 133
admission вход *m* fkhot 82
Africa Африка *f* **ah**freekah 146
after после **pos**lee 15, 77, 143, 153
afternoon, in the после обеда **pos**lee ah**b^{y}eh**dah 151
afterwards потом pah**tom** 153
again ещё (раз) ee**shch^{y}o** (rahs) 96, 136
against против **prot**teef 15
age возраст *m* **voz**rahst 149
ago назад nah**zaht** 149, 151
air conditioning кондиционер *m* kahndeetsiah**n^{y}ehr** 23, 28
airmail авиапочта ahveeah**poch^{y}**tah, авиа **ah**veeah 133
airplane самолёт *m* sahmah**l^{y}ot** 65
airport аэропорт *m* ighrah**port** 65
air terminal аэровокзал *m* ighrahvahg**zahl** 65
alarm clock будильник *m* boo**deel^{y}**neek 121
alcohol алкоголь *m* ahlkah**gol^{y}** 37
all всё fs^{y}o 103
allergy аллергия *f* ahl^{y}**ehr**gee^{y}ah 141
already уже oo**zheh** 15
also тоже **to**zheh 15
always всегда fseeg**dah** 15
ambulance скорая помощь *f* **skor**rah^{y}ah **pom**mahshch^{y} 79, 154
American американец *m* ahmeeree**kah**neets, американка *f* ahmeeree**kahn**kah 93; американский ahmeeree**kahns**keey 126
amount сумма *f* **soom**mah 62, 131
anaesthesia наркоз *m* nahr**kos** 144; обезболивание *nt* ahbeez**bo**leevahnee^{y}eh 145
analgesic болеутоляющая таблетка *f* boleeootahl^{y}**ah^{y}**ooshch^{y}ah^{y}ah tah**bl^{y}eht**kah 109
and и ee 15
animal животное *nt* zhiv**vot**nah^{y}eh 85
ankle лодышка *f* lah**dish**kah 139
another другой droo**goy** 61, 123
answer, to отвечать ahtvee**ch^{y}aht^{y}** 136
antibiotic антибиотик *m* ahnteebee**o**tteek 143
antiques антиквариат *m* ahnteekvahree**aht** 83
antique shop антикварный магазин *m* ahntee**kvahr**niy mahgah**zeen** 98
antiseptic антисептический ahnteeseep**tee**ch^{y}eeskeey 109, 140
anyone кто-нибудь **kto**neebood^{y} 12, 16

anything что-нибудь **shto**neebood[y] 17, 24, 25, 101, 103, 114
apart from кроме **krom**[y]eh 15
appartment квартира *f* kvahr**tee**rah 154
appendicitis аппендицит *m* ahpeendee**tsit** 142
appetizer закуска *f* zah**koos**kah 41
apple яблоко *nt* [y]**ah**blahkah 52, 63, 120
appointment, to make записаться zahpee**saht**[y]sah 30, 137, 145; *(person)* договориться (с) dahgahvah**reet**[y]sah (s) 131
apricot абрикос *m* ahbree**koss** 52
April апрель *m* ah**pr[y]ehl[y]** 150
archaelogy археология *f* ahrkheeah**loggee**[y]ah 83
architect архитектор *m* ahrkhee**t[y]ehk**tahr 83
architecture архитектура *f* ahrkheeteek**too**rah 83
arm рука *f* roo**kah** 138, 139
arrival прибытие *nt* pree**bi**ttee[y]eh 65
arrive, to прийти pree**ytee** 68, 130; приехать pree[y]**eh**khaht[y] 11; *(plane)* прилетать preelee**taht[y]** 65
art искусство *nt* ees**koost**vah 83
artery артерия *f* ahr**t[y]eh**ree[y]ah 138
art gallery картинная галерея *f* kahr**teen**nah[y]ah gahleer[y]**eh**[y]ah 81, 98
article предмет *m* preed**m[y]eht** 101
artist художник *m* khoo**dozh**neek 83
ashtray пепельница *f* **p[y]eh**peel[y]neetsah 27, 36
Asia Азия *f* **ah**zee[y]ah 146
ask for, to просить prah**sseet**[y] 25, 136; *(order)* заказать zahkah**zaht[y]** 61
aspirin аспирин *m* ahspee**reen** 109
asthma астма *f* **ahst**mah 141
at у oo, в v 15
athletics лёгкая атлетика *f* **l[y]okh**kah[y]ah ahtl**[y]eh**teekah 89
at least по крайней мере pah **krigh**neey **m[y]eh**ree 24
at once немедленно neem[y]**eh**dleennah 31
attention внимание *nt* vnee**mah**nee[y]eh 154
August август *m* **ahv**goost 150
aunt тётя *f* **t[y]ot**[y]ah 93
Australia Австралия *f* ahfs**trah**lee[y]ah 146
Austria Австрия *f* **ahfs**tree[y]ah 146
automatic автоматический ahftahmah**tee**ch[y]eeskeey 124
autumn осень *f* **o**sseen[y] 150
avenue проспект *m* prahs**p[y]ehkt** 81, 154
awful ужасный oo**zhahs**niy 84, 94

B

baby ребёнок *m* ree**b[y]on**nahk 24, 111
babysitter приходящая няня *f* preekhah**d[y]ah**shch[y]ah[y]ah **n[y]ah**n[y]ah 27
back спина *f* spee**nah** 138, 141
back, to be/go/get вернуться veer**noot**[y]sah 21, 77, 80, 136
bacon бекон *m* b[y]eh**kon** 47
bad плохой plah**khoy** 14
badly плохо **plo**khah 11, 14, 95
bag сумка *f* **soom**kah 18, 103
baggage багаж *m* bah**gahsh** 18, 21, 26, 31, 71
baggage check камера хранения *f* **kah**meerah khrah**n[y]eh**nee[y]ah 67, 71
baker's булочная *f* **boo**lahch[y]nah[y]ah 98
balance *(account)* баланс *m* bah**lahnss** 131
balcony балкон *m* bahl**kon** 23
ball *(inflated)* мяч *m* m[y]ahch[y] 128
ballet балет *m* bahl**[y]eht** 87
ball-point pen шариковая ручка *f* **shah**reekahvah[y]ah **rooch**[y]kah 104
banana банан *m* bah**nahn** 52, 63
bandage гигиенический бинт *m* geegee[y]eh**nee**ch[y]eeskeey beent 109
Band-Aid пластырь *m* **plahs**tir[y] 109
bangle браслет *m* brahs**l[y]eht** 121
bank *(finance)* банк *m* bahnk 130
banknote купюра *f* koop**[y]oo**rah 130
bar бар *m* bahr 33; *(chocolate)* плитка *f* **pleet**kah 63
barber парикмахерская *f* pahreek**mah**kheerskah[y]ah 30
bath(room) ванная *f* **vahn**nah[y]ah 23, 25, 27
bathing cap купальная шапочка *f* koo**pahl[y]**nah[y]ah **shah**pahch[y]kah 116

bathing suit купальник *m* koo**pahl**ʸneek 116
bathrobe купальный халат *m* koo**pahl**ʸniy khah**laht** 116
bath towel банное полотенце *nt* **bahn**nahʸeh pahlah**tʸehn**tseh 27
battery батарейка *f* bahtah**rʸay**kah 119, 125; *(car)* аккумулятор *m* ahkoomoolʸ**ah**tahr 75, 78
be, to быть bitʸ 160; находиться nahkhah**deet**ʸsah 76, 81
beach пляж *m* plʸahsh 90
beans *(green)* фасоль *f* fah**sol**ʸ 50
beard борода *f* bahrah**dah** 31
beautiful красивый krah**ssee**viy 14; *(it is)* красиво krah**ssee**vah, прекрасно pree**krahs**nah 84
beauty salon косметический кабинет *m* kahsmʸeh**tee**chʸeeskeey kahbee**nʸeht** 30, 98
bed кровать *f* krah**vaht**ʸ 23, 24, 144; постель *f* pahs**tʸehl**ʸ 142, 144
beef говядина *f* gah**vʸah**deenah 47
beer пиво *nt* **pee**vah 40, 55, 56, 58
beet(root) свёкла *f* **svʸok**lah 50
before *(time)* до do 153; перед **pee**reet 143
begin, to начинаться nahchʸee**naht**ʸsah 80, 86
beginning начало *nt* nah**chʸah**lah 87, 150
behind за zah 15
bell *(electric)* звонок *m* zvah**nok** 144
below внизу vnee**zoo** 62
belt пояс *m* **po**ʸahss, ремень *m* ree**mʸehn**ʸ 117
bend *(road)* поворот *m* pahvah**rot** 79
berth полка *f* **pol**kah 71
better лучше **looch**ʸsheh 14, 25, 101
beware осторожно ahstah**rozh**nah 154
bicycle велосипед *m* veelahsee**pʸeht** 74
big большой bahlʸ**shoy** 14, 59, 91, 101
bill счёт *m* shchʸot 31, 62, 102; *(banknote)* купюра *f* koo**pʸoo**rah 130
billion *(Am.)* миллиард *m* meellee**ahrt** 148
binoculars бинокль *m* bee**nokl**ʸ 123
bird птица *f* **ptee**tsah 85
birthday день рождения *m* dʸehnʸ rahzh**dʸeh**neeʸah 151, 152
biscuits *(Br.)* печенье *nt* pee**chʸehn**ʸeh 53, 63, 120
bite *(wound)* укус *m* oo**koos** 139
bitter горький **gor**ʸkeey 61
black чёрный **chʸor**niy 105, 113
bladder мочевой пузырь *m* mahchʸee**voy** poo**zir**ʸ 138
blanket одеяло *nt* ahdeeʸ**ah**lah 27
bleed, to кровоточить krahvahtah**chʸeet**ʸ 145
blister волдырь *m* vahl**dir**ʸ 139
blood кровь *f* krovʸ 142
blood pressure давление *nt* dahv**lʸeh**neeʸeh 141, 142
blood transfusion переливание крови *nt* peereelee**vah**neeʸeh **kro**vee 144
blouse блузка *f* **bloos**kah 116
blow dry, to сушить феном soo**shit**ʸ **fʸeh**nahm 30
blue синий **see**neey 105, 113
blusher румяна *pl* roo**mʸah**nah 110
boat лодка *f* **lot**kah 74
body тело *nt* **tʸeh**lah 138
boil нарыв *m* nah**rif**, фурункул *m* foo**roon**kool 139
bone кость *f* kostʸ 138
book книга *f* **knee**gah 12, 104
book, to заказать zahkah**zaht**ʸ 134
booking office предварительная продажа билетов *f* preedvah**ree**teelʸnahʸah prah**dah**zhah beelʸ**eh**tahf 67
bookshop книжный магазин *m* **kneezh**niy mahgah**zeen** 98, 104
boot сапог *m* sah**pok** 118
born, to be родиться rah**deet**ʸsah 150
botanical gardens ботанический сад *m* bahtah**nee**chʸeeskeey saht 81
botany ботаника *f* bah**tah**neekah 83
bottle бутылка *f* boo**til**kah 17, 55, 56, 120
bottle-opener штопор *m* **shto**ppahr 106
boulevard бульвар *m* boolʸ**vahr** 81, 154
bowel кишка *f* keesh**kah** 138
box коробка *f* kah**rop**kah 106, 120; *(theatre)* ложа *f* **lo**zhah 88
boy мальчик *m* **mahl**ʸchʸeek 112

boyfriend друг *m* drook 93
bra бюстгальтер *m* bʸooz**khahl**ʸtehr 116
bracelet браслет *m* brahs**lʸeht** 121
brake тормоз *m* **tor**mahs 78
bread хлеб *m* khlʸehp 37, 38, 63, 64
break, to сломать(ся) slah**mahtʸ**(sah) 139, 145
breakdown авария *f* ahv**ah**reeʸah 78
breakdown van буксирный автомобиль *m* book**seer**niy ahftahmah**beelʸ** 78
breakfast завтрак *m* **zahf**trahk 24, 26, 34, 38
breast грудь *f* groodʸ 138
breathe, to дышать di**shahtʸ** 141
bridge мост *m* most 85
briefs трусы *pl* troo**ssi**, трусики *pl* **troo**seekee 116
bring, to принести preenees**tee** 13, 36, 53, 55, 56, 71; *(someone)* привести preevees**tee** 95
British англичанин *m* ahnglee**chʸah**neen, англичанка *f* ahnglee**chʸahn**kah 93
broken сломан **slom**mahn 29, 123, 140
brooch брошь *f* broshʸ, брошка *f* **brosh**kah 121
brother брат *m* braht 93
brown коричневый kah**reechʸ**neeviy 113
bruise ушиб *m* oo**ship** 139
brush щётка *f* **shchʸot**kah 111
build, to построить pah**stro**eetʸ 83
building здание *nt* **zdah**neeʸeh 81, 83
bulb лампочка *f* **lahm**pahchʸkah 28, 119
Bulgaria Болгария *f* bahl**gah**reeʸah 146
burn ожог *m* ah**zhok** 139
burn out, to *(bulb)* перегореть peereegahr**ʸeht**ʸ 28
bus автобус *m* ahf**to**bbooss 11, 18, 19, 65, 67, 73
business дела *nt/pl* dee**lah** 16, 131
bus stop остановка автобуса *f* ahstah**nof**kah ahf**to**bboossah 73, 80
busy занят(а) **zah**neet(ah) 96
but но noh 15
butane gas газ в баллонах *m* gahs v bah**lon**nahkh 32, 106
butcher's мясной магазин *m* mees**noy** mahgah**zeen** 98
butter масло *nt* **mahs**lah 37, 38
button пуговица *f* **poo**gahveetsah 29, 117
buy, to купить koo**peet**ʸ 20, 68, 82, 100, 104, 121, 123, 132

C

cabbage капуста *f* kah**poos**tah 50
cabin *(ship)* каюта *f* kah**ʸoo**tah 74; *(tel.)* кабина *f* kah**bee**nah 134
cafeteria кафетерий *m* kahfee**tʸeh**reey 33
cake торт *m* tort 54; пирожное *nt* pee**rozh**nahʸeh 53
cake shop кондитерская *f* kahn**dee**tʸehrskahʸah 33, 98
calculator счётная машинка *f* **shchʸot**nahʸah mah**shin**kah 105
calendar календарь *m* kahleen**dahr**ʸ 104
call *(phone)* разговор *m* rahzgah**vor** 134, 136
call, to *(give name)* называть nahziv**vaht**ʸ 11; *(phone)* позвонить pahzvah**neet**ʸ 78, 136, 155; *(summon)* вызвать **viz**vahtʸ 79
camera фотоаппарат *m* fotahahpah**raht** 124, 125
camera shop магазин фототоваров *m* mahgah**zeen** fottotah**vah**rahf 98
camp, to устроить стоянку oos**tro**eetʸ stah**ʸahn**koo 32
campbed складная кровать *f* sklahd**nah**ʸah krah**vaht**ʸ 106
camping кемпинг *m* **kehm**peeng 32, 106
can *(tin)* банка *f* **bahn**kah 120
can *(to be able)* мочь mochʸ 13, 160
Canada Канада *f* kah**nah**dah 146
Canadian канадец *m* kah**nah**deets, канадка *f* kah**naht**kah 93
canal канал *m* kah**nahl** 85
cancel, to отказаться ahtkah**zaht**ʸsah 65
candle свечка *f* **svʸehchʸ**kah 106
candy конфеты *pl* kahn**fʸeh**ti, карамель *f* kahrah**mʸehlʸ** 64
can opener консервный нож *m* kahn**sʸehr**vniy nosh 106
cap кепка *f* **kʸehp**kah 116
capital *(finance)* капитал *m* kahpee**tahl** 131

car машина *f* mah**shi**nnah 19, 20, 26, 32, 75, 76, 79
carat карат *m* kah**raht** 121
caravan караван *m* kahrah**vahn** 32
carburettor карбюратор *m* kahrb^{y}oo**rah**tahr 78
cardigan вязаный жакет *m* **v^{y}ah**zahniy zhah**k^{y}eht** 116
car hire прокат машин *m* prah**kaht** mah**shin** 20
car park автостоянка *f* ahftahstah**^{y}ahn**kah 77
car rental прокат машин *m* prah**kaht** mah**shin** 20
car wash автомойка *f* ahftah**moy**kah 76
carriage вагон *m* vah**gon** 70
carrot(s) морковь *f* mahr**kov^{y}** 50
carton *(of cigarettes)* блок (сигарет) *m* blok (seegah**r^{y}eht**) 17
case *(camera, etc.)* футляр *m* footl**^{y}ahr** 123, 125
cash, to *(check)* разменять rahzmee**n^{y}aht^{y}** 130
cash desk касса *f* **kahs**sah 103
cassette кассета *f* kah**ss^{y}eh**tah 127, 128
castle замок *m* **zah**mahk 81
catalogue каталог *m* kahtah**lok** 82
catch, to *(taxi)* поймать pigh**maht^{y}** 19
cathedral собор *m* sah**bor** 81, 84
Catholic католический kahtah**lee**ch^{y}ehskeey 84
caution берегись beeree**gees^{y}** 154
caviar икра *f* ee**krah** 41, 42, 63, 127
cemetery кладбище *nt* **klahd**beeshch^{y}eh 81
centre центр *m* tsehntr 19, 21, 73, 76, 81
century век *m* v^{y}ehk, столетие stahl**^{y}eh**tee^{y}eh 149
ceramics керамика *f* kee**rah**meekah 83, 127
certificate свидетельство *nt* svee**d^{y}eh**teel^{y}stvah 144
chain *(jewellery)* цепочка *f* tseh**poch^{y}**kah 121
chair стул *m* stool 106
champagne *(sparkling wine)* шампанское *nt* shahm**pahns**kah^{y}eh 55
change *(money)* мелочь *f* **m^{y}eh**lahch^{y} 130; сдача *f* **zdah**ch^{y}ah 62
change, to поменять pahmee**n^{y}aht^{y}** 61, 65, 123; *(money)* обменять ahbmee**n^{y}aht^{y}** 18, 129, 130; *(trains)* делать пересадку **d^{y}eh**laht^{y} peeree**saht**koo 68, 72, 73
charge плата *f* **plah**tah 136
cheap дешёвый dee**shov**viy 14, 101
check чек *m* ch^{y}ehk 131; *(restaurant)* счёт *m* shch^{y}ot 62
check, to проверить prah**v^{y}eh**reet^{y} 75, 123; *(luggage)* отправить aht**prah**veet^{y} 71
check book чековая книжка *f* **ch^{y}eh**kahvah^{y}ah **kneesh**kah 131
check card чековая карточка *f* **ch^{y}eh**kahvah^{y}ah **kahr**tahch^{y}kah 130
check in, to *(airport)* регистрировать багаж reegeestree**rah**vaht^{y} bah**gahsh** 65
checking out *(departure)* отъезд *m* aht**^{y}ehzd** 31
check out, to уехать oo**^{y}eh**khaht^{y} 31
checkup *(medical)* исследование *nt* eessl**^{y}eh**dahvahnee^{y}eh 142
cheek щека *f* shch^{y}ee**kah** 138
cheese сыр *m* sirr 38, 43, 63, 120
chemist's аптека *f* ahpt**^{y}eh**kah 98, 108
cheque чек *m* ch^{y}ehk 131
cheque book чековая книжка *f* **ch^{y}eh**kahvah^{y}ah **kneesh**kah 131
cherry черешня *f* ch^{y}eer**^{y}ehsh**n^{y}ah 52; *(sour)* вишня *f* **veesh**n^{y}ah 52
chess *(game, set)* шахматы *pl* **shahkh**mahti 127, 128
chewing gum жвачка *f* **zhvahch^{y}**kah 126
chicken курица *f* **koo**reetsah 44, 49
child ребёнок *m* ree**b^{y}o**nnahk 61, 139
children дети *pl* **d^{y}eh**tee 24, 82, 93
children's doctor педиатр *m* peedee**ahtr** 137
China Китай *m* kee**tigh** 146
chocolate шоколад *m* shahkah**laht** 54, 63
chocolates шоколадные конфеты *f/pl* shahkah**lahd**ni^{y}eh kahn**f^{y}eh**ti 63, 120
choose, to выбрать **vi**braht^{y} 35
chop котлета *f* kahtl**^{y}eh**tah 47

Christmas Рождество *nt* rahzhdeest**vo** 152
church церковь *f* **tsehr**kahf^{y} 81, 84
cigar сигара *f* see**gah**rah 126
cigarette сигарета *f* seegahr^{y}**eh**tah 17, 95, 126
cigarette case портсигар *m* portsee**gahr** 121
cigarette lighter зажигалка *f* zahzhi**gahl**kah 121, 126
cine camera кинокамера *f* keenah**kah**meerah 124
cinema кино *nt* kee**no** 86, 96
circus цирк *m* tsirk 87
city город *m* **go**rraht 81, 154
city centre центр города *m* tsehntr **go**rrahdah 81
classical классический klah**ssee**ch^{y}eeskeey 128
clean чистый **ch^{y}ees**tiy 14
clean, to *(room)* убрать oo**braht^{y}** 29; *(clothes)* почистить pah**ch^{y}ees**teet^{y} 29
clinic поликлиника *f* pahlee**klee**neekah 137, 145
clips клипсы *m/pl* **kleep**si 121
cloakroom гардероб *m* gahrdee**rop** 88
clock часы *pl* ch^{y}e**ssi** 119, 121
close, to закрываться zahkri**vvaht^{y}**sah 11, 82, 108, 132
closed закрыто zah**kri**ttah 154
cloth ткань *f* tkahn^{y} 118
clothes одежда *f* ah**d^{y}ehzh**dah 116
clothing одежда *f* ah**d^{y}ehzh**dah 112
cloud облако *nt* **o**blahkah 94
coat пальто *nt* pahl^{y}**to** 116
coffee кофе *m* **ko**fee 38, 54, 60, 63
cold холодный khah**lod**niy 14, 61; *(it is)* холодно **kho**llahdnah 13
cold *(illness)* простуда *f* prah**stoo**dah 108
cologne тройной одеколон *m* trigh**noy** ahdeekah**lon** 110
colour цвет *m* tsv^{y}eht 103, 113
colourful яркий ^{y}**ahr**keey 113
comb расчёска *f* rahs**ch^{y}os**kah 111
come, to приехать pree^{y}**eh**khaht^{y} 16, 25; прийти preey**tee** 95, 137
comedy комедия *f* kah**m^{y}eh**dee^{y}ah 86
common *(frequent)* употребительный oopahtree**bee**teel^{y}niy 154
compartment купе *m* koo**peh** 71
complaint жалоба *f* **zhah**lahbah 61
concert концерт *m* kahn**tsehrt** 86, 87
concert hall концертный зал *m* kahn**tsehrt**niy zahl 81, 87
condom презерватив *m* preezeervah**teef** 109
conductor *(orchestra)* дирижёр *m* deeree**zhor** 87
confectioner's кондитерская *f* kahn**deet^{y}**ehrskah^{y}ah 98
confirm, to подтвердить pahttveer**deet^{y}** 65
confirmation подтверждение *nt* pahttveerzh**d^{y}eh**nee^{y}eh 23
congratulate, to поздравлять pahzdrah**vl^{y}aht^{y}** 152
connection *(plane, train)* пересадка *f* peeree**saht**kah 65, 68
constipation запор *m* zah**por** 140
consulate консульство *nt* **kon**sool^{y}stvah 156
contact lens контактная линза *f* kahn**tahkt**nah^{y}ah **leen**zah 123
contagious заразный zah**rahz**niy 142
contain, to содержать sahdeer**zhaht^{y}** 37
contraceptive противозачаточное средство *nt* prahteevahzah**ch^{y}ah**tahch^{y}nah^{y}eh **sr^{y}ehtst**vah 109
contract договор *m* dahgah**vor**, контракт *m* kahn**trahkt** 131
control контроль *m* kahn**trol^{y}** 16
convent монастырь *m* mahnah**stir^{y}** 81
cookies печенье *nt* pee**ch^{y}eh**n^{y}eh 63, 120
corkscrew штопор *m* **shto**ppahr 106
corner угол *m* **oo**gahl 21, 36, 77
cost расходы *m/pl* rahs**kho**ddi 131
cost, to стоить **sto**eet^{y} 69, 79, 80, 133, 136
cottage дача *f* **dah**ch^{y}ah 85
cotton бумажная ткань *f* boo**mahzh**nah^{y}ah tkahn^{y} 114; *(plant)* хлопок *m* **khlo**pahk 115
cotton wool вата *f* **vah**tah 109
cough кашель *m* **kah**shehl^{y} 108
cough, to кашлять **kahshl^{y}**aht^{y} 142
country страна *f* strah**nah** 92, 146
countryside деревня *f* deer^{y}**ehv**n^{y}ah 85

course *(language)* курс *m* koors 16
cramp судорога *f* **soo**dahrahgah, спазма *f* **spahz**mah 141
crayon карандаш *m* kahrahn**dahsh** 104
cream *(pharm.)* мазь *f* mahz^y 109; *(toiletry)* крем *m* kr^{y}ehm 110; *(food)* сливки *pl* **sleef**kee 43, 54
credit card кредитная карточка *f* kree**deet**nah^{y}ah **kahr**tahch^{y}kah 20, 31, 62, 102, 130
crockery посуда *f* pah**ssoo**dah 107
crossing *(by sea)* переправа *f* peeree**prah**vah 74; *(street)* переход *m* peeree**khot** 154
crossroads перекрёсток *m* peeree**kr^{y}os**tahk 77
cruise круиз *m* kroo**ees** 74
cucumber огурец *m* ahgoo**r^{y}ehts** 42, 50, 63
cuisine кухня *f* **kookh**n^{y}ah 35
cup чашка *f* **ch^{y}ahsh**kah 36, 54, 55, 107
currency валюта *f* vah**l^{y}oo**tah 129
currency exchange обмен валюты *m* ahb**m^{y}ehn** vah**l^{y}oo**ti 18, 129
curtain занавес *m* **zah**nahv^{y}ehs 28
curve *(road)* поворот *m* pahvah**rot** 79
customs таможня *f* tah**mozh**n^{y}ah 16, 17, 102
cut *(wound)* порез *m* pah**r^{y}ehs** 139
cut, to *(hair)* постричься pah**streech^y**sah 30
cutlery прибор *m* pree**bor** 106, 107
cutlet котлета *f* kaht**l^{y}eh**tah 47
cystitis цистит *m* tsis**teet** 142

D

dairy молочная *f* mah**loch^y**nah^{y}ah 98
dance, to танцевать tahntseh**vaht^y** 87, 88, 96
dangerous опасный ah**pahss**niy 79, 155
dark тёмный **t^{y}om**niy 56, 101, 113; *(it is)* темно teem**no** 25
date *(day)* число *nt* ch^{y}ees**lo** 25, 151; *(appointment)* свидание *nt* svee**dah**nee^{y}eh 95; *(fruit)* финик *m* **fee**neek 52
daughter дочь *f* doch^y 93
day день *m* d^{y}ehn^y 16, 20, 24, 32, 80, 90, 151
day off выходной день *m* vikhad**noy** d^{y}ehn^y 151
December декабрь *m* dee**kahbr^y** 150
decision решение *nt* ree**sheh**nee^{y}eh 25, 102
deck *(ship)* палуба *f* **pah**loobah 74
declaration *(customs)* декларация *f* deeklah**rah**tsi^{y}ah 17
declaration form бланк декларации *m* blahnk deeklah**rah**tsi^{y}ee 17
declare, to *(customs)* объявить ahb^{y}ee**veet^y** 17
deep глубокий gloo**bo**keey 91, 142
delicatessen гастроном *m* gahstrah**nom** 98
delicious *(meal)* вкусно **fkoos**nah 62
deliver, to отправить aht**prah**veet^y 102
delivery доставка *f* dah**stahf**kah 102
dentist зубной врач *m* zoob**noy** vrahch^y 98, 145
denture протез *m* prah**tehs** 145
deodorant дезодорант *m* deezahdah**rahnt** 110
department *(shop)* отдел *m* aht**d^{y}ehl** 100
department store универмаг *m* ooneev^{y}ehr**mahk** 81, 98
departure *(plane)* вылет *m* **vil**^{y}eht 65
deposit залог *m* zah**lok** 20
deposit, to *(bank)* внести на счёт vnees**tee** nah shch^{y}ot 131
dessert десерт *m* dees**^{y}ehrt** 36, 53
detour *(traffic)* объезд *m* ahb**^{y}ehzd** 79
diabetes диабет *m* deeah**b^{y}eht** 141
diabetic диабетик *m* deeah**b^{y}eh**teek 37
dialling code код(города) *m* koht (**go**rrahdah) 135
diamond бриллиант *m* breelee**ahnt** 122
diapers пелёнки *pl* pee**l^{y}on**kee 111
diarrhoea понос *m* pah**noss** 140
diary записная книжка *f* zahpees**nah**^{y}ah **kneesh**kah 104
dictionary словарь *m* slah**vahr^y** 12, 104
diet диета *f* dee**^{y}eh**tah 37

difficult трудный **trood**niy 14
difficulty трудность *f* **trood**nahst^{y} 28, 102
dining car вагон-ресторан *m* vah**gon**-reestah**rahn** 68, 70
dining room столовая *f* stah**lov**vah^{y}ah 27
dinner ужин *m* **oo**zhin 34, 94
direct прямой pree**moy** 65, 69
director *(theatre)* режиссёр *m* reezhiss^{y}**or** 86
disabled инвалид *m* eenvah**leet** 82
discotheque дискотека *f* deeskaht^{y}**eh**kah 88
disease болезнь *f* bahl^{y}**ehzn**^{y} 142
dish блюдо *nt* **bl^{y}oo**dah 36, 37, 40
disinfectant дезинфицирующее средство *nt* deezeenfeet**si**roo-^{y}ooshch^{y}eh^{y}eh **sr^{y}ehts**tvah 109
diversion *(traffic)* объезд *m* ahb^{y}**ehzd** 79
do, to делать **d^{y}eh**laht^{y} 139
doctor врач *m* vrahch^{y} 15, 79, 137, 143, 144, 155
doctor's office кабинет врача *m* kahbee**n^{y}eht** vrah**ch^{y}ah** 137
dog собака *f* sah**bah**kah 154
doll кукла *f* **kook**lah 128
dollar доллар *m* **dol**lahr 17, 18, 102, 130
door дверь *f* dv^{y}ehr^{y} 15, 28, 72
double bed двуспальная кровать *f* dvoo**spahl^{y}**nah^{y}ah krah**vaht^{y}** 23
double room номер на двоих *m* **no**mmeer nah dvah**eekh** 19, 23
downtown центр города *m* tsehntr **go**rrahdah 81
dress платье *nt* **plaht**^{y}eh 116
dressing gown халат *m* khah**laht** 116
drink напиток *m* nah**pee**tahk 40, 55, 58, 60, 61, 63
drink, to пить peet^{y} 35, 36, 55
driving licence (водительские) права *nt/pl* (vah**deet**^{y}ehl^{y}skee^{y}eh) prah**vah** 16, 20
drugstore аптека *f* ahpt^{y}**eh**kah 98, 108
dry сухой soo**khoy** 30, 56, 111
dry cleaner's химчистка *f* kheem**ch^{y}eest**kah 29, 98
duty *(customs)* пошлина *f* **posh**leenah 17
dye *(hair)* окраска *f* ah**krahs**kah 30

E
each каждый **kahzh**diy 143
ear ухо *nt* **oo**khah (*pl* уши **oo**shi) 138
early рано **rah**nah 14, 31, 153
earring серьга *f* seer^{y}**gah** 121
east восток *m* vahs**tok** 77
Easter Пасха *f* **pahs**khah 152
easy лёгкий **l^{y}okh**keey 14
eat, to есть ^{y}ehst^{y} 36, 37, 144
egg яйцо *nt* ^{y}eey**tso** 38, 42, 63, 120
eight восемь **vo**sseem^{y} 147
eighteen восемнадцать vahsseem**naht**saht^{y} 147
eighty восемьдесят **vo**sseem^{y}deess^{y}aht 148
elastic резинка *f* ree**zeen**kah 117
elastic bandage эластичный бинт *m* ehlahs**teech^{y}**niy beent 109
Elastoplast пластырь *m* **plahs**tir^{y} 109
elbow локоть *m* **lo**kkaht^{y} 138
electric shop магазин электротоваров *m* mahgah**zeen** ehl^{y}ehktrah-tah**vah**rahf 98, 119
electricity электричество *nt* ehleek**tree**ch^{y}ehstvah 32
electronic электронный ehleek**tron**niy 125, 128
elevator лифт *m* leeft 27, 100
eleven одиннадцать ah**dee**nahtsaht^{y} 147
embarkation point пристань *f* **pree**stahn^{y} 74
embassy посольство *nt* pah**sol^{y}st**vah 155
emergency крайний случай *m* **krigh**neey **slooch**^{y}igh 155
emergency exit запасной выход *m* zahpahs**noy vi**khaht 27, 99, 154
empty пустой poos**toy** 14
end конец *m* kahn^{y}**ehts** 15, 150
engaged *(phone)* занятый **zah**neetiy 136
England Англия *f* **ahn**glee^{y}ah 134, 146
English английский ahn**gleeys**keey; по-английски pah ahn**gleeys**kee 12, 16, 17, 80, 82, 84, 104, 126, 135, 137; англичанин *m* ahnglee**ch^{y}ah**neen, англичанка *f* ahnglee**ch^{y}ahn**kah 93
enjoy, to нравиться **nrah**veet^{y}sah 62, 92

enough достаточно dah**stah**tahch^{y}-nah 14
enquiry booth справки *f/pl* **sprah**fkee, справочное бюро *nt* **sprah**vahch^{y}nah^{y}eh b^{y}**ooro** 134
entrance вход *m* fkhot 15, 67, 72, 99, 154
envelope конверт *m* kahn**v^{y}ehrt** 27, 105, 132
equipment оборудование *nt* ahbah**roo**dahvahnee^{y}eh 106; снаряжение *nt* snahree**zheh**nee^{y}eh 91
eraser резинка *f* ree**zeen**kah 105
escalator эскалатор *m* ehskah**lah**tahr 100
estimate *(cost)* предварительная смета *f* preedvah**ree**teel^{y}nah^{y}ah **sm^{y}eh**tah 131
Europe Европа *f* eev**rop**pah 146
evening вечер *m* **v^{y}eh**ch^{y}eer 10, 88, 95, 96, 151
evening dress вечернее платье *nt* vee**ch^{y}ehr**nee^{y}eh **plah**t^{y}eh 116
every каждый **kahzh**diy 143
everything всё fs^{y}o 24, 31, 62
exchange, to обменять ahbmee**n^{y}aht^{y}** 103
exchange rate валютный курс *m* vahl^{y}**oot**niy koors 18, 130
excursion экскурсия *f* ehks**koor**see^{y}ah 80
excuse, to простить prahs**teet^{y}**, извинить eezvee**neet^{y}** 10
exercise book тетрадь *f* tee**trahd^{y}** 105
exhaust pipe выхлоп *m* **vi**khlahp 78
exhibition выставка *f* **vi**stahfkah 81
exit выход *m* **vi**khaht 67, 72, 99
expenses расходы *m/pl* rahs**kho**ddi 131
expensive дорогой dahrah**goy** 14, 19, 24, 101, 121
express экспресс ehks**pr^{y}ehss** 133
expression *(term)* выражение *nt* virah**zheh**nee^{y}eh 100, 131
expressway автомагистраль *f* ahftahmahgees**trahl^{y}** 76
eye глаз *m* glahs 138, 139
eye drops глазные капли *f/pl* glahzni^{y}eh **kah**plee 109
eyesight зрение *nt* **zr^{y}eh**nee^{y}eh 123
eye specialist глазной врач *m* glahz**noy** vrahch^{y} 137

F

fabric *(cloth)* ткань *f* tkahn^{y}, материал *m* mahteeree**ahl** 114, 115
face лицо *nt* lee**tso** 138
face powder пудра *f* **poo**drah 110
facilities удобства *nt/pl* oo**dopst**vah 32
factory завод *m* zah**vot**, фабрика *f* **fah**breekah 81
fair ярмарка-выставка *f* **^{y}ahr**mahrkah-**vi**stahfkah 81
fall *(autumn)* осень *f* **o**sseen^{y} 150
fall, to упасть oo**pahst^{y}** 139
family семья *f* seem**^{y}ah** 93, 144
far далеко dahlee**ko** 14, 100
fare цена *f* tsin**nah** 69
farm ферма *f* **f^{y}ehr**mah 85
fat *(meat)* жир *m* zhirr 37
father отец *m* aht**^{y}ehts** 93
February февраль *m* feev**rahl^{y}** 150
fee *(doctor)* плата *f* **plah**tah 144
feeding bottle детский рожок *m* **d^{y}ehts**keey rah**zhok** 111
feel, to чувствовать себя **ch^{y}oost**vahvaht^{y} see**b^{y}ah** 140, 142, 144
fever жар *m* zhahr 140
few мало **mah**lah 14; *(a)* несколько **n^{y}ehs**kahl^{y}kah 14
field поле *nt* **pol**^{y}eh 85
fifteen пятнадцать peet**nah**tsaht^{y} 147
fifth пятый **p^{y}ah**tiy 149
fifty пятьдесят peedee**ss^{y}aht** 147
fill in, to заполнить zah**pol**neet^{y} 26
filling *(tooth)* пломба *f* **plom**bah 145
filling station заправочная станция *f* zah**prah**vahch^{y}nah^{y}ah **stahn**tsi^{y}ah 75
film *(cinema)* фильм *m* feel^{y}m 86; *(camera)* плёнка *f* **pl^{y}on**kah 124, 125
filter фильтр *m* feel^{y}tr 125, 126
find, to найти nigh**tee** 11, 12, 21, 76, 84, 100, 137
fine хорошо khahrah**sho**, прекрасно pree**krahs**nah 10, 25
finger палец *m* **pah**leets 138
Finland Финляндия *f* feenl**^{y}ahn**dee^{y}ah 146
fire пожар *m* pah**zhahr** 155; *(bonfire)* костёр *m* kahs**t^{y}or** 32
first первый **p^{y}ehr**viy 149

first-aid kit аптечка *f* ahpt^{y}**ehch**^{y}-kah 106
first course первое *nt* **p^{y}ehr**vah^{y}eh 36
first name имя *nt* **ee**m^{y}ah 25
fish рыба *f* **rib**bah 40, 45, 46
fish, to ловить рыбу lah**veet**^{y} ribboo 90
fishing рыбная ловля *f* **rib**nah^{y}ah **lov**l^{y}ah 90
fishmonger's рыбный магазин *m* ribniy mahgah**zeen** 98
fit, to сидеть seed^{y}**eht**^{y} 115
fitting room примерочная *f* preem^{y}**eh**rahch^{y}nah^{y}ah 115
five пять p^{y}aht^{y} 147
fix, to заделать zahd^{y}**eh**laht^{y} 75
flash вспышка *f* **fspish**kah 125
flashlight карманный фонарик *m* kahr**mahn**niy fah**nah**reek 106
flat tyre прокол *m* prah**kol** 75, 78
flight полёт *m* pahl^{y}**ot** 65; *(trip)* рейс *m* rayss 65
floor этаж *m* eh**tahsh** 27; *(ground)* пол *m* poll 15
florist's цветочный магазин *m* tsvee**toch**^{y}niy mahgah**zeen** 98
flour мука *f* moo**kah** 37
flower цветок *m* tsvee**tok** 85
flu грипп *m* greep 142
fluid жидкость *f* **zhit**kahst^{y} 75, 123
fog туман *m* too**mahn** 94
follow, to следовать **sl^{y}eh**dahvaht^{y} 77
food еда *f* ee**dah** 61,106; питание *nt* pee**tah**nee^{y}eh 111
foot нога *f* nah**gah** 138
football футбол *m* foot**bol** 89
for для dl^{y}ah 15
forest лес *m* l^{y}ehss 15, 85
forget, to забыть zah**bit**^{y} 61
fork вилка *f* **veel**kah 36, 61, 107
form *(document)* бланк *m* blahnk 17, 133; анкета *f* ahn**k^{y}eh**tah 25
fortress крепость *f* **kr^{y}eh**pahst^{y} 81
forty сорок **sor**rahk 147
fountain фонтан *m* fahn**tahn** 81
fountain pen авторучка *f* ahftah**rooch**^{y}kah 105
four четыре ch^{y}ee**ti**ree 147
fourteen четырнадцать ch^{y}ee**tir**nahtsaht^{y} 147
fourth четвёртый ch^{y}eet**v^{y}or**tiy 149
frame *(glasses)* оправа *f* ah**prah**vah 123
France Франция *f* **frahn**tsi^{y}ah 146
free свободный svah**bod**niy 14, 36, 80, 95; бесплатный bees**plaht**niy 82
French bean фасоль *f* fah**sol**^{y} 50
fresh свежий **sv^{y}eh**zhiy 61
Friday пятница *f* **p^{y}aht**neetsah 151
friend приятель *m* pree^{y}**ah**teel^{y} 95
from от aht 15
frost мороз *m* mah**ros** 94
fruit фрукты *pl* **frook**ti 40, 52, 63
fruit juice фруктовый сок *m* frook**tov**viy sok 37, 38, 60, 63
frying pan сковородка *f* skahvah**rot**kah 106
full полный **pol**niy 14, 20, 24, 69, 75
full board полное содержание *nt* **pol**nah^{y}eh sahdeer**zhah**nee^{y}eh 24
fur coat шуба *f* **shoo**bah 116
fur hat меховая шапка *f* meekhah**vah**^{y}ah **shahp**kah 116, 127
furniture мебель *f* **m^{y}eh**b^{y}ehl^{y} 83
furrier's магазин меховых изделий *m* mahgah**zeen** meekhah**vikh** eezd^{y}**eh**leey 98

G

gallery галерея *f* gahleer^{y}**eh**^{y}ah 81, 98
game игра *f* ee**grah** 128
garage гараж *m* gah**rahsh** 26; *(repairs)* станция обслуживания *f* **stahn**tsi^{y}ah ahp**sloo**zhivahnee^{y}ah 78
garden(s) сад *m* saht 81, 85
gas газ *m* gahs 155
gasoline бензин *m* been**zeen** 20, 75
gastritis гастрит *m* gah**street** 142
gauze марля *f* **mahr**l^{y}ah 109
general общий **ob**shch^{y}eey 27, 100, 108, 134, 137
general practitioner терапевт *m* teerah**p^{y}ehft** 137
genitals половые органы *m/pl* pahlah**vi**^{y}eh **or**gahni 138
geology геология *f* geeah**lo**ggee^{y}ah 83
Germany Германия *f* geer**mah**nee^{y}ah 146
get, to *(find)* достать dah**staht**^{y} 11, 32, 89; *(fetch)* вызвать **viz**vaht^{y} 21, 137; *(obtain)* получить pahlooch^{y}**eet**^{y} 108

get off, to сходить skhah**deet**ʸ 72, 73
get to, to проехать prahʸ**eh**khahtʸ 65; доехать dahʸ**eh**khahtʸ 76
get up, to вставать fstah**vaht**ʸ 144
get well, to поправляться pahprahvlʸ**aht**ʸsah 152
gift подарок *m* pah**dah**rahk 17, 121
girl девочка *f* **d**ʸ**eh**vahchʸkah 112, 128
girlfriend подруга *f* pah**droo**gah 93
give, to дать dahtʸ 13, 61, 63, 75, 123, 130, 131, 140
glass стакан *m* stah**kahn** 36, 55, 56
glasses очки *pl* ahchʸ**kee** 123
glove перчатка *f* peer**ch**ʸ**aht**kah 116
glue клей *m* klʸay 105
go, to идти eet**tee** 11, 72, 73, 160; пойти pigh**tee** 87, 96; *(by car)* ехать ʸ**eh**khahtʸ 76
go away, to уходить ookhah**deet**ʸ 155
gold золото *nt* **zol**lahtah 121, 122
golden золотистый zahlah**tees**tiy 113
good хороший khah**ro**shiy 14, 35, 96, 100, 101; добрый **do**briy 10
goodbye до свидания dah svee**dah**neeʸah 10
gram грамм *m* grahm 57, 120
grammar book учебник *m* oochʸ**ehb**neek 105
grandfather дедушка *m* **d**ʸ**eh**dooshkah 93
grandmother бабушка *f* **bah**booshkah 93
grapes виноград *m* veenah**graht** 52
grapefruit грейпфрут *m* **gr**ʸ**ayp**froot 52
gray серый **s**ʸ**eh**riy 113
graze ссадина *f* **ssah**deenah 139
greasy жирный **zhir**niy 30, 111
great отлично aht**leech**ʸnah 95
Great Britain Великобритания *f* veeleekahbree**tah**neeʸah 146
green зелёный zeelʸ**o**nniy 113
green bean фасоль *f* fah**sol**ʸ 44, 50
greengrocer's овощной магазин *m* ahvahshchʸ**noy** mahgah**zeen** 98
greeting приветствие *nt* preev**ʸehtst**veeʸeh 10, 152
grey серый **s**ʸ**eh**riy 113
grocery бакалея *f* bahkahl**ʸeh**ʸah, продукты *m/pl* prah**dook**ti 98, 120
group группа *f* **groop**pah 82

guide гид *m* geet 80
guidebook путеводитель *m* pooteevah**dee**teelʸ 82, 104, 105
gums *(teeth)* десна *f* dees**nah** 145
gynaecologist гинеколог *m* geenee**ko**llahk 137, 141

H

hair волосы *m/pl* **vo**llahsi 30, 111
hairbrush щётка (для волос) *f* **shch**ʸ**ot**kah (dlʸah vah**loss**) 111
haircut стрижка *f* **streesh**kah 30
hairdresser's парикмахерская *f* pahreek**mah**kheerskahʸah 27, 30, 98
hair dryer фен *m* fʸehn 119
hairspray лак *m* lahk 30, 111
hairstyle причёска *f* pree**ch**ʸ**os**kah 30
half половина *f* pahlah**vee**nah 149
half an hour полчаса polchʸee**ssah** 153
hall porter портье *m* pahr**t**ʸ**eh**, швейцар *m* shvigh**tsahr** 26
ham ветчина *f* veetchʸee**nah** 38, 41, 47, 63
hammer молоток *m* mahlah**tok** 106
hand рука *f* roo**kah** 138
handbag сумочка *f* **soo**mahchʸkah 155
handicrafts ремёсла *nt/pl* reem**ʸos**lah 83
handkerchief носовой платок *m* nahssah**voy** plah**tok** 116
handmade ручная работа *f* roochʸ**nah**ʸah rah**bo**tah 114
hanger вешалка *f* **v**ʸ**eh**shahlkah 27
happy счастливый shchʸahst**lee**viy 152
harbour гавань *m* **gah**vahnʸ 74, 81; порт *m* port 81
hard жёсткий **zhost**keey 66, 69; твёрдый **tv**ʸ**or**diy 123
hat шляпа *f* **shl**ʸ**ah**pah 116
have, to есть ʸehstʸ 20, 79, 100, 110, 114, 118, 160
have to, to *(must)* надо **nah**dah 72, 73, 77
hay fever сенная лихорадка *f* seen**nah**ʸah leekhah**raht**kah 108
he он onn 159
head голова *f* gahlah**vah** 138, 139, 141
headache головная боль *f* gahlahv**nah**ʸah bolʸ 108

headlights фары *pl* **fah**ri 78
health здоровье *nt* zdah**rov**^{y}eh 57
heart сердце *nt* **s^{y}ehr**tseh 138
heart attack сердечный приступ *m* seer**d^{y}ehch^y**niy **pree**stoop 141
heating оттопление *nt* ahtah**pl^{y}eh**nee^{y}eh 23, 28
heavy тяжёлый tee**zhol**liy 14, 101
heel каблук *m* kah**blook** 118
helicopter вертолёт *m* veertah**l^{y}ot** 74
hello! здравствуйте! **zdrahst**vooyt^{y}eh 10; *(phone)* алло! ah**l^{y}o** 135
help помощь *f* **pom**mahshch^y 155
help! на помощь! nah **pom**mahshch^y 155
help, to помочь pah**moch^y** 13, 78
here здесь zd^{y}ehs^y 14; *(here is)* вот vot 14, 16
herring сельдь *f* s^{y}ehl^{y}d^y, селёдка *f* seel**^{y}ot**kah 42, 45
high высокий vis**so**keey 141
high season разгар сезона *m* rahz**gahr** see**zon**nah 150
hill холм *m* kholm 85
hire прокат *m* prah**kaht** 20
hire, to взять напрокат vz^{y}aht^y nahprah**kaht** 19, 20, 90, 91, 106
history история *f* ees**to**ree^{y}ah 83
hole дырка *f* **dir**kah 29
holiday праздник *m* **prahz**neek 151, 152
holidays отпуск *m* **ot**poosk 16, 151
honey мёд *m* m^{y}ot 38, 59
hope, to надеяться nah**d^{y}eh**^{y}aht^{y}sah 96
horse racing бега *pl* bee**gah**, скачки *pl* **skahch^y**kee 89
hospital больница *f* bahl^y**nee**tsah 15, 99, 144
hot горячий gah^{y}r**^{y}ahch**^{y}eey 14; жарко **zhahr**kah 25, 94
hotel гостиница *f* gah**stee**neetsah 19, 21, 22, 26, 30, 73, 80, 96, 102
hotel pass пропуск *m* **prop**poosk 22
hot water горячая вода *f* gahr**^{y}ahch**^{y}ah^{y}ah vah**dah** 23, 28
hour час *m* ch^{y}ahss 77, 80, 90, 143, 153
house дом *m* dom 83, 154
how как kahk 11
how far как далеко kahk dahlee**ko** 11, 76, 85
how long как долго kahk **dol**gah, сколько времени skol^{y}kah **vr^{y}eh**meenee 11, 24
how many сколько **skol^y**kah 11
how much сколько **skol^y**kah 11, 24
hundred сто sto 148
Hungary Венгрия *f* **v^{y}ehn**gree^{y}ah 146
hungry *(I am)* мне хочется есть mn^{y}eh **kho**ch^{y}eetsah ^{y}ehst^y 13, 35
hunt, to пойти на охоту pigh**tee** nah ah**kho**ttoo 90
hurry, to be in a спешить spee**shit^y** 21
hurt, to болеть bahl**^{y}eht^y** 140, 142, 145; *(oneself)* повредить pahvree**deet^y** 139
husband муж *m* moosh 10, 92, 93

I

I я ^{y}ah 159
ice лёд *m* l^{y}ot 56, 94
ice cream мороженое *nt* mah**ro**zhehnah^{y}eh 53, 63
icon икона *f* ee**ko**nnah 83, 127
ill больной bahl^y**noy** 140, 155
illness болезнь *f* bahl**^{y}ehzn^y** 140
immediately незамедлительно neezahmee**dleet**^{y}ehl^{y}nah 137
important важно **vahzh**nah 13
in в v, на nah 15
included включён fkl^{y}oo**ch^{y}on** 20, 24, 31, 62, 80
India Индия *f* **een**dee^{y}ah 146
indigestion расстройство желудка *nt* rahs**stroyst**vah zhi**loot**kah 141
inexpensive недорогой needahrah**goy** 124
infection заражение *nt* zahrah**zheh**nee^{y}eh 140; воспаление *nt* vahspahl**^{y}eh**nee^{y}eh 141
inflammation воспаление *nt* vahspahl**^{y}eh**nee^{y}eh 142
inflation инфляция *f* eenfl**^{y}ah**tsi^{y}ah 131
information bureau справки *pl* **sprahf**kee, спавочное бюро *nt* **sprah**vahch^{y}nah^{y}eh b^{y}oo**ro** 99, 134, 154
injection укол *m* oo**kol**, инъекция *f* een**^{y}ehk**tsi^{y}ah 142, 144
injured раненый **rah**neeniy 79
injury травма *f* **trahv**mah, повреждение *nt* pahvreezhd**^{y}eh**nee^{y}eh 139

ink чернила *pl* ch^{y}eer**nee**lah 105
insect bite укус насекомого *m* oo**kooss** nahsee**ko**mmahvah 108
insect repellent средство от комаров *nt* **sr^{y}ehts**tvah aht kahmah**rof** 109
insurance страхование *nt* strahkhah**vah**nee^{y}eh 20
interest процент *m* prah**tsehnt** 131
interest, to интересовать eenteereessah**vaht^y** 83, 96
interesting интересно eenteer^y**ehs**nah 84
international международный meezhdoonah**rod**niy 129, 133, 135
interpreter переводчик *m* peeree**vod**ch^{y}eek 131
interrupt, to прервать preer**vaht^y** 135
intersection перекрёсток *m* peeree**kr^{y}os**tahk 77
into в v 15
Intourist office бюро Интуриста *nt* b^{y}ooro eentoo**rees**tah 19, 80
introduce, to познакомить pahznah**ko**mmeet^y 92
introduction *(social)* знакомство *nt* znah**komst**vah 92
investment капиталовложение *nt* kahpeetahlahvlah**zheh**nee^{y}eh 131
invitation приглашение *nt* preeglah**sheh**nee^{y}eh 94
invite, to пригласить preeglah**seet^y** 94, 95
invoice счёт *m* shch^{y}ot, фактура *f* fahk**too**rah 131
iodine йод *m* ^{y}ot 109
Ireland Ирландия *f* eer**lahn**dee^{y}ah 146
Irish ирландец *m* eer**lahn**deets, ирландка *f* eer**lahnt**kah 93
iron *(laundry)* утюг *m* oot^y**ook** 119
iron, to погладить pah**glah**deet^y 29
Italy Италия *f* ee**tah**lee^{y}ah 146

J
jacket куртка *f* **koort**kah 116; *(man)* пиджак *m* peed**zhahk** 116
jam джем *m* dzhehm, варенье *nt* vahr^y**ehn**^{y}eh 38, 59, 120
January январь *m* een**vahr^y** 150
Japan Япония *f* ee**po**nee^{y}ah 146
jaundice желтуха *f* zhil**too**khah 142
jaw челюсть *f* **ch^{y}eh**l^{y}oost^y 138
jeans джинсы *pl* **dzhin**si 116
jersey вязаная кофта *f* **v^{y}ah**zahnah^{y}ah **kof**tah 116
jeweller's ювелирный магазин *m* ^{y}oovee**leer**niy mahgah**zeen** 99, 121
jewellery ювелирные изделия *pl* ^{y}oovee**leer**ni^{y}eh eez**d^{y}eh**lee^{y}ah 121
joint сустав *m* soo**stahf** 138
journey путешествие *nt* pootee**shehst**vee^{y}eh 74
juice сок *m* sok 38, 60
July июль *m* ee^y**ool^y** 150
jumper *(sweater)* свитер *m* **svee**tehr 116
June июнь *m* ee^y**oon^y** 150
just *(only)* только **tol^y**kah 16, 37

K
kefir *(sour milk)* кефир *m* kee**feer** 43, 60, 63
kerosene керосин *m* keerah**seen** 106
kettle чайник *m* **ch^{y}igh**neek 119
key ключ *m* kl^{y}ooch^y 27, 155
kidney почка *f* **poch^y**kah 138
kilo(gram) килограмм *m* keelah**grahm** 120
kilometre километр *m* keelah**m^{y}ehtr** 20, 79
kind любезно l^{y}oo**b^{y}ehz**nah 95
knee колено *nt* kahl^y**eh**nah 138
kneesocks гольфы *pl* **gol^y**fi 116
knife нож *m* nosh 36, 61, 107
know, to знать znaht^y 16, 24, 96
kopeck копейка *f* kahp^y**ay**kah 129, 132, 154
Kremlin Кремль *m* kr^{y}ehml^y 81

L
lake озеро *nt* **o**zeerah 23, 81, 85, 90
lamb молодая баранина *f* mahlah**dah**^{y}ah bah**rah**neenah 47
lamp лампа *f* **lahm**pah 27, 106, 119
lantern фонарь *m* fah**nahr^y** 106
large большой bahl^y**shoy** 20, 101, 118; крупный **kroop**niy 101, 130
last прошлый **prosh**liy 149, 151; последний pah**sl^{y}ehd**neey 68
last name фамилия *f* fah**mee**lee^{y}ah 25
late поздно **poz**nah 14, 153
late, to be опаздывать ah**pahz**divaht^y 69

later позже pah**pozz**heh 136
laugh, to смеяться smeey**aht**ysah 95
laundry *(place)* прачечная *f* **prah**chyeechynahyah 23, 29, 99; *(clothes)* бельё *nt* beely**o** 29
law courts суд *m* soot 81
laxative слабительное *nt* slah**bee**teelynahyeh 109
leather кожа *f* **ko**zhah 114, 118
leave, to уехать ooy**eh**khahty 31; отходить ahtkhah**deet**y 68, 69, 74; оставить ah**stah**veety 26, 96, 155
left налево nahly**eh**vah 21, 77
left, to be остаться ah**staht**ysah 87, 88
left-luggage office камера хранения *f* **kah**meerah khrahny**eh**neeyah 18, 67, 71
leg нога *f* nah**gah** 138
lemon лимон *m* lee**mon** 37, 38, 52, 59, 63
lend, to одолжить ahdahl**zhit**y 78
lens *(glasses)* стекло *nt* stee**klo** 123; *(camera)* объектив *m* ahbyeek**teef** 125
less меньше my**ehn**ysheh 14
letter письмо *nt* peesy**mo** 28, 132, 133
letter box почтовый ящик *m* pahchy**to**vviy y**ah**shchyeek 132
letter of credit аккредитив *m* ahkkreedee**teef** 130
library библиотека *f* beebleeahty**eh**kah 81, 99
licence *(permit)* разрешение *nt* rahzree**sheh**neeyeh 90
lie down, to ложиться lah**zhit**ysah 142
life belt спасательный круг *m* spah**sah**teelyniy krook 74
life boat спасательная лодка *f* spah**sah**teelynahyah **lot**kah 74
lifeguard спасательная команда *f* spah**sah**teelynahyah kah**mahn**dah 91
lift лифт *m* leeft 27, 100
light *(weight)* лёгкий ly**okh**keey 14, 53, 101; *(colour)* светлый svy**eht**liy 101, 113
light свет *m* svyeht 28, 71, 124
light, to разжечь rahz**zhehch**y 32
lighter зажигалка *f* zahzhi**gahl**kah 126
lightning молния *f* **mol**neeyah 94
like, to хотеть khahty**eht**y 13, 20, 23, 62, 96, 103; *(take pleasure)* нравиться **nrah**veetysah 25, 61, 92, 102, 112, 113
line линия *f* **lee**neeyah 72, 136
lip губа *f* goo**bah** 138
lipstick губная помада *f* goob**nah**yah pah**mah**dah 110
listen, to слушать **sloo**shahty 128
literature литература *f* leeteerah**too**rah 83
litre литр *m* leetr 75, 120
little (a) мало **mah**lah 14
live, to жить zhity 83
liver печень *f* **p**y**eh**chyehny 138
local национальный nahtsiah**nahl**y-niy 36, 40; местный my**ehst**niy 69
long *(time)* долго **dol**gah 134, 135; длинный **dleen**niy 115, 116
look, to смотреть smahtry**eht**y 100
look for, to искать ees**kaht**y 13
look out! осторожно ahstah**rozh**nah 155
loose *(clothes)* широкий shir**ro**keey 115
lose, to потерять pahteery**aht**y 123, 155
loss *(finance)* убыток *m* oo**bit**tahk 131
lost, to be заблудиться zahbloo**deet**ysah 13, 155
lost property office бюро находок *nt* byoo**ro** nah**kho**ddahk 67, 155
lot *(a)* много **mno**ggah 14
loud *(voice)* громко **grom**kah 135
love, to любить lyoo**beet**y 160
lovely прекрасный pree**krahs**niy 94
low низкий **nees**keey 141
luck *(success)* удача *f* oo**dah**chyah, успех *m* oospy**ehkh** 152
luggage багаж *m* bah**gahsh** 17, 18, 26, 31, 71
luggage trolley тележка *f* teely**ehsh**kah 18
lunch обед *m* ahby**eht** 15, 34, 80
lungs лёгкие *pl* ly**okh**keeyeh 138

M

machine машина *f* mah**shin**nah 115
magazine журнал *m* zhoor**nahl** 105
magnifying glass лупа *f* **loo**pah 123
maid горничная *f* **gor**neechynahyah 26
mail почта *f* **poch**ytah 28

mail, to отправить aht**prah**veet[y] 28
mailbox почтовый ящик *m* pahch[y]**tov**viy [y]**ah**shch[y]eek 132
main главный **glahv**niy 80
make, to делать **d[y]eh**laht[y] 131
make-up косметика *f* kahs**m[y]eh**teekah 110
man мужчина *m* moo**shch[y]ee**nah 112
manager директор *m* deer[y]**ehk**tahr 26
manicure маникюр *m* mahnee**k[y]oor** 30
many много **mnog**gah 14
map схема *f* **skh[y]eh**mah 19, 105; план *m* plahn 105; карта *f* **kahr**tah 76, 105
March март *m* mahrt 150
market рынок *m* **rin**nahk 81, 99
marmalade варенье *nt* vahr[y]**ehn**[y]eh 38, 59
married *(man)* женат zheh**naht** 93; *(woman)* замужем **zah**moozhehm 93
mascara тушь для ресниц *f* toosh[y] dl[y]ah rees**neets** 110
mass *(church)* служба *f* **sloozh**bah 84
match спичка *f* **speech**[y]kah 106, 126; *(sport)* соревнование *nt* sahreevnah**vah**nee[y]eh, матч *m* mahtch[y] 89
material материал *m* mahteeree**ahl** 114
matinée дневной спектакль *m* dneev**noy** speek**tahkl[y]** 88
mattress матрас *m* mah**trahss** 106
May май *m* migh 150
may *(can)* мочь moch[y] 13, 160
meal питание *nt* pee**tah**nee[y]eh 24; еда *f* ee**dah** 143
mean, to значить **znah**ch[y]eet[y] 11, 26
measles корь *f* kor[y] 142
measure, to снять мерку sn[y]aht[y] **m[y]ehr**koo 113
meat мясо *nt* **m[y]ah**ssah 40, 47, 48, 61
mechanic механик *m* mee**khah**neek 78
medical certificate медицинское свидетельство *nt* meedeet**sins**kah[y]eh sveed[y]**eh**teel[y]stvah 144
medicine медицина *f* meedeet**si**nnah 83; лекарство *nt* lee**kahrst**vah 143
meet, to встретиться fstr[y]**eh**teet[y]sah 96
melon дыня *f* **din**[y]ah 52
memorial памятник *m* **pah**meetneek, мемориал *m* meemahree**ahl** 81
mend, to заделать zah**d[y]eh**laht[y] 75; *(clothes)* заштопать zah**shtop**paht[y] 29
menu меню *nt* meen**[y]oo** 36, 37, 39, 40
message, to take передать peeree**daht[y]** 136
metre метр *m* m[y]ehtr 115
metro метро *nt* mee**tro** 72
middle середина *f* seeree**dee**nah 88, 150
midnight полночь *f* **pol**nahch[y] 153
milk молоко *nt* mahlah**ko** 15, 38, 59, 60, 63
milliard миллиард *m* meellee**ahrt** 148
million миллион *m* meellee**on** 148
mineral water минеральная вода *f* meenee**rahl**[y]nah[y]ah vah**dah** 55, 60, 63
minute минута *f* mee**noo**tah 21, 69, 134, 153
mirror зеркало *nt* **z[y]ehr**kahlah 115, 123
miss, to не хватать nee khvah**taht[y]** 18, 29, 61
mistake, to make ошибаться ahshi**baht**[y]sah 31, 61, 62, 102
monastery монастырь *m* mahnahs**tir**[y] 81
Monday понедельник *m* pahnee**d[y]ehl**[y]neek 151
money деньги *pl* **d[y]ehn**[y]gee 130, 155; валюта *f* vahl**[y]oo**tah 129
month месяц *m* **m[y]eh**sseets 16, 150
monument памятник *m* **pah**meetneek 81
moon луна *f* loo**nah** 94
more больше **bol**[y]sheh 14
morning утро *nt* **oo**trah 10, 15, 151
mosque мечеть *f* mee**ch[y]eht[y]** 84
mother мать *f* maht[y] 93
motor двигатель *m* **dvee**gahteel[y], мотор *m* mah**tor** 78
motor boat моторная лодка *f* mah**tor**nah[y]ah **lot**kah 74, 91

motor cycle мотоцикл *m* mahtah**tsikl** 74
motorship теплоход *m* teeplah**khot** 74
motorway автомагистраль *f* ahftahmahgees**trahl^y** 76
mountain гора *f* gah**rah** 23, 85
moustache усы *pl* **oo**ssi 31
mouth рот *m* rot 138, 142
move, to двинуть **dvee**noot^y 139
movie фильм *m* feel^{y}m 86
movie camera кинокамера *f* keenah**kah**meerah 124
movies кино *nt* kee**no** 86, 96
much много **mno**ggah 14
muscle мышца *f* **mish**tsah 138, 140
museum музей *m* mooz^y**ay** 15, 81
mushrooms грибы *pl* gree**bi** 41, 50
music музыка *f* **moo**zikah 83, 128
must, to должен (должна) **dol**zhehn (dahlzh**nah**) 31, 95, 142
mustard горчица *f* gahr**ch^{y}ee**tsah 37, 63, 120
mutton *(meat)* баранина *f* bah**rah**neenah 47
my мой moy 159
myself сам, сама sahm, sah**mah** 120

N

nail *(human)* ноготь *m* **no**ggaht^y 110
nail polish лак для ногтей *m* lahk dl^{y}ah nahg**t^{y}ay** 110
name фамилия *f* fah**mee**lee^{y}ah 23, 25, 79, 131, 133
napkin салфетка *f* sahl**f^{y}eht**kah 36
nappies пелёнки *pl* peel^y**on**kee 111
narrow узкий **oos**keey 118; *(it is)* тесно **t^{y}ehs**nah 25
nationality гражданство *nt* grahzh**dahnst**vah 25
natural history естествознание *nt* eest^{y}ehstvah**znah**nee^{y}eh 83
nausea тошнота *f* tahshnah**tah** 108
near близко **blees**kah 14
nearby поблизости pah**blee**zahstee 35, 77, 84, 91, 98
nearest ближайший blee**zhigh**shiy 72, 75, 78, 104, 108, 132, 134
neck шея *f* **sheh**^{y}ah 30, 138
necklace ожерелье *nt* ahzhir^y**ehl**^{y}eh 121
need, to нужен (нужна) **noo**zhehn (noozh**nah**) 19, 20, 29, 118, 125
needle иголка *f* ee**gol**kah 27
nephew племянник *m* pleem^y**ahn**neek 93
nerve нерв *m* n^{y}ehrf 138
nervous system нервная система *f* **n^{y}ehrv**nah^{y}ah seest^y**eh**mah 138
never никогда neekahg**dah** 15
new новый **no**vviy 14
newspaper газета *f* gah**z^{y}eh**tah 14, 104
newsstand газетный киоск *m* gah**z^{y}eht**niy kee**osk** 67, 99, 104
New Year Новый Год *m* **no**vviy got 152
next будущий **boo**dooshch^{y}eey 149, 151; следующий **sl^{y}eh**doo^{y}ooshch^{y}eey 65, 68, 72, 73, 95, 151
next to около **o**kkahlah 15, 77
nice *(weather)* хороший khah**ro**shiy 94
niece племянница *f* pleem^y**ahn**neetsah 93
night ночь *f* noch^y 10, 151
nightclub ночной клуб *m* nahch^y**noy** kloop 88
nightdress ночная рубашка *f* nahch^y**nah**^{y}ah roo**bahsh**kah 116
nine девять **d^{y}eh**veet^y 147
nineteen девятнадцать deeveet**nah**tsaht^y 147
ninety девяносто deevee**no**stah 148
no нет n^{y}eht 10
nobody никто neek**to** 15
noisy шумно **shoom**nah 25
nonsmoker некурящий *m* neekoor^y**ah**shch^{y}eey 66
noon полдень *m* **pol**deen^y 153
normal нормальный nahr**mahl^y**niy 30
north север *m* **s^{y}eh**veer 77
North America Северная Америка *f* **s^{y}eh**veernah^{y}ah ahm^y**eh**reekah 146
nose нос *m* noss 138
nosebleed кровотечение из носа *nt* krahvahtee**ch^{y}eh**nee^{y}eh eez **no**ssah 141
not не nee 15
notebook записная книжка *f* zahpees**nah**^{y}ah **kneesh**kah 105
note paper почтовая бумага *f* pahch^y**to**vvah^{y}ah boo**mah**gah 105
nothing ничего neech^{y}ee**vo** 15
notice *(sign)* объявление *nt* ahb^{y}ee**vl^{y}eh**nee^{y}eh 154

notify, to сообщать sahahp**shchʸaht**ʸ 144
November ноябрь *m* nahʸ**ahbr**ʸ 150
now сейчас see**chʸahss** 15
number номер *m* **no**mmeer 25, 65, 134, 135, 136; число *nt* chʸees**lo** 147
nurse медсестра *f* meetsees**trah** 144
nut орех *m* ahrʸ**ehkh** 52

O

observatory обсерватория *f* ahpsʸehrvah**to**reeʸah 81
occupation профессия *f* prah**fʸeh**sseeʸah 25
occupied занятый **zah**neetiy 14
October октябрь *m* ahkt**ʸahbr**ʸ 150
office бюро *nt* bʸooro 19, 67, 80
oil (растительное) масло *nt* (rahs**tee**teelʸnahʸeh) **mahs**lah 37, 75, 111
oily жирный **zhir**niy 30, 111
old старый **stah**riy 14
olive маслина *f* mahs**lee**nah 41
on на nah 15
once (один)раз (ah**deen**) rahs 143, 149
one один ah**deen** 147
one-way *(ticket)* в один конец v ah**deen** kahn**ʸehts** 65, 69
on foot пешком peesh**kom** 76, 85
onion лук *m* look 42, 50
only только **tol**ʸkah 15, 24, 80, 88
on time вовремя **vo**vrʸehmʸah 68, 153
open открытый aht**kri**ttiy 14, 82
open, to открываться ahtkri**vaht**ʸ-sah 11, 82, 108, 130, 132; открыть aht**krit**ʸ 17, 70, 130, 142
opera опера *f* **o**ppeerah 87
opera house оперный театр *m* oppeerniy tee**ahtr** 81, 87
operation операция *f* ahpeer**ah**tsiʸah 144
operator телефонистка *f* teeleefah**neest**kah 26
operetta оперетта *f* ahpeerʸ**eh**ttah 87
opposite напротив nah**pro**tteef 77
optician оптика *f* **op**teekah 99, 123
or или **ee**lee 15
orange оранжевый ah**rahn**zhiviy 113
orange апельсин *m* ahpeelʸ**seen** 52, 63
orchestra оркестр *m* ahr**kʸehstr** 87
order *(goods)* заказ *m* zah**kahs** 40, 102
order, to *(meal, goods)* заказать zahkah**zaht**ʸ 61, 102, 103
other другой droo**goy** 58, 60, 74, 101
our наш nahsh 159
out of stock распродано rahs**pro**ddahnah 103
outlet *(electric)* розетка *f* rah**zʸeht**kah 27
oval овальный ah**vahl**ʸniy 101
overnight сутки *pl* **soot**kee 24
overtaking обгон *m* ahb**gon** 79

P

packet пачка *f* **pahchʸ**kah 120, 126
pain боль *f* bolʸ 140, 141, 143, 144
painkiller болеутоляющее средство *nt* boleeootah**lʸah**ʸooshchʸehʸeh **srʸehtst**vah 140
paint, to писать pee**ssaht**ʸ 83
paintbox краски *f/pl* **krahs**kee 105
painter живописец *m* zhivvah**pee**sseets, художник *m* khoo**dozh**neek 83
painting живопись *f* **zhi**vvahpeesʸ 83
pair пара *f* **pah**rah 116
palace дворец *m* dvahr**ʸehts** 81
palpitations сердцебиение *nt* sʸehrtsehbeeʸ**eh**neeʸeh 141
pancake блин *m* bleen 42, 63
panties трусики *pl* **troo**sseekee 116
pants *(trousers)* брюки *pl* **brʸoo**kee 116
paper бумага *f* boo**mah**gah 105
paraffin *(fuel)* керосин *m* keerah**seen** 106
parcel посылка *f* pah**ssil**kah 132
parents родители *pl* rah**dee**teelee 93
park парк *m* pahrk 81
park, to поставить машину pah**stah**veetʸ mah**shi**nnoo 26, 77
parking стоянка *f* stahʸ**ahn**kah 77, 79
part часть *f* chʸahstʸ 138
party *(social gathering)* вечеринка *f* veechʸee**reen**kah 95
pass *(mountain)* перевал *m* peeree**vahl** 85

passing *(car)* обгон *m* ahb**gon** 79
passport паспорт *m* **pahs**pahrt 16, 17, 25, 26, 124, 130, 133, 155
paste *(glue)* клей *m* kl^{y}ay 105
pastry shop кондитерская *f* kahn**dee**t^{y}ehrskah^{y}ah 99
path тропинка *f* trah**peen**kah 85
patient пациент/пациентка *m/f* pahtsi^y**ehnt**/pahtsi^y**ehnt**kah 144
pay, to платить plah**teet^y** 17, 31, 62, 102, 103, 136
payment оплата *f* ah**plah**tah 102; платёж *m* plah**t^{y}osh** 131
peas горох *m* gah**rokh** 50
peach персик *m* **p^{y}ehr**seek 52, 120
pear груша *f* **groo**shah 52
pearl жемчуг *m* **zhehm**ch^{y}ook 121, 122
pen ручка *f* **rooch^y**kah 105
pencil карандаш *m* kahrahn**dahsh** 105
pendant кулон *m* koo**lon** 121
penicilline пенициллин *m* peeneetsi**lleen** 143
penknife перочинный ножик *m* peerah**ch^{y}een**niy **no**zhik 106
pensioner пенсионер *m* p^{y}ehns^{y}ah**n^{y}ehr** 82
people люди *pl* **l^{y}oo**dee 92
pepper перец *m* **p^{y}eh**reets 37, 38, 64
per cent процент *m* prah**tsehnt** 149
performance спектакль *m* speek**tahkl^y** 86
perfume духи *pl* doo**khee** 110, 127
perfumery парфюмерия *f* pahrf^{y}oomee**ree**^{y}ah 99, 108
perhaps может быть **mo**zheht bit^y 15
period *(monthly)* менструация *f* meenstroo**ah**tsi^{y}ah 141
permanent wave перманент *m* p^{y}ehrmah**n^{y}ehnt** 30
person человек *m* ch^{y}eelah**v^{y}ehk** 32
personal личный **leech^y**niy 17
petrol бензин *m* been**zeen** 20, 75
photo фотография *f* fahtah**grah**fee^{y}ah 124, 125
photocopy фотокопия *f* fahtah**ko**ppee^{y}ah 131
photographer *(shop)* фотография *f* fahtah**grah**fee^{y}ah 99, 124
phrase фраза *f* **frah**zah 12
phrasebook разговорник *m* rahzgah**vor**neek 12, 105
pick up, to *(person)* заехать за zah^y**eh**khaht^y zah 80, зайти за zigh**tee** zah 96
picnic пикник *m* **peek**neek 62
picture картина *f* kahr**tee**nah 83
picture, to take фотографировать fahtahgrah**fee**rahvaht^y, снимать snee**maht^y** 82, 84, 124
piece кусок *m* koo**ssok** 120; *(luggage)* место *nt* **m^{y}ehs**tah 18
pill противозачаточная пилюля *f* prahteevahzah**ch^{y}ah**tahch^{y}nah^{y}ah peel**^{y}oo**lah 141
pillow подушка *f* pah**doosh**kah 27
pin булавка *f* boo**lahf**kah 121
pineapple ананас *m* ahnah**nahss** 52
pink розовый **ro**zahviy 113
pipe трубка *f* **troop**kah 126
place место *nt* **m^{y}ehs**tah 25, 70, 76
plane самолёт *m* sahmah**l^{y}ot** 65
planetarium планетарий *m* plahnee**tah**reey 81
plaster *(cast)* гипс *m* geeps 140
plastic пластмасса *f* plahst**mahs**sah 107
plate тарелка *f* tah**r^{y}ehl**kah 37, 61, 107
platform *(station)* платформа *f* plaht**for**mah 67, 68, 69, 70
play *(theatre)* пьеса *f* **p^{y}eh**ssah 86
play, to играть ee**graht^y** 86, 87, 89, 90
playground площадка для игр *f* plah**shch^{y}aht**kah dl^{y}ah eegr 32
please пожалуйста pah**zhahl**stah 10
pleasure удовольствие *nt* oodah**vol^{y}st**vee^{y}eh 96
plug *(electric)* штепсель *m* **sht^{y}ehps**^{y}ehl^y 29, 119
plum слива *f* **slee**vah 52
pneumonia воспаление лёгких *nt* vahspahl**^{y}eh**nee^{y}eh **l^{y}okh**keekh 142
pocket карман *m* kahr**mahn** 117
pocket calculator карманная счётная машинка *f* kahr**mahn**nah^{y}ah **shch^{y}ot**nah^{y}ah mah**shin**kah 105
poison отрава *f* ah**trah**vah, яд *m* ^{y}aht 109, 155
poisoning отравление *nt* ahtrahv**l^{y}eh**nee^{y}eh 142
Poland Польша *f* **pol^y**shah 146
police милиция *f* mee**lee**tsi^{y}ah 79, 99, 155

police station отделение милиции *nt* ahtdeel^y**eh**nee^{y}eh meel**ee**tsi^{y}ee 99, 155
pork свинина *f* svee**nee**nah 47
port порт *m* port 74
porter носильщик *m* nah**seel**^{y}-shch^{y}eek 18, 26, 71
portion порция *f* **por**tsi^{y}ah 37, 61
post *(letters)* почта *f* **poch**^{y}tah 28
post, to отправить aht**prah**veet^y 28
postage stamp (почтовая) марка *f* (pahch^y**to**vvah^{y}ah) **mahr**kah 28, 132
postcard открытка *f* aht**krit**kah 105, 132
poste restante до востребования dah vahs**tr**^{y}**eh**bahvahnee^{y}ah 133
poster плакат *m* plah**kaht** 127
post office почта *f* **poch**^{y}tah 19, 99, 132; *(main)* почтамт *m* pahch^y**tahmt** 132
potato картофель *m* kahr**to**feel^y 50
pottery керамика *f* kee**rah**meekah 83
poultry птица *f* **ptee**tsah 49
pound *(money)* фунт *m* foont 17, 18, 102, 130
powder пудра *f* **poo**drah 110
prefer, to предпочитать preetpahch^{y}ee**taht**^{y} 101
pregnant беременна beer^y**eh**meennah 141
prepare, to приготовить preegah**to**veet^y 108
prescribe, to прописать prahpee**ssaht**^{y} 143
prescription рецепт *m* ree**tsehpt** 108, 143
present подарок *m* pah**dah**rahk 121
press stud кнопка *f* **knop**kah 117
pressure давление *nt* dahvl^y**eh**-nee^{y}eh 75, 141, 142
pretty мило **mee**lah 84
price цена *f* tsi**nnah** 20, 80
processing *(photo)* проявление *nt* praheevl^y**eh**nee^{y}eh 125
profit доход *m* dah**khot**, прибыль *f* **pree**bil^y 131
programme программа *f* prah**grahm**mah 88
Protestant протестантский praht^{y}ehs**tahnts**keey 84
provide, to найти nigh**tee** 131
public holiday праздник *m* **prahz**neek 152
public telephone телефон-автомат *m* teelee**fon**-ahftah**maht** 134
public transport общественный транспорт *m* ahb**shch**^{y}**ehst**-v^{y}enniy **trahns**pahrt 72
pull, to *(muscle)* растянуть rahstee**noot**^{y} 140
pullover свитер *m* **svee**tehr 112, 116; пуловер *m* poolo**v**veer 116
puncture прокол *m* prah**kol** 75
purchase покупка *f* pah**koop**kah, купля *f* **koo**pl^{y}ah 131
pure чистый **ch**^{y}**ees**tiy 115
put, to поставить pah**stah**veet^y 24, 71
pyjamas пижама *f* pee**zhah**mah 117

Q

quality качество *nt* **kah**ch^{y}eestvah 103, 114
quantity количество *nt* kah**lee**ch^{y}eestvah 14, 103
quay набережная *f* **nah**beer^{y}ehzhnah^{y}ah 154
question вопрос *m* vah**pross** 11, 108, 134
quick(ly) быстро **bi**strah 14, 155
quiet тихий **tee**kheey 23

R

radiator *(car)* радиатор *m* rahdee**ah**tahr 78
radio радио *nt* **rah**deeo 23, 28; *(set)* приёмник *m* pree^y**om**neek 119
radish редиска *f* ree**dees**kah 42, 50
railway station вокзал *m* vahg**zahl** 19, 21, 67
rain дождь *m* doshch^y 94
raincoat плащ *m* plahshch^y 117
raisin(s) изюм *m* eez^y**oom** 52, 64
rash сыпь *f* sip^y 139
rate *(exchange)* курс *m* koors 18, 130
razor бритва *f* **breet**vah 110
razor blades лезвия *nt/pl* **l**^{y}**ehz**vee^{y}ah 110
read, to читать ch^{y}ee**taht**^{y} 12
ready готовый gah**to**vviy 29, 118, 123, 125, 145
real настоящий nahstah^y**ah**shch^{y}eey 121
receipt чек *m* ch^{y}ehk 103
reception регистрация *f* reegee**strah**tsi^{y}ah 23

receptionist администратор *m* ahdmeenee**strah**tahr 26
recommend, to посоветовать pahsahv**ʸeh**tahvahtʸ 36, 41, 55, 80, 137; порекомендовать pahreekahmeendah**vahtʸ** 40, 86, 87
record *(disc)* пластинка *f* plahs**teen**kah 127, 128
record player проигриватель *m* prah**ee**greevahteelʸ 119
rectangular прямоугольный prʸahmahoo**gol**ʸniy 101
red красный **krahs**niy 55, 56, 113
Red Square Красная площадь *f* **krahs**nahʸah **plo**shchʸeedʸ 73, 82
reduction скидка *f* **skeet**kah 24, 82
refund, to pay вернуть деньги veer**nootʸ** **dʸehn**ʸgee 103
regards привет *m* preev**ʸeht** 152
register, to *(luggage)* отправить aht**prah**veetʸ 71
registered *(mail)* заказной zahkahz**noy** 133
registration регистрация *f* reegees**trah**tsiʸah 25
registration form анкета для приезжающих *f* ahn**kʸeh**tah dlʸah preeʸeez**zhah**ʸooshchʸeekh 25, 26
religious service богослужение *nt* bahgahsloo**zheh**neeʸeh 84
rent, to взять напрокат vzʸahtʸ nahprah**kaht** 19, 20, 90, 91, 106
rental прокат *m* prah**kaht** 20
repair(s) ремонт *m* ree**mont** 79, 118, 125, 154
repair, to починить pahchʸee**neetʸ** 29, 118, 119, 121, 123, 125, 145
repeat, to повторить pahftah**reetʸ** 12
report, to *(a theft)* заявить zahee**veetʸ** 155
reservation *(seat)* плацкарта *f* plahts**kahr**tah 69, 70
reservations office предварительная продажа билетов *f* preedvah**ree**teelʸnahʸah prah**dah**zhah beel**ʸeh**tahf 67
reserve, to заказать zahkah**zahtʸ** 23, 36, 88
reserved заказано zah**kah**zahnah 154
rest остальное *nt* ahstahlʸ**no**ʸeh 130
restaurant ресторан *m* reestah**rahn** 19, 32, 34, 35, 36, 96; кафе *nt* kah**feh** 33

return *(ticket)* туда и обратно too**dah** ee ah**braht**nah 65, 69
return, to *(give back)* возвратить vahzvrah**teetʸ** 103
revolution революция *f* reevah**lʸoo**tsiʸah 152
rheumatism ревматизм *m* rʸehvmah**teezm** 141
rib ребро *nt* ree**bro** 138
ribbon лента *f* **lʸehn**tah 105
rice рис *m* reess 40, 44, 51
right направо nah**prah**vah 21, 77; *(correct)* правильный **prah**veelʸniy 12, 14
ring *(finger)* кольцо *nt* kahlʸ**tso** 121
river река *f* ree**kah** 85, 90
road дорога *f* dah**ro**ggah 76, 77, 85
road assistance ГАИ *f* **gah**ee 78
road map карта дорог *f* **kahr**tah dah**rok** 105
road sign дорожный знак *m* dah**rozh**niy znahk 77, 79
roast beef ростбиф *m* **rost**beef 47
roll *(bread)* булочка *f* **boo**lahchʸkah 38, 64
room комната *f* **kom**nahtah 19, 29; номер *m* **no**mmeer 23, 24, 25, 26; *(space)* место *nt* **mʸehs**tah 32
rope верёвка *f* veer**ʸof**kah 107
rouble рубль *m* rooblʸ 18, 101, 103, 129, 130, 154
rouge румяна *f* room**ʸah**nah 110
round круглый **kroog**liy 101
round *(game)* игра *f* ee**grah** 90
roundtrip *(ticket)* туда и обратно too**dah** ee ah**braht**nah 65, 69
route дорога *f* dah**ro**ggah 85
rowing гребля *f* **grʸeh**blʸah 89
rowing-boat лодка *f* **lot**kah 91
rubber *(material)* резина *f* ree**zee**nah 118; *(eraser)* резинка *f* ree**zeen**kah 105
rug ковёр *m* kahv**ʸor** 127
ruins развалины *f/pl* rahz**vah**leeni 82
ruler линейка *f* leen**ʸay**kah 105
Russia Россия *f* **rahssi**ʸah 146
Russian русский **roos**keey 16, 35, 113; по-русски pah **roos**kee 11, 12, 95; *(language)* русский язык *m* **roos**keey ee**zik** 16
Russian course курсы русского языка *m/pl* **koor**si **roos**kahvah eezi**kah** 16

DICTIONARY

S

safe сейф *m* sayf 26
safety pin английская булавка *f* ahn**gleeys**kahʸah boo**lahf**kah 110
sailing-boat парусная лодка *f* **pah**roosnahʸah **lot**kah 91
salad салат *m* sah**laht** 40, 42
sale продажа *f* prah**dah**zhah 131
salmon сёмга *f* **sʸom**gah 42, 45, 63
salt соль *f* solʸ 37, 38, 64
same такой же tah**koy** zheh 118
samovar самовар *m* sahmah**vahr** 59, 127
sand песок *m* pee**ssok** 90
sandal сандалия *f* sahn**dah**leeʸah 118
sandwich *(open)* бутерброд *m* booteer**brod** 63
Saturday суббота *f* soo**bo**ttah 151
saucer блюдце *nt* **blʸoo**tseh 107
sausage колбаса *f* kahlbah**ssah** 41, 64; *(frankfurter)* сосиска *f* sah**sees**kah 38, 64
say, to сказать skah**zahtʸ** 160
scarf шарф *m* shahrf 117
school holidays каникулы *pl* kah**nee**kooli 151
scissors ножницы *pl* **nozh**neetsi 107, 110
Scotland Шотландия *f* shat**lahn**deeʸah 146
screwdriver отвёртка *f* ahtv**ʸort**kah 107
sculptor скульптор *m* **skoolʸ**ptahr 83
sculpture скульптура *f* skoolʸp**too**rah 83
sea море *nt* **mor**ʸeh 23, 85
seafood дары моря *pl* dah**ri** **mor**ʸah 40, 45
season время года *nt* **vrʸeh**mʸah **go**ddah, сезон *m* see**zon** 150
seat место *nt* **mʸehs**tah 70, 88
seat reservation плацкарта *f* plahts**kahr**tah 69, 70
second второй ftah**roy** 149
second секунда *f* see**koon**dah 153
secretary секретарша *f* seekree**tahr**shah 27, 131
section отдел *m* aht**dʸehl** 104
see, to *(look at)* посмотреть pahsmah**trʸehtʸ** 12, 25, 89
sell, to продать prah**dahtʸ** 100
send, to послать pah**slahtʸ** 132, 133; прислать pree**slahtʸ** 31, 78

sentence предложение *nt* preedlah**zheh**neeʸeh 12
separately отдельно aht**dʸehlʸ**nah 62
September сентябрь *m* seent**ʸahbrʸ** 150
serious серьёзно seer**ʸoz**nah 139
service обслуживание *nt* ahp**sloo**zhivvahneeʸeh 23, 62, 100
service bureau бюро обслуживания *nt* bʸ**ooro** ahp**sloo**zhivvahneeʸah 22, 27
serviette салфетка *f* sahl**fʸeht**kah 36
setting lotion фиксатор *m* feek**sah**tahr 30, 111
seven семь sʸehmʸ 147
seventeen семнадцать seem**nah**tsahtʸ 147
seventy семьдесят **sʸehm**deesseet 148
sew, to пришить pree**shitʸ** 29
shampoo шампунь *m* shahm**poonʸ** 30, 111
shape размер *m* rahz**mʸehr** 103
share *(finance)* акция *f* **ahk**tsiʸah 131
sharp острый **os**triy 140
shave, to побрить(ся) pah**breetʸ**(sah) 31
shaver (электро)бритва *f* (ehlʸehktrah)**breet**vah 27, 119
she она ah**nah** 159
shine *(sun)* светить svee**teetʸ** 94
ship корабль *m* kah**rahblʸ**, судно *nt* **sood**nah 74
shirt рубашка *f* roo**bahsh**kah 117
shoe туфля *f* **too**flʸah, ботинок *m* bah**tee**nahk 118
shoelace шнурок *m* shnoo**rok** 118
shoemaker's *(repairs)* ремонт обуви *m* ree**mont** **o**boovee 99, 118
shoe polish гуталин *m* gootah**leen** 118
shoes обувь *f* **o**boovʸ 118
shoe shop магазин обуви *m* mahgah**zeen** **o**boovee 99
shop магазин *m* mahgah**zeen** 32, 98, 100
shopping покупки *pl* pah**koop**kee 97
shop window витрина *f* vee**tree**nah 100, 112

Словарь

shopping centre торговый центр *m* tahr**gov**viy tsehntr 99
short коротко **ko**rrahtkah 30, 115, 116
shoulder плечо *nt* plee**ch^{y}o** 138
show представление *nt* preetstah**vl^{y}eh**nee^{y}eh 86
show, to показать pahkah**zaht^y** 76, 100, 101, 103, 119, 124
shower душ *m* doosh 23, 32
shut закрытый zah**kri**ttiy 14
sick *(ill)* больной bahl^y**noy** 140, 155
sickness *(illness)* болезнь *f* bah**l^{y}ehzn^y** 140
side бок *m* bok 30
side dish гарнир *m* gahr**neer** 40
sightseeing tour экскурсия *f* ehks**koor**see^{y}ah 80
sign *(notice)* надпись *f* **naht**pees^y 154
sign, to подписать(ся) pahtpee**ssaht^y**(sah) 26, 130
sign up, to записаться zahpee**ssaht^y**sah 80
signature подпись *f* **pot**pees^y 25
silk шёлк *m* sholk 114
silver *(colour)* серебряный seer^y**eh**breeniy 113
silver серебро *nt* seeree**bro** 121, 122
simple простой prahs**toy** 124
since с s 15, 150
sing, to петь p^{y}eht^y 87
single *(ticket)* в один конец v ah**deen** kah**n^{y}ehts** 65, 69
single room номер на одного *m* **no**mmeer nah ahdnah**vo** 19, 23
sister сестра *f* sees**trah** 93
sit down, to присесть prees**^{y}ehst^y** 95
six шесть shehst^y 147
sixteen шестнадцать shees**naht**tsaht^y 147
sixty шестьдесят sheesdee**s^{y}aht** 147
size размер *m* rahz**m^{y}ehr** 112, 113, 124; *(shoes)* номер *m* **no**mmeer 118
skates коньки *pl* kahn^y**kee** 91
skis лыжи *pl* **li**zhi 91
ski, to ходить на лыжах khah**deet^y** nah **li**zhahkh 91
skin кожа *f* **ko**zhah 138
skirt юбка *f* ^{y}**oop**kah 117
sky небо *nt* **n^{y}eh**bah 94
sled санки *pl* **sahn**kee 91
sleep, to спать spaht^y 144
sleeping bag спальный мешок *m* **spahl^y**niy mee**shok** 107
sleeping-car спальный вагон *m* **spahl^y**niy vah**gon** 68, 69, 71
sleeping pill снотворное *nt* snah**tvor**nah^{y}eh 109, 143
sleeve рукав *m* roo**kahf** 116, 142
slide *(photo)* слайд *m* slighd 124
slip комбинация *f* kahmbee**nah**tsi^{y}ah 117
slipper тапка *f* **tahp**kah, тапочка *f* **tah**pahch^{y}kah 118
slowly медленно **m^{y}eh**dleennah 12, 14, 135
small маленький **mah**leen^{y}keey 14, 20, 37, 101, 118, 121
smoke, to курить koo**reet^y** 95, 126, 154
smoker курящий *m* koo**r^{y}ah**shch^{y}eey 66
snack bar буфет *m* boo**f^{y}eht** 33, 67, 70
snap fastener кнопка *f* **knop**kah 117
snow снег *m* sn^{y}ehk 94
soap мыло *nt* **mi**llah 27, 111
soccer футбол *m* foot**bol** 89
sock носок *m* nah**ssok** 117
socket *(outlet)* розетка *f* rah**z^{y}eht**kah 27
soft мягкий **m^{y}ahkh**keey 66, 69, 123
sold out *(theatre)* распродано rahs**pro**ddahnah 88
sole подмётка *f* pahd**m^{y}ot**kah 118
soloist солист *m* sah**leest**, солистка *f* sah**leest**kah 87
someone кто-нибудь **kto**-neebood^y 31
something что-нибудь **shto**-neebood^y 36, 53, 55, 108, 113; что-то **shto**-tah 29, 139
somewhere где-нибудь **gd^{y}eh**-neebood^y 88
son сын *m* sinn 93
song песня *f* **p^{y}ehs**n^{y}ah 128
soon скоро **sko**rrah 15
sorry *(I'm)* простите, извините prah**steet**^{y}eh, eezvee**neet**^{y}eh 10
sort *(kind)* сорт *m* sort 120
soup суп *m* soop 44
sour cream сметана *f* smee**tah**nah 35, 41, 42, 43

south юг *m* ʸook 77
South Africa Южная Африка *f* ʸ**oozh**nahʸah **ah**freekah 146
South America Латинская Америка *f* lah**teens**kahʸah ah**mʸeh**reekah 146
souvenir сувенир *m* soovee**neer** 127
souvenir shop магазин сувениров *m* mahgah**zeen** soovee**nee**rahf 99
Soviet Union *(USSR)* Союз Советских Социалистических Республик (СССР) *m* saʸ**oos** sahvʸ**ehts**keekh sahtsiahlees**tee**chʸeeskeekh rees**poo**bleek (ehs ehs ehs ehr) 146
Spain Испания *f* ees**pah**neeʸah 146
spare part запчасть *f* zahp**chʸahst**ʸ 79
spare tyre запасное колесо *nt* zahpahs**no**ʸeh kahlee**sso** 75
spark(ing) plug свеча *f* svee**chʸah** 76
speak, to говорить gahvah**reet**ʸ 12, 16, 84, 134, 135, 137
speaker *(loudspeaker)* громкоговоритель *m* gromkahgahvah**ree**teelʸ 119
special особый ah**sso**bbiy 37
spectacle case футляр для очков *m* footlʸ**ahr** dlʸah ahchʸ**kof** 123
speed скорость *f* **sko**rrahstʸ 79
spell, to сказать по буквам skah**zaht**ʸ pah **book**vahm 12, 135
spend, to истратить ees**trah**teetʸ 101
spine позвоночник *m* pahzvah**noch**ʸneek 138
spoon ложка *f* **losh**kah 37, 61, 107
sport(s) спорт *m* sport 89
sporting goods shop спорттовары *m/pl* sporttah**vah**ri 99
sports jacket спортивная куртка *f* spahr**teev**nahʸah **koort**kah 117
spring *(season)* весна *f* vees**nah** 150; *(water)* источник *m* ees**toch**ʸneek 85
square квадратный kvah**draht**niy 101
square площадь *f* **plo**shchʸeedʸ 82
stadium стадион *m* stahdee**on** 82
stain пятно *nt* peet**no** 29
stainless steel нержавеющая сталь *f* neerzhahvʸ**eh**ʸooshchʸahʸah stahlʸ 107, 122
stalls *(theatre)* партер *m* pahrtʸ**ehr** 88
stamp *(postage)* (почтовая) марка *f* (pahchʸ**to**vvahʸah) **mahr**kah 28, 127, 132
star звезда *f* zveez**dah** 94
start, to начинаться nahchʸee**naht**ʸsah 80, 86
starter *(appetizer)* закуска *f* zah**koos**kah 36, 40, 41
station *(railway)* вокзал *m* vahg**zahl** 19, 21, 67; *(underground)* станция *f* **stahn**tsiʸah 72
stationer's культтовары *m/pl* koolʸttah**vah**ri 99, 104
statue статуя *f* **stah**tooʸah 82
stay, to пробыть prah**bit**ʸ 16, 24, 26
steak бифштекс *m* beef**shtehks** 47
steal, to украсть oo**krahst**ʸ 155
steamboat пароход *m* pahrah**khot** 74
steppe степь *f* stʸehpʸ 85
sting укус *m* oo**koos** 139
sting, to ужалить oo**zhah**leetʸ 139
stitch, to *(clothes)* зашить zah**shit**ʸ 29, 118
stock, out of распродано rahs**pro**ddahnah 103
stocking чулок *m* chʸoo**lok** 117
stomach живот *m* zhi**vot**, желудок *m* zhi**loo**dahk 138, 141
stools кал *m* kahl 142
stone камень *m* **kah**meenʸ 122; галька *f* **gahl**ʸkah 90
stop *(bus)* остановка *f* ahstah**nof**kah 73
stop, to остановиться ahstahnah**veet**ʸsah 21, 68
stop thief! держи вора! deer**zhi** **vo**rrah 155
store *(shop)* магазин *m* mahgah**zeen** 99
storm буря *f* **boo**rʸah 94
stove печка *f* **p**ʸ**ehch**ʸkah 107
straight ahead прямо **pr**ʸ**ah**mah 21, 77
strange странно **strahn**nah 84
street улица *f* **oo**leetsah 15, 25, 77, 82, 154
streetcar трамвай *m* trahm**vigh** 67, 73
street map план города *m* plahn **go**rrahdah 19, 105

string верёвка *f* veer^{y}**of**kah 105

strong сильный **seel**^{y}niy 143; крепкий **kr^{y}ehp**keey 126

student студент *m* stoo**d^{y}ehnt**, студентка *f* stoo**d^{y}ehnt**kah 82, 93

study, to учиться oo**ch^{y}eet**^{y}sah 93

sturdy крепкий **kr^{y}ehp**keey 101

subway *(railway)* метро *nt* mee**tro** 19, 67, 72

suede замша *f* **zahm**shah 114, 118

sugar сахар *m* **sah**khahr 37, 38, 54

suit *(man/woman)* костюм *m* kahs**t^{y}oom** 117

suitcase чемодан *m* ch^{y}eemah**dahn** 17, 18

summer лето *nt* **l^{y}eh**tah 150

sun солнце *nt* **son**tseh 94

sunburn солнечный ожог *m* **sol**neech^{y}niy ah**zhok** 108

Sunday воскресенье *nt* vahskree**s^{y}eh**n^{y}eh 151

sunglasses тёмные очки *m/pl* **t^{y}om**ni^{y}eh ahch^{y}**kee** 123

sunshade *(beach)* зонтик *m* **zon**teek 91

sunstroke солнечный удар *m* **sol**neech^{y}niy oo**dahr** 141

supermarket универсам *m* ooneev^{y}ehr**sahm** 99

supplement доплата *f* dah**plah**tah 69

suppositories свечи *pl* **sv^{y}eh**ch^{y}ee 109

surgeon хирург *m* khee**roork** 144

surgery *(consulting room)* кабинет врача *m* kahbee**n^{y}eht** vrah**ch^{y}ah** 137

surgery hours приёмные часы *pl* pree**^{y}om**ni^{y}eh ch^{y}ee**ssi** 137, 145

swallow, to глотать glah**taht**^{y} 143

sweater свитер *m* **svee**tehr 117

sweatshirt спортивный пуловер *m* spahr**teev**niy poo**lo**veer 117

Sweden Швеция *f* **shv^{y}eh**tsi^{y}ah 146

sweet *(food)* сладкий **slaht**keey 56, 61

sweets *(candy)* конфеты *pl* kahn**f^{y}eh**ti, карамель *f* kahrah**m^{y}ehl^{y}** 64

sweet corn кукуруза *f* kookoo**roo**zah 50

sweetener сахарин *m* sahkhah**reen** 37

swell, to опухнуть ah**pookh**noot^{y} 139

swelling опухоль *f* **o**ppookhahl^{y} 139

swim, to плавать **plah**vaht^{y} 90, 91; купаться koo**paht**^{y}sah 91

swimming плавание *nt* **plah**vahnee^{y}eh 90

swimming pool бассейн *m* bah**ss^{y}ayn** 32, 90

swimming trunks плавки *pl* **plahf**kee 117

swimsuit купальник *m* koo**pahl**^{y}neek 117

switch *(light)* выключатель *m* **vikl**^{y}ooch^{y}aht^{y}ehl^{y} 29

switchboard operator телефонистка *f* teeleefah**neest**kah 26

Switzerland Швейцария *f* shveey**tsah**ree^{y}ah 146

synagogue синагога *f* seenah**go**ggah 84

synthetic синтетика *f* seen**teh**teekah 115

system система *f* sees**t^{y}eh**mah 138

T

table стол *m* stoll 15, 107; *(restaurant)* столик *m* **sto**leek 36, 61

tablet таблетка *f* tah**bl^{y}eht**kah 109, 143

taiga тайга *f* tigh**gah** 85

take, to взять vz^{y}aht^{y} 18, 21, 71, 102; *(time)* занять времени zah**n^{y}aht^{y}** **vr^{y}eh**meenee 79, 102, 115

taken занято **zah**neetah 70

tangerine мандарин *m* mahndah**reen** 52

tap *(water)* кран *m* krahn 28

tape recorder магнитофон *m* mahgneetah**fon** 119

tart пирог *m* pee**rok** 53

taxi такси *m* tahk**see** 18, 19, 21, 31, 67

tea чай *m* ch^{y}igh 38, 59, 60, 64, 71, 120

team команда *f* kah**mahn**dah 89

tearoom чайная *f* **ch^{y}igh**nah^{y}ah 34, 59

teaspoon чайная ложка *f* **ch^{y}igh**nah^{y}ah **losh**kah 107, 143

telegram телеграмма *f* teelee**grahm**mah 133

telegraph office телеграф *m* teelee**grahf** 99, 133

DICTIONARY

Словарь

telephone телефон *m* teelee**fon** 14, 28, 134, 136
telephone, to позвонить pahzvah**neet^y** 78, 134
telephone booth телефон-автомат *m* teelee**fon**-ahftah**maht** 134
telephone call разговор *m* rahzgah**vor** 134, 136
telephone number номер *m* **no**mmeer 134, 135, 136; телефон *m* teelee**fon** 136
television *(set)* телевизор *m* teelee**vee**zahr 23, 28, 119
tell, to сказать skah**zaht^y** 11, 13, 72, 73, 76
temperature температура *f* teempeerah**too**rah 90, 140, 142
temple храм *m* khrahm 82
temporarily временно **vr^{y}eh**meennah 145
ten десять **d^{y}eh**seet^y 147
tendon сухожилие *nt* sookhah**zhi**lee^{y}eh 138
tennis теннис *m* **t^{y}ehn**nees 89, 90
tent палатка *f* pah**laht**kah 32, 107
terminus конечная остановка *f* kah**n^{y}ehch^y**nah^{y}ah ahstah**nof**kah 73
terrace терраса *f* teer**rah**sah 36
terrible страшно **strahsh**nah, ужасно oo**zhahs**nah 84
tetanus столбняк *m* stahlb**n^{y}ahk** 140
thank you спасибо spah**ssee**bah 10
that то toh 100
theatre театр *m* tee**ahtr** 82, 86
theft кража *f* **krah**zhah 155
their их eekh 159
then тогда tahg**dah** 15
there там tahm 14
thermometer термометр *m* teer**mo**m^{y}ehtr, градусник *m* **grah**doosneek 109, 144
they они ah**nee** 159
thief вор *m* vor 155
thigh бедро *nt* bee**dro** 138
thin тонкий **ton**keey 114
thing вещь *f* v^{y}ehshch^y 18
think, to думать **doo**maht^y 92, 94
third третий **tr^{y}eh**teey 149
third треть *f* tr^{y}eht^y 149
thirsty *(I am)* мне хочется пить mn^{y}eh **kho**ch^{y}eetsah peet^y 13, 35
thirteen тринадцать tree**nah**tsaht^y 147
thirty тридцать **tree**tsaht^y 147
this это **eh**tah 100
thousand тысяча **ti**ssеech^{y}ah 148
thread нитка *f* **neet**kah 27
three три tree 147
throat горло *nt* **gor**lah 138
through через **ch^{y}ee**rees 15
thunder гром *m* grom 94
thunderstorm гроза *f* grah**zah** 94
Thursday четверг *m* ch^{y}eet**v^{y}ehrk** 151
ticket билет *m* bee**l^{y}eht** 65, 69, 74, 87, 88, 89
ticket office билетная касса *f* bee**l^{y}eht**nah^{y}ah **kah**ssah 19, 67
tie галстук *m* **gahl**stook 117
tight *(clothes)* узко **oos**kah 115
tights колготы *pl* kahl**go**tti 117
time время *nt* **vr^{y}eh**m^{y}ah 80, 134 *(occasion)* раз *m* rahs 95, 143, 149
time, in/on вовремя **vo**vr^{y}ehm^{y}ah 68, 153
timetable *(train)* расписание поездов *nt* rahspee**sah**nee^{y}eh paheez**dof** 68
tin *(can)* банка *f* **bahn**kah 120
tin opener консервный нож *m* kahn**s^{y}ehrv**niy nosh 107
tire шина *f* **shin**nah 75, 76, 78
tired устал(а) oo**stahl**(ah) 13
to к k 15
toast гренки *pl* green**kee** 41
tobacco табак *m* tah**bahk** 126
tobacconist's табак *m* tah**bahk** 99, 126
today сегодня see**vo**dn^{y}ah 29, 69, 151
toe палец ноги *m* **pah**leets nah**gee** 138
toilet *(lavatory)* туалет *m* tooah**l^{y}eht**, уборная *f* oo**bor**nah^{y}ah 23, 27, 32, 67, 154
toilet paper туалетная бумага *f* tooah**l^{y}eht**nah^{y}ah boo**mah**gah 111
toiletry туалетные принадлежности *pl* tooa**l^{y}eht**ni^{y}eh preenah**dl^{y}ehzh**nahstee 110
toilet water одеколон *m* ahdeekah**lon** 111
tomato помидор *m* pahmee**dor** 42, 50, 64, 120
tomato juice томатный сок *m* tah**maht**niy sok 60

tomb могила *f* mah**gee**lah, усыпальница *f* oosi**pahl^y**neetsah 82
tomorrow завтра **zahf**trah 29, 137, 151
tongs клещи *pl* **kl^{y}eh**shch^{y}ee 107
tongue язык *m* ee**zik** 138
tonsils миндалины *pl* meen**dah**leeni 138
too *(much)* слишком **sleesh**kahm 14; *(also)* тоже **to**zheh 15
tool kit набор инструментов *m* nah**bor** eenstroo**m^{y}ehn**tahf 107
tools инструменты *pl* eenstroo**m^{y}ehn**ti 78
tooth зуб *m* zoop 145
toothache зубная боль *f* zoob**nah**^{y}ah bol^y 145
toothbrush зубная щётка *f* zoob**nah**^{y}ah **shch^{y}ot**kah 111
toothpaste зубная паста *f* zoob**nah**^{y}ah **pahs**tah 111
top, at the сверху **sv^{y}ehr**khoo 30, 145
torch *(flashlight)* карманный фонарик *m* kahr**mahn**niy fah**nah**reek 107
touch, to трогать **tro**gaht^y 154
tour экскурсия *f* ehks**koor**see^{y}ah 74, 80
towards к k 15
towel полотенце *nt* pahlah**t^{y}ehn**tseh 27, 111
tower башня *f* **bahsh**n^{y}ah 82
town город *m* **go**rraht 19, 21, 25, 70, 76
town centre центр города *m* tsehntr **go**rrahdah 21, 76, 82
tow truck буксирный автомобиль *m* book**seer**niy ahftahmah**beel^y** 78
toy игрушка *f* ee**groosh**kah 128
toy shop магазин игрушек *m* mahgah**zeen** ee**groo**shehk 99, 128
track *(station)* путь *m* poot^y 67
traffic движение *nt* dvee**zheh**nee^{y}eh 79
traffic light светофор *m* sveetah**for** 77
trailer караван *m* kahrah**vahn** 32
train поезд *m* **po**eezd 66, 68, 69
tram трамвай *m* trahm**vigh** 67, 73
tranquillizer успокоительное *nt* oospahkah**ee**teel^{y}nah^{y}eh 109, 143
transfer *(bank)* перевод *m* peeree**vot** 131
translate, to перевести peereevees**tee** 12
transport транспорт *m* **trahns**pahrt 72
travel agency бюро путешествий *m* b^y**oo**ro pootee**shehst**veey 99
travel guide путеводитель *m* pooteevah**dee**t^{y}ehl^y 104, 105
traveller's cheque дорожный чек *m* dah**rozh**niy ch^{y}ehk 18, 62, 130
travelling bag сумка *f* **soom**kah 18
travel sickness морская болезнь *f* mahrs**kah^y**ah bah**l^{y}ehzn^y** 108
treatment лечение *nt* lee**ch^{y}eh**nee^{y}eh 143
tree дерево *nt* **d^{y}eh**reevah 85
trip путешествие *nt* pootee**shehst**vee^{y}eh 74; путь *m* poot^y 152
trolley тележка *f* teel^y**ehsh**kah 18
trolleybus троллейбус *m* trahl^y**ay**booss 73
trousers брюки *pl* **br^{y}oo**kee 117
try, to пробовать **pro**bbahvaht^y 58; *(clothes)* померить pah**m^{y}eh**reet^y 115
T-shirt майка *f* **migh**kah 117
Tuesday вторник *m* **ftor**neek 151
Turkey Турция *f* **toor**tsi^{y}ah 146
turn, to повернуть pahveer**noot^y** 21
turn очередь *f* **o**ch^{y}eereed^y 145
turn on, to включить fkl^{y}oo**ch^{y}eet^y** 71
turn out, to выключить vikl^{y}ooch^{y}eet^y 71
twelve двенадцать dvee**nah**tsaht^y 147
twenty двадцать **dvah**tsaht^y 147
two два dvah 147
typewriter (пишущая) машинка *f* (**pee**shooshch^{y}ah^{y}ah) mah**shin**kah 27, 105
tyre шина *f* **shin**nah 75, 76, 78

U

ugly некрасивый neekrah**see**viy 14; безобразный b^{y}ehzah**brahz**niy 84
umbrella зонтик *m* **zon**teek 91, 117
uncle дядя *m* **d^{y}ah**d^{y}ah 93
unconscious, to be потерять сознание pahteer^y**aht^y** sahz**nah**nee^{y}eh 139
under под paht 15

underground *(railway)* метро *nt* mee**tro** 67, 72
underpants трусы *pl* troo**ssi** 117
undershirt майка *f* **migh**kah 117
understand, to понимать pahnee**maht^{y}** 12, 16, 101, 135
underwear нижнее бельё *nt* **neezh**nee^{y}eh beel^{y}**o** 117
undress, to раздеться rahz**d^{y}eht^{y}**sah 142
United States Соединённые Штаты Америки (США) *pl* sighdee**n^{y}onni**^{y}eh **shtah**ti ahm**^{y}eh**reekee (s-shah) 146
university университет *m* ooneev^{y}ehrseet**^{y}eht** 82
until до dah 15
upper верхний **v^{y}ehrkh**neey 71
upset stomach расстройство желудка *nt* rahs**stroyst**vah zhi**loot**kah 108
urgent срочно **sroch^{y}**nah 13, 145
urine моча *f* mah**ch^{y}ah** 142
use пользование *nt* **pol^{y}**zahvahnee^{y}eh 17
use, to пользоваться **pol^{y}**zahvaht^{y}sah 32
useful полезный pahl**^{y}ehz**niy 15
USSR СССР ehs ehs ehs ehr 146
usually обычно ah**bich^{y}**nah 143

V

vacancy свободный номер *m* svah**bod**niy **nom**meer 23
vacation отпуск *m* **ot**poosk 151
vaccination прививка *f* pree**veef**kah 140
vacuum flask термос *m* **tehr**mahs 107
vaginal infection воспаление влагалища *nt* vahspahl**^{y}eh**nee^{y}eh vlah**gah**leeshch^{y}ah 141
valley долина *f* dah**lee**nah 85
value стоимость *f* **sto**eemahst^{y}, цена *f* tsin**nah** 131
veal телятина *f* teel**^{y}ah**teenah 47
vegetables овощи *pl* **o**vvahshch^{y}ee 40, 50
vegetable store овощной магазин *m* ahvahshch**^{y}noy** mahgah**zeen** 99
vegetarian вегетарианский veegeetahree**ahn**skeey 37
vein вена *f* **v^{y}eh**nah 138
venereal disease венерическая болезнь *f* veenee**reech^{y}**eeskah^{y}ah bahl**^{y}ehzn^{y}** 142
very очень **och^{y}**een^{y} 15
vest майка *f* **migh**kah 117; *(Am.)* жилет *m* zhil**^{y}eht** 117
veterinarian ветеринар *m* veeteereen**ahr** 99
video cassette видео-кассета *f* **vee**deho-kah**ss^{y}eh**tah 119, 128
video recorder видеомагнитофон *m* veedehomahgneetah**fon** 119
view вид *m* veet 23, 25
village село *nt* see**lo**, деревня *f* deer**^{y}ehv**n^{y}ah 76, 85
vinegar уксус *m* **ook**soos 37
visa виза *f* **vee**zah 16
visit, to осмотреть ahsmah**tr^{y}eht^{y}** 84; навестить nahvees**teet^{y}** 95
visiting hours часы посещений *m/pl* ch^{y}ee**ssi** pahssee**shch^{y}eh**neey 144
vitamin pills витамины *pl* veetah**mee**ni 109
vodka водка *f* **vot**kah 57, 58, 127
voltage напряжение *nt* nahpree**zheh**nee^{y}eh 27
vomit, to рвать rvaht^{y} 140

W

waistcoat жилет *m* zhil**^{y}eht** 117
wait, to ждать zhdaht^{y} 21, 108, 134, 135, 145
waiter официант *m* ahfee**tsiahnt** 26, 36
waiting room зал ожидания *m* zahl ahzhi**ddah**nee^{y}ah 67
waitress официантка *f* ahfee**tsiahnt**kah 26; девушка *f* **d^{y}eh**vooshkah 36
wake, to разбудить rahzboo**deet^{y}** 27, 71
wall стена *f* stee**nah** 85
wallet бумажник *m* boo**mahzh**neek 155
want, to хотеть khaht**^{y}eht^{y}** 13, 160
war война *f* vigh**nah** 15
warm тёплый **t^{y}o**pliy 94
wash, to вымыть **vi**mmit^{y} 76; *(clothes)* стирать stee**raht^{y}** 29, 115
washing powder стиральный порошок *m* stee**rahl^{y}**niy pahrah**shok** 107
watch часы *pl* ch^{y}ee**ssi** 121, 122

watchmaker's часовая мастерская *f* chʸeessah**vah**ʸah mahsteers**kah**ʸah 99
watchstrap браслет для часов *m* brahsl**ʸeht** dlʸah chʸee**ssof** 122
water вода vah**dah** *f* 15, 23, 28, 32, 75, 90, 143
waterfall водопад *m* vahdah**paht** 85
watermelon арбуз *m* ahr**boos** 52
wave волна *f* vahl**nah** 91
we мы mi 159
weather погода *f* pah**go**ddah 94
wedding ring обручальное кольцо *nt* ahbroo**chʸahl**ʸnahʸeh kahl**ʸtso** 121
Wednesday среда *f* sree**dah** 151
week неделя *f* need**ʸeh**lʸah 16, 20, 24, 80, 92, 151
weekday будний день *m* **bood**neey dʸehnʸ 151
weekend конец недели *m* kahn**ʸehts** need**ʸeh**lee, викенд *m* vee**kehnt** 89, 151
well хорошо khahrah**sho** 10, 14, 115
west запад *m* **zah**paht 77
what что shto 11
wheel колесо *nt* kahlee**sso** 78
when когда kahg**dah** 11
where где gdʸeh 11
where from откуда aht**koo**dah 56, 92, 133, 146
where to куда koo**dah** 11
which какой kah**koy** 11
white белый **bʸeh**liy 55, 56, 113
who кто kto 11
whole целый **tseh**liy 143
why почему pahchʸee**moo** 12
wide широкий shir**ro**keey 118
wife жена *f* zhin**nah** 10, 92, 93, 152
wig парик *m* pah**reek** 111
wind ветер *m* **vʸeh**teer 94
window окно *nt* ahk**no** 28, 36, 70; *(shop)* витрина *f* vee**tree**nah 100, 112
windscreen/shield ветровое стекло *nt* veetrah**vo**ʸeh stee**klo** 76
wine вино *nt* vee**no** 17, 55, 56
winter зима *f* zee**mah** 150
wish пожелание *nt* pahzhil**lah**neeʸeh 152
wish, to желать zhil**lahtʸ** 152
with с s 15
withdraw, to *(bank)* снять со счёта snʸahtʸ sah **shchʸo**ttah 130
without без bʸehs 15
woman женщина *f* **zhehn**shchʸeenah 112
wonderful чудесный chʸood**ʸeh**sniy 96
wood *(forest)* лес *m* lʸehss 85
wool шерсть *f* shehrstʸ 114, 115
word слово *nt* **slo**vvah 12, 15, 133
work, to работать rah**bo**ttahtʸ 93; *(function)* действовать **dʸayst**vahvahtʸ, работать rah**bo**ttahtʸ 28, 119, 125
working day рабочий день *m* rah**bo**chʸeey dʸehnʸ 151
worse хуже **khoo**zheh 14
wound рано *f* **rah**nah 139
wrap, to завернуть zahveer**nootʸ** 103
wristwatch ручные часы *pl* roochʸ**ni**ʸeh chʸee**ssi** 122
write, to написать nahpee**ssahtʸ** 12, 101
writing pad блокнот *m* blahk**not** 105
writing paper бумага для писем *f* boo**mah**gah dlʸah **pee**sseem 27
wrong неправильный nee**prah**veelʸniy 14, 135, 136

X

X-ray рентген *m* rʸehntg**ʸehn** 140

Y

year год *m* got 149
years лет *pl* lʸeht 150
yellow жёлтый **zhol**tiy 113
yes да dah 10
yesterday вчера fchʸee**rah** 151
yet ещё ee**shchʸo** 15, 16, 24
you ты, вы ti, vi 159
young молодой mahlah**doy** 14
your твой tvoy, ваш vahsh 159
youth hostel молодёжная турбаза *f* mahlah**dʸozh**nahʸah toor**bah**zah 22

Z

zero ноль nolʸ 147
zip(per) молния *f* **mol**neeʸah 117
zoo зоопарк *m* zah**pahrk** 82
zoology зоология *f* zahlo**ggee**ʸah 83

Русское оглавление

Авария 78
Автобус 73
Адрес 133
Алфавит 6
Аптека 108

Багаж 18, 71
Балет 87
Банк 129, 130
Билеты 67, 87
Болезнь 140
Больница 144

Вино 55
Водка 57
Вокзал 67, 69
Вопросы 11
Врач 137
Времена года 150
Время 153

Гинеколог 141
Год и возраст 149
Гостиница 22
  заказ номера 19
  отъезд 31
  регистрация 23, 25
  телефон – почта 28
  трудности 28
Грамматика 157

Деловые выражения 131
День и число 151
Деревня 85
Десерт 53
Диета 37
Дискотека 88
Достопримечательности 80, 81

Жалобы 61, 103

Завтрак 38
Закуски 41
Заправочная станция 75
Зимний спорт 91
Знакомства 92
Зубной врач 145

Игрушки 128

Камни 122
Качество 14
Квас 59
Кемпинг 32, 106
Кино 86
Книжный магазин 104
Количество 14
Концерт 87
Крайний случай 155
Культтовары 104

Лечение 143

Магазины 98
Машина 75
  авария 78
  дорожные знаки 79
  несчастный случай 79
  прокат 20
  ремонт 79
  стоянка 77
Меню 39, 40
Месяцы 150
Метро 72
Молочные продукты 43
Мясо 47

Надписи 154
Напитки 55, 60
Несчастный случай 79, 139
Ночной клуб 88

Обмен валюты 18, 129
Обувь 118

Общественный транспорт 72
автобус 73
метро 72
трамвай 73
Объявления 154
Овощи 50
Одежда 112, 116
размер 112
ткани 114
цвета 113
Опера 87
Оптика 123
Отдых 86

Парикмахерская 30
Пароход 74
Парфюмерия 108
Паспортный контроль 16
Пиво 56
Пикник 62
Пластинки 127
Пляж 90
Погода 94
Поезд 66
билеты 69
справки 67
Покупки 97
Полезные адреса 98
Посуда 107
Почта 28, 132
Праздники 152
Прачечная 29
Прибор 107
Приветствия 10, 152
Приглашения 94
Приезд 16
Пропажи и находки 155
Продукты 63, 120
Прокат машин 20
Птица 49

Размер 112
Ремонт 79, 118
Ресторан 33
Русская кухня 35
Рыба 45

Салат 42
Самолёт 65
Свидания 95
Семья 93
Сладкие блюда 53
Словарь 162
Сокращения 154
Спальный вагон 71
Спорт 89
Справки 67
Страны 146
Сувениры 127
Суп 44
Счёт 62
Сыр 43

Табак 126
Такси 21
Таможня 17
Театр 86
Телеграммы 133
Телефон 134
Трамвай 73
Туалетные принадлежности 110

Фотография 124, 125
Фрукты 52

Химчистка 29

Цвета 113
Цирк 87

Чай 59
Части тела 138
Часы 121
Числа 147

Электротовары 119
Экскурсии 80

Ювелирные изделия 121

SWEDEN
FINLAND
Stockholm
Helsinki
BALTIC SEA
St. Petersburg
ESTONIA
Novgorod
LATVIA
Yaroslavl
LITHUANIA
Smolensk
MOSCOW
Nizhni Novgorod
Kazan
Minsk
POLAND
Warsaw
BELARUS
Brest
RUSSIA
Volga
Kiev
Kharkov
Don
UKRAINE
Volgograd
Dnepr
MOLDAVIA
Odessa
RUMANIA
Rostov-on-Don
Bucharest
Yalta
CASPIAN SEA
BULGARIA
BLACK SEA
GEORGIA
AZER-BAIJAN
Ankara
ARMENIA
TURKEY